2

All Against the Collar

Contents

List of Illustrations

Introduction

I write this book because a publisher asked me to. It is years late and I am still uneasy about it. When first asked, I said I was too young to do a memoir. The editor said, 'Let us put it this way. You may become less interesting later on.'

Trade union officers do not write books. Or hardly ever. Since the end of World War Two, I can trace only four union officers who have written books and one of these confined himself to novels of working-class life! Why is this? They normally spend more than twenty years in a position of influence in the community but, unless they combine this with a political career, they promptly disappear from public view at sixty-five. In some unions they even have to retire at fifty-five: the Civil Service unions are full of black holes because of this – and it has undoubtedly contributed to leadership problems there with ultra-right and ultra-left factions having more room to manoeuvre.

I was a professional trade union officer for forty-two years, although I adopted the 'professional' prefix only after ten years of becoming what I considered proficient – and finding that I did not want to go back or do anything else. And during that time I wrote or co-wrote eight books. Why? As a national officer or general secretary of a significant trade union – and I was general secretary of ASTMS for twenty-eight years and also president of the Trades Union Congress – there are a tremendous amount of stimuli at work all of the time. I could not help being immensely excited by this. But I am also coloured to a marked degree by that old Welsh teaching and preaching urge. I wanted to propagate ideas.

My first book happened almost by chance. Aneurin Bevan was the sparkplug, using his adoring property developer, Howard Samuel, to commission it. Howard helped finance *Tribune*, for which I was writing articles in the fifties, and, when Michael Foot was the editor, he gave Christmas parties to thank the staff. I was at one held in the Café Royal in Regent Street in the mid-1950s and amazed Aneurin Bevan with the story that the mineworkers' pension fund held the lease. I ventured that the developing pension funds and their managers would reinforce the British power elite. 'Have you been making a study of this?' 'Well, I have a box of cross-indexed cards.' 'Howard! This young comrade has got a book in him.' 'We'll publish it.' Howard had recently bought McGibbon and Kee, under the management of Reg Davis-Poynter. I saw them together in Great Portland Street with my little box and they gave me a contract for £100 (£50 down). So my first book, *Power at the Top*, was conceived. It was a straightforward and rather dense argument seeking to show that the nationalising Acts of the 1945–50 Labour government had no effect upon the class structure and power relationships in British society.

The second, *Power Behind the Screen*, was another lengthy argument directed at a single point. It sought to establish that the independent television contracting companies were not the show-business organisations that they seemed to be but were simple extensions of existing financial power. Reg Davis-Poynter had the idea for the book. Alas, Howard Samuel was a distressed man and disappeared into the sea, leaving, I am told, a substantial sum of cheques in his clothes on the beach.

Other books followed, developing my ideas on unions and power structures; I tell the story behind them in the following pages. This book, however, is more personal. It is a stream of observations and memories filtered through the brain of a happily left-wing radical who happened to have been a union officer for more than forty-two years. With no tradition of the average trade union official writing books or articles, anyone who does is seen to be unrepresentative and distrusted, and certainly this book is untypical, a highly individualistic and idiosyncratic look at unions. In it, I return again and again to incomes policy, for this I believe will be critically important for a future Labour government.

It is also, of course, about me. I am not arrogant, in spite of what my dear friend Ian Mikardo has written, but I have been influenced by the leader who declared: 'I have only made one mistake. Briefly, twenty years ago, I thought I was wrong on an important issue. I was only wrong about my being wrong.' I do not think I have been wrong about important issues *at the time*. I adjusted my views on the European Economic Community, incomes policies and unilateral nuclear disarmament over thirty years. Of course, my timing has sometimes been wrong, or blurred or out of phase. Often beaten in an engagement or abandoned by allies, I have still known what was right for *me* to do. It was not always correct and I have repeatedly made the error of equating all movements around me with my own efforts. But I believe that I *made* some things happen and shaped some perceptions. Individuals do matter. The impact of ideas upon other opinion-formers matters.

The British unions' influence on national affairs peaked under the Wilson and Callaghan governments. The TUC's influence was mainly useful and benign but the 'Winter of Discontent' (I think I first coined the phrase, not Larry Lamb) soured it all and created a situation where strident Conservative right-wing policies could flourish on a national minority vote and a Labour government could lose a confidence vote in spite of Michael Foot cajoling MPs (and union leaders to persuade MPs) in the House of Commons leader's room. Moss Evans, then General Secretary of the Transport Workers Union, and I said we would try. I would think the decent Gerry Fitt (now Lord Fitt) has often regretted his abstention on the vote on 28 March 1979.

The Left in the unions got it wrong and the seeds for Mrs Thatcher's counter-revolution were germinated. This book is about this and other mistakes and consequences – ageing unions, ageing arguments in an ageing discarded workforce – all against a background of the best, though often poorly directed, Labour government intentions. The last decade has seen a right-wing governmental attack based on a hatred of democratic institutions. I am still surprised at hearing the popular legend inside the union that Margaret Thatcher was a member of one of our founder unions when it was really a Communist club. In these years I have become so fascinated by the growing and then the failing dynamic of the British unions and so attached to their essential *goodness* that my criticisms insist upon being marshalled. I believe that the very *identity* of some trade unions (let alone their social purpose) is still being menaced by their lack of leadership, understanding and sheer mechanical efficiency. They are also so competitive between themselves as to resemble the great takeover international mega-corporations. They have no long-range perspective as unions; in their traditional disdain of theory they merely pick up and half-digest the more resistant parts of yesterday's analysis. There are no schools of thought, only current disputants. Without a theology, there is no priesthood and no continuity of line. What will happen if new ideas are not being developed?

This book is, however, not intended as open-heart surgery on the unions, nor as a chronicle of my own difficulties and defeats – my friends will remind me of those. It tells of my professional experiences, how I achieved some of the successes I did. But echoing Archie Rice in John Osborne's *The Entertainer*, 'Don't clap too hard – it's a very old building. Well, I 'ave a go, don't I? I do – I 'ave a go.'

1

Background
and Bias

To start, I want to disclose my biases so that you may take them into shrewd account. First and most important, although now sharply diluted, I am Welsh, from that strip of the narrow South Wales coastal plain where the literary societies and chapels bred politicians and exported them like guided missiles to the rest of the United Kingdom.

As I got older, the feeling of Welshness permeated me more and more. As a willow far from water throws out a taproot, so mine goes all the way back to the Ruhr-like industrialisation of the Port Talbot-Neath-Swansea coal and steel complex. I am partly liberated from this now as I write this on a beautiful beach in the Pacific basin but my dreams all recall the small room of 4 Maes-y-Cwrt Terrace where I was born or the house along the street which my maternal grandfather owned.

The cultural pattern of the industrial coastal plain from Llanelli to Cardiff was being shattered by the hammer blows of Anglicisation and mechanisation when I was born in the General Strike year of 1926 and our terraced house was not far from the blast furnaces, close to the shuffling shunts of the floodlit marshalling yard and the sulphurous coke ovens. This was my birthplace, on 2 May. Would it not have been glorious to have been born on 1 May 1926? Alas, my mother was not political and did not force her pelvic girdle to have me out on May Day.

My father was a trade unionist, an apathetic trade unionist. An unwilling clerical worker, he had always wanted to be an

1

electrician. He had not trained for it, he did not know anything about it, but all his life he hankered after being an electrician. Why he did not manage it I never quite knew. Lack of money to support an apprenticeship?

He had gone into the saloon, lathering the customers in Taibach when he was eleven, then into the mill at thirteen. He once said, 'I was an assistant inspector in the copper works for two years,' and I knew that he had worked long night-shifts in a tinplate works because he had a favourite gruesome story about how 'the big fly-wheel went round and round and round and it broke this man up so that it took hours getting his pieces out'. There was some sort of trade union demarcation trouble: they stopped making copper tube, he lost the job.

My father's unemployment bit bone-deep. It scarred my mother's use of the words 'safe' and 'security' for the rest of her married life. She often reminded me and my brother Tom: 'See that dresser there . . . your dad made that. Until then we had orange boxes.' There was a hint of an estrangement with her father (called in Welsh 'Tad') over it all. 'A big Liberal', he was the seventh member of the local Co-operative Society and its first treasurer. (I first thought of calling this chapter '1393' – my mam's Co-op number.) As a young girl my mother used to be sent to the bank on Mondays with a shawl wrapped around the gladstone bag by her mother in case of robbers, sometimes carrying up to three hundred tiny gold sovereigns. Tad was a foreman-fitter in the Duffryn engine yard, and was also a harbour master. No wonder he owned three terraced houses and a huge moustache cup.

My mother recalled that 'he did two jobs sometimes and had two pays but he didn't get your father a job until I ran after him. I will never forget it – I caught him up in the park, the George V Memorial Park (before our house), and said, "You know Sam hasn't had a job;. can't you get him one, now?" He did it that week. Your father went to work on the GWR [Great Western Railway Company]. Steady on the railway then, it was a good steady job.' He developed a good handwriting and became the 'good writer' for the whole terrace; all the wills came from Sam Jenkins. Miriam Jenkins always wanted her sons in steady jobs, secure from unemployment, an attitude that influenced me for a few years, until I broke away.

My father ended up as a timekeeper on the Great Western Railway. I would go with him on the afternoon shift and hand out the brass tags to the engine drivers which proved they had reported for duty. I found six of these in the Flea Market in New Orleans thirty years later. Of course I bought them.

It was not a 'union' household, although there was always a pile of the *Railway Clerk* on the windowsill. (My brother Tom, six years older than me, would become the Railway Clerks' Association's General Secretary decades later.) After my father's death in 1952, I found in a dressing-table drawer a copy of the 1926 agreement between the railway unions and the main-line railway companies. This arrogantly recorded that the three unions had been wrong in calling their members out in support of a General Strike and made it an agreed formula that workers would only be recalled when 'the traffic offered', and reserving a company's right to proceed against anyone alleged to have been violent or intimidating. An inactive unionist he may have been, but the personal injury done to my father by that document was kept alive for twenty-five years.

A Welsh child can never make friends with his parents, and therefore the interchange of information along the oral channels of friendship is never really possible. But ten years after my father's death, I tape-recorded my mother's answers to dozens of questions about herself and her girlhood, her courtship and marriage. We dug up the distant, grey, almost invisible aunts who had kept a stall in the Aberavon market, selling meat and lavabread, and the Jenkins family coming to Port Talbot to work in a brick yard. The long-dead Jenkins uncles were so rude, quarrelsome and boisterous that they were named after their trade, 'the bricks'. Quick to take offence, hasty to fight, their nickname still hangs about down there, so much so that BBC television made a programme about them many decades later.

My paternal grandfather was called Dai Te or David the Tea, because he bought it in bulk and sold it from his house in North Street near the river, long razed for a concrete jungle by-pass. He was 'a lovely singer although he went to Welsh church and not Chapel'. A member of the local hospital management committee (what organisation elected him?), he was an Independent Labour Party supporter when my mother met him in 1915. 'What are we but Labour, all of us, we are all Labour,' he said to her. Although voting ILP whenever he could, he belonged to the Conservative Club ('because the dog breeders went there').

Perhaps he was a poacher too. He certainly had a gun. My mother recalled my father often talking about the time when they had a good feed on the swan his father brought home from the Baglan moors – fifty years later the site of a major petrochemical complex.

He was in the old Volunteers and went away for training every year. His brother had belonged, too. This brother was a shadowy figure whose photograph stared down from a North Street wall in a red-tinted uniform with a white belt and a white pillbox strapped to the side of his head. He went to fight in the Boer War and was buried on the veldt.

Like many South Wales mining and maritime towns, the streets were named after the casual and bloody encounters of an imperial trading nation. Inkerman Terrace, Balaclava Row (until I was twelve I had a stubborn belief that all the Balaclava helmets in the world were named after that street) and Gallipoli Field, which was the terminus for the Whit Monday combined Sunday schools walk through the town, when small boys changed to long trousers for the first time and sang 'Onward Christian Soldiers' before going to blancmange, three kinds of cake and kiss-in-the-ring at their own Chapel vestry fields. These were our bar mitzvahs. How would we know about them? Aberavon had one Jewish family. Not one of us knew that the real Gallipoli existed as an actual place where Welshmen had died in an out-generalled, incompetently supplied army, although ANZAC service would be revered in Australia and New Zealand for the next seventy years for loyalty and bravery.

My mother sent me off to see Madam Miriam Joseph James, a locally famed troupe-trainer and 'elocutionist'. She sat me at the piano, heard me, and suggested I try singing, starting with learning the words of 'Count Your Blessings, One by One'. I stopped attending and she reproached my mother in the Co-op grocery department. 'After all it's only half-a-crown a term.'

4

My mother was chagrined – as if she could not find that amount to improve her younger son. Neither were to know that I would be invited to leave the Sir Robert B. Byass Tinplate Works Male Voice Choir in 1942 for singing flat. But Madam Joseph James and her tap-dancing, singing infants sailed through the war like a cheerful fleet, entertaining hospitals and giving relief to chapels.

On our holidays, my mother remembered, 'We went as far as it was allowed on your father's free passes.' There was the time I was put to sleep on a Brighton boarding-house floor and my ear was blooded by a rat in the night; the foreign landlady, in contrition, gave us her bronze clip-bound family bible. And a tension-filled return from Blackpool with 'two shillings between us – when we got the wrong ferry across the Mersey'. Another Railway Clerk member fixed the tickets in 1936.

Through the thread of her answers time and again ran the resentment that some 'union men' some time prevented my father from being 'what he always wanted, an electrician'. So, he 'wrote hymns, he was always writing hymns. Do you remember pumping that harmonium we bought him in Neath – was it the day the Queen came?'

There I was back in the heart of it, growing up almost in the shadow of the Duffryn Calvinist Methodist Chapel (printed on all the cups, saucers and plates). I really knew only Methodists (our God was a jealous God), although I later found out about the Water Street Baptists and the Congregationalists and the Wesleyans, if not very much. I since admired the minority group from a split chapel which after a long-forgotten theological dispute built a new chapel in the old way, in stone, as high as any, but flattened like an upended sandwich, on an elongated plot between a Jewish dentist and a draper ('We wanted to make our witness on a main road').

But, in chapel, I learned to use words and then to carry ideas on them. The English language became a fascinating and explorable rabbit warren, partly because I helped to teach small children. On Sunday afternoon, by the time I became eleven, I had to go to a corner of the vestry and teach five- to seven-year-olds the Welsh alphabet – especially the ffs, lls and dds (no xs and zs for us) – from varnished wooden boards with a handy finger-hole at the top. In the morning I would have had to learn a fresh verse in Welsh from the Old Testament: this had to be repeated to the class teacher before the lesson started. We all had to bring our verses in.

There was always an atmosphere of disputation and elucidation. The theologians preferred Welsh and when, reluctantly, they were forced into English by the ignorance of their listeners, they inlaid it with softer Welsh. This was teaching, simply. Oratory came in the evening service from masters of the *hwyl*. One of these looked rather like a caped picture of the legendary David Lloyd George. He was the minister, T.J. Morgan. He wrote my first job testimonial and I recall the main point was that I came from a 'pious family'. Short and stout, with thick, long, silver-grey hair, he was an expert preacher and a mass exciter. When I went back to the Duffryn Calvinist Methodist Chapel with Sir Harry Secombe for his 'Highway' television programme, I could feel his presence and I stood in his pulpit and prickled with respect.

In sermons he would pick a situation, a subject, a phrase, and start to handle it. Slowly he would build up a verbal heightening, magnifying the philosophical defects of the devil's work on the situation. He had an initially bland, flat and calm delivery, broken yet fluid, but as he preached his face got very red over a high white collar, and sets of long-phrased rhythms started cycling. The originally offending phrase would start to become alien (even if it was as familiar as 'fed-up') as it broke up in his mouth. 'Fe-e-ed *up*?' he would shout like a pistol shot. He would be swaying around by now in the high mahoganay pulpit and liltingly changing the speed, tone and style of his word-groups until, towards the climax, sections would almost, not quite, be sung. The man achieved self-exaltation at this stage (fuelled by the musical 'A-mens' from the deacon's Big Seat). He and the congregation had then a common pulse-rate, a common metabolism, and this is the entry and union that every Welsh political speaker is *always* feeling for.

Aneurin Bevan and George Thomas had it. They preferred to convert by speaking than writing: they liked the houselights up, the need to see – and flux – the audiences' faces. This may explain why there are so few penetrating Welsh political authors: writing as compared to courting a live meeting is too soilitary. This is the atmosphere of disputation and projection in which I grew, absorbing like a sponge the religious puritanism, politics and suppressed sensuality which gives the Welsh their Celtic flame.

Expression has always mattered to me. Over the decades in meetings and at dinner tables, jotting on menu cards and agendas, I have been trying to capture those sentences, those thoughts, of other officials, that snap on the lights for me. After all, I am a Celt and we Welsh people are continually having our senses excited by words and movements, drab to others, which illuminate the truth for us.

I only realised my Welshness, truly, when I went back to bury my father in 1952. I had then been away for five years. The feeling became painfully clear, as I watched rather like on a scratched, flickering newsreel, the file of people coming through the house to see my mother. They had not forgotten their much earlier working-class habits, and it was as if it was still a financial penalty to bury the dead. When they sympathised with her, they dropped money into her lap until the handkerchief she was holding there, which was rolled and balled up with tears, was half covered by a pile of moving, clinking silver that was being dropped into her lap in order to 'make what we feel real and genuine, like . . .'

The old minister was dead by now and, theological-college fresh, the new one came in through the glass scullery door with all the weight and authority of the 'we have got a rich Chapel here you know' around him as a mantle. 'We were sorry, s-o s-o-r-r-y to lose your father, he was a good man. Chapel auditor.'

They buried him the next day, carrying the coffin in a long, black-tie, white-shirted darkly-uniformed procession that strung itself out along the waste-blackened river Ffrwydwyllt. Before we had gone half-way the mists moved across from the tops of our desiccated-plateau mountains and the rain drizzled down. It got heavier, and by the time we reached the churchyard gates the railwaymen's blue uniforms were bulky and shiny with the water that sopped its way from collar to trousers.

But as their boots struck the flags of the cemetery pathway, the leading deacon started to sing bass and everyone else joined in so quickly that it was like a breaker that suddenly forms a few yards from the shore. It rolled up into the trees and startled the rooks, who flew out noisily and angrily and circled around and around as they put the coffin in the clayey grave, while the railwaymen dropped lumps of mud on to it with sticky, friendly, feeling hands.

By this time I knew that my taproot ran 180 miles due west, but somewhere it had a kink. I had made a local break in this ingrown community, though only later did this seem important. For a long time I did not question my everyday assumption that I was different, separated off from the atmosphere, now long gone, in which I grew until I was twenty-one years old. It took me years to find out that there had been traces of political tradition in my family, to realise that I carried faint memories of sporadic, working-class activity and some bitter class resentments. My great-grandfather lost a leg tunnelling for coal, under the sands of the Morfa Beach, and his son, my paternal grandfather, was a shearer in the Vivian's tinplate works where they rolled the red-hot steel by hand and their fingers split open in the winter. But none of this past seemed real to me despite my own early industrial experience.

I had left the Port Talbot County School in the spring holiday of 1940 just before I was fourteen years old, to go to work. Since I had 'passed the scholarship' my parents were fined £5 by the Glamorgan education authority for taking me out of school and sending me off to work. This also happened to my older brother Tom (who coincidentally also became a trade union General Secretary – of the Transport Salaried Staffs Association which succeeded the Railway Clerks' Association – perhaps after seeing how much I was enjoying life as a union organiser). I remember going to the Charing Cross Hotel to see him waiting to go in for a clerical job interview. He got the job and climbed the ladder.

It was my second cousin Mary, a pretty ringleted girl who lived alongside us in Maes-y-Cwrt Terrace, who said she could get me an interview in the new aluminium alloy sheet plant, recently built alongside the blackplate and manganese steel works of industrialist Sir Robert B. Byass. So off I went to see the works manager, Charles H. Cunniffe, on a Saturday morning in April 1940, wearing my red-ribboned school blazer and cap (with a metal badge for the House of Tudor on it). 'I'll give you a test,' he said. 'Write this down: "The farmer was in the field sowing. His wife was in the house sewing. So they were both . . .".' Precociously, I said I would need a composite word. I got the job.

I started in the test house of the 5L3 aluminium sheet plant, bought myself a white coat and started measuring the hardness and tensile strength of aluminium alloys. My first payslip, very elongated in a brown envelope, was for 16s 8d. (The test house girls were all mobilised to go to the timekeeper's office on a Friday morning to fill the packets for all the workers.) I was the only boy and the girls' butt, especially as I was obviously fascinated by two pretty blondes named Pearl and Ruby, who were identical twins.

But Charlie Cunniffe was watching over me. He paid my fees and train fares twice a week to go to the Swansea Technical College to study metallurgy. He therefore almost killed me. This was the time of sustained Luftwaffe raids on Swansea and Mount Pleasant Hill, the road to the College, came under heavy incendiary bombing and machine-gunning. I remember spending hours in a train in Swansea station waitng for the 'All Clear' after a particularly vicious raid. He also stopped my attempt to become a cadet officer in the Navy, claiming I was in a reserved occupation; he was very cross about my attempt to leave him. At fourteen I was the youngest student ever enrolled for the City and Guilds course. But I passed the examination and there I was a Shift Chemist, later to rise to the dizzy heights of Day Chemist and, at eighteen, to Chief Chemist.

In this time I was seriously gashed several times because sheet metal is difficult to handle without gloves. Also, as the Day Book recorded, 'This is the end of my report. I have been gassed.' So I had. I still have the stitch marks on my forehead from falling from the roof of a furnace when I had been repairing a thermocouple. My cousin Eunice, renowned for having had five fiancés, nursed me and I got an extra ration of milk – allegedly to deal with the carbon monoxide. I also lost some of my teeth as a result of us having to check the acid baths which descaled the hot rolled blackplate; we used pipettes in which one sucked up the acid. I am surprised now that any of us had *any* teeth left.

I certainly learned there, from the shop stewards who first told me of 'incentives' for workers and of the casual, yet organised sexual encounters on the night-shift, when perspiring nubile girls on roller-flattening machines might spend only a few hours on them and the rest of the time in the huge railway pantechnicons on the line that ran beside the furnaces. In the wartime night-shift camaraderie, their piece-work payments did not suffer: on the contrary. I had no concept of earthy working-class sex. When an experienced old roller (probably all of forty years) flicked a match between the breasts of a girl stacker, I simply marvelled at his skill.

During this period the manager of the Co-operative Insurance Society lent me an introduction to Marx and another to Machiavelli. I never looked back. He reminded me of this at a London Caxton Hall meeting denouncing the EEC more than twenty years later.

The wartime period was culture starved, entertainment starved: so some of the local schoolteachers and clergymen set up a debating society in Port Talbot called the Forum. I was on the committee and we invited famous speakers. Desmond Bernal came, Julian Huxley, C.E.M. Joad, who stayed at the best Port Talbot Hotel, the Walnut Tree, and after the crowded meeting came down to supper with the committee with one toe peeping out of a tattered slipper. We were shocked. They got £50 and expenses, which was enormous in those days, but we filled chapels at half a crown a head.

I had joined the Labour Party (the first in my immediate family to do so) at fourteen and agitated for libertarian causes. I treasure an agenda for a ward committee meeting for December 1945 where I was to move two motions: 'That British troops throughout the world be used only to safeguard British interest and not to uphold any reactionary imperialistic system of a Foreign power. This is with special reference to Java and Indo-China from which we should immediately withdraw our military government as such.' And, secondly, 'That we immediately set at liberty all Spanish Republican refugees at present held in this country in concentration camps. Further, that we terminate diplomatic relations with Franco's Spain.' I lost both.

I had some encouragements. The Welsh National Eisteddfod did not take place during the Second World War years because the Bards only permitted it in times of peace. They would meet and cry out 'A Oes Heddwch' ('Is there Peace?'). Unless the answer was affirmative there was no eisteddfod. So a Workers Eisteddfod was established and my rolling mill manager, the great E.G. Davies, encouraged me to submit an essay. It won the first prize in Cardiff, which was only thirty miles away from home but I was so delighted that I sent a telegram to Port Talbot telling my mother that I had won. And the efficiency of the Post Office in those days was such that it arrived there hours before I returned.

My essay was about the girls in the rolling mills, wearing their pinnies and their California Poppy perfume and handling great pieces of aluminium alloy through the rollers. I had referred to them as 'gaily caparisoned' and the mill manager did not believe there was such a word. They were a very smiling, sweaty lot and the scene was very colourful. Alas, one day a piece of metal was misjudged through one of the great rollers and it slewed around, cutting a young woman almost in half; the mill was drenched with her blood.

I submitted an essay the next year and won the joint first prize. So I was interested in writing, or as it was known in South Wales schools, 'composition'. When VE Day came there was a town competition for what young people would want to see in the future. I won that as well. I have always been fascinated with persuasive language, something which would help me when it came to trying to open consciousness and organise hundreds of thousands of white-collar workers twenty-five years on.

I became a temperance campaigner, deeply impressed by a full-time teetotalism lecturer in the classrooms who would drop a worm in a jam-jar of pure alcohol and say 'See!'. I did some lay preaching in the valleys in their cause, and was recruited at sixteen into the Association of Scientific Workers (AScW) by a London metallurgist who came to work in a light alloys plant

11

where I first learned about X-ray diffraction. I still have prints of my hand. I'll probably die of the radiation.

A union Branch Secretary in the same year as my recruitment, I was a member of a national AScW union committee by the time I was nineteen. Money from our members used to come to me in Hanbury's pastille tins left hurriedly by lads, who had been told by the works managers to give up union dues collection or else . . . They all left to a man. This was the first time I felt a cold, soggy punch in my belly. I did believe, however primitively, in solidarity – and we were all so exploited.

By this time I had given up the chapel. My rationale was that shift work did not permit it, but what did you do as a – very young – individual if your employers said 'I want you 7 to 5 instead of 9 to 5'? You went in. For no more money. I was deeply under the influence of the arguments and fears of the community in which I lived. When I was ten at the Central Boys' School another boy told me about Dic Penderyn ('named after a little bird – his voice was so sweet') unjustly hanged for the death of a Redcoat in the riots against English landlordism in Newport and allegedly buried in St Mary's churchyard ('the day the real murderer confessed – in Australia – a cross grew up in grass on his grave: it does it every year. Come and look for it?'). Most of the energy of the Nonconformist Welsh derives from their fear of slothfulness and certainty of spiritual and fleshly guilt.

As the protégé of the formidable and engaging works director Charlie Cunniffe, I moved with him to three different factories in these years up to 1947. A cripple who nevertheless raised a Home Guard company, he got an MBE (as a result of Sir Stafford Cripps visiting his aluminium alloy plant when he was Minister of Aircraft Production). At the antiquated Eaglebush Tinplate Works in Neath, where I became the night-shift foreman, he told me one day, 'Only two things matter.' He tapped the crystal of his wristwatch, 'Time'; he gestured with his hands 'and these'. He was fascinated by hands. He got me to take photographs of the hands of the rollermen, which were plowed with greasy lines that had cracked open the top layer of skin to show the pink flesh underneath. The rollermen worked hard, their hands became too hot, they plunged them into water and this in the end destroyed the suppleness of the skin. He supplied me with salt tablets for them to take to counteract the effect but they preferred beer so the remedy did not work. My grandfather's hands must have been like this. But this was a point that did not seem at all real to me in Charlie Cunniffe's office with the drying prints pinned up around the walls.

Charlie Cunniffe had me earning £9 a week in 1946 when the '£5 a week man' was the aristocrat of South Wales labour and it was to his great distaste – he was appalled at the idea of 'staff' joining a union – that I was the South Wales treasurer of the AScW, a job I had had since I was seventeen because no one else wanted it. He preferred pay bargaining and promotions through the rampant Freemason structure in South Wales.

I had been the prime agent for a newspaper advertisement for a 'staffs' meeting at the Port Talbort YMCA. (I never had back the £4 I paid for it.) Hardly anybody came. The officials present almost outnumbered the audience but I was fascinated by the way all the officials took out their diaries at the end of the meeting and found it difficult to find a time when to meet again. They were so busy. I did not even have a diary.

An ultimatum about my amateur work in organising white-collar staffs in the works in Port Talbort and Neath ripened my urge to move. A letter was on my desk one night: desist (and probably be promoted) or go. Other managements had 'had a word' and a manager from my own works had been stopped from entering another simply because of me. At least, he said so. He was so senior a local Freemason, I doubt if anyone would have dreamed of stopping him. Without obvious merit, he effortlessly took on management posts, although basically illiterate. So I looked for jobs even more actively.

My chance came with Harry Knight, General Secretary of the Association of Supervisory Staffs, Executives and Technicians, who had arrived at ASSET from the then ostracised National Union of Public Employees after Ian Mikardo had successfully moved a motion of censure at the 1945 Annual Conference on the entire National Executive Council and the then General Secretary. They all resigned, although the discredited General Secretary Tom Agar many years later briefly found a way onto the National Executive Committee of the Labour Party via one of its esoteric constituencies. Unusually, the Metal Box Company, which owned Eaglebush, had allowed Harry Knight to address their white-collar staffs around the country, though with their works manager in the chair at the meetings. At the Eaglebush Tinplate Works we had the formidable Charlie Cunniffe in the chair, and after Harry had spoken out, habitually jingling coins in his trouser pocket, and put his recruitment literature on the table, Charlie glowered around and no one went forward to pick it up. Except me.

I then went with Harry over the railway bridge (where I would tape a BBC 'One Pair of Eyes' twenty years later) and we waited in the rain for a bus back to Port Talbot. ASSET could not afford a car. He questioned my audacity in helping. I told him of my membership of the Association of Scientific Workers, which was, almost vainly, trying to recruit the draughtsmen. In the drizzle, in the lamplight, Harry said, 'We have a vacancy in Birmingham for a bright young man, why not apply?' My heart jumped as I saw the chance to join the 'diary men'.

I still remember shivering at the bus stop on the Mount in Taibach and murmuring into the turned-up collar of my blue Civil Defence greatcoat (a treasured relic of having been an air-raid messenger warden) the magic words 'Assistant Midlands Divisional Officer of the Association of Supervisory Staffs, Executives and Technicians'. This was the job for which I applied, a metallurgist with minor qualifications and only twenty years old, although I said I was about to be twenty-one – the minimum qualifying age.

The National Executive Council selected me – remarkably – as the youngest full-time trade union officer ever appointed in the United Kingdom. They had two goes at it, as the snows in the terrible winter of 1946–47 aborted the first selection interviews in Birmingham. My chief advocate on the selection committee was Harry Knight, although my friend Ian Mikardo, as ASSET member who had been elected as MP for Reading in 1945, later claimed that he had me appointed. 'Mik' remembered my appointment as 'freakish. We had a Lord Mayor in for it, but it was so cold we voted and went home.'

That night in February 1947 I went back to my job as the foreman on the night-shift at the Eaglebush Tinplate Works to work out my week's notice and to say goodbye. I was leaving the furnacemen, the rollers, behinders and doublers in the antiquated hot tinpot works. To become a trade union official was to make a major status jump: 'You'll soon forget all about us, boyo.'

My last individual contribution to the private sector in Britain was to steal a truck-load of coal to keep the Metal Box Company in business. In the bitterly cold, prolonged winter of that year, the Eaglebush Tinplate Works were faltering. The boilers were cooling, the flywheel was slowing and the workers would have to be sent home. As their foreman I had reconnoitred and found a truck of precious coal just off the blocked main railway line. So I took a team of tin workers and stokers out into the siding and we uncoupled and pushed a truck down into the works to feed the boilers. We should not have done it because there was a primitive rationing system in place. (Manny Shinwell as the Labour government's Minister of Fuel and Power got all the blame and the sack for the ferociously icy conditions.) But I kept the engine going and the low-cost, inefficiently coated plate from the hot tinpots flowed into the Metal Box manufacturing plant alongside. The lads, enormously hard-working in their loose dark-blue Welsh flannel shirts, had their money: the public had its food cans. I mentioned the exploit to Charlie Cunniffe, who may – or may not – have done something about it.

I was anyway feeling light-hearted. I knew I was off, leaving the hot dirty mills and tinpots. I had never been unemployed. I had never been in want. I was a qualified technician and I was becoming a trade union official of my own choice, based on a deliberate decision and a fortuitous encounter, some luck, some energy.

It must have been the English that Harold Laski had in mind when he complained, 'Nothing is more striking than the way in which we train the sons of the rich or well-born men to habits of authority, while the children of the poor are trained to habits of deference.'

I was not. In my case another working-class Celt was homing in on the Anglo-Saxons, burdened by ill-absorbed theology and hoping to get some formal training, but determined to move events and succeed.

2

The Wage Freeze
Watershed

I arrived in Birmingham on 28 February 1947, with two new Co-op suits and £28, full of passionate enthusiasm and very green. An older trade union official met me at the barrier in Birmingham's Snow Hill Station and as we left in the bus, he introduced my new world by saying, 'You must remember that it is your bread and butter now.' This was my first introduction to professionalism as a trade union officer. I really did not know anything about it all. Like most trade union appointees (even those twenty years older), I was totally untrained and had no real concept of what work had to be done – let alone how to do it.

For the first six months, operating from a one-room office in Corporation Street, I worried that it would emerge that I was too young to have been eligible to be appointed and feared that I would be sacked. ASSET, with its tiny office staff (all eleven of us), at that time claimed 11,000 members, of whom perhaps 8,000 were paying. But ASSET had grand pretensions. It proclaimed that 'the foreman is the forgotten man in industry', the same slogan used a generation later for so-called 'middle management'. All gone now.

ASSET had an odd history and like many small organisations attracted colourful and corrupt charlatans, for ever being involved in internal feuding and inquiries into itself. When, less than fourteen years later, I was unanimously selected as General Secretary of a slowly changing union, I radically warmed and

16

speeded up the process of change. We needed it. The 'foreman's union' had originally been formed by railway workshop supervisors in 1917 and even forty years later I would address meetings of bowler-hatted men with gold watch-chains and waxed moustaches.

In 1947 Clement Attlee's Labour government, after its landslide victory at the end of the war, was putting through its sweeping programme of nationalisation and new social services against a background of post-war economic problems made more acute by the ending of the US 'Lend-lease' aid and now the prolonged icy winter of 1946–47. The coal mines had been nationalised at the start of the year and the railways were due to follow in January 1948. Faced by fuel and food shortages and rising inflation, the Chancellor of the Exchequer, Sir Stafford Cripps, introduced draconian measures to curb wages and spending. The Conservative Party, though still demoralised, was starting to research and draft: part of the older top echelon of trade union leaders had moved across on to the new public corporation boards. The Labour Attorney-General, Sir Hartley Shawcross, was saying that 'we are the masters now'.

In many ways the lower levels of trade union administrators saw themselves as agents of Labour ministers. This was not very often put into words, but I can recall the district secretary of a craft union saying in the Birmingham Trades Council, in an argument against a strike, 'Look, this used to be all right, but *our* people are in there now and we have got to back them up.' This had the effect of cooling down wage arguments.

As I trudged, badly fed, around the streets of Midland cities, living first in a garret with a gas ring, using surplus pressurised 'bombs' left over from the Burma war to keep down the bed bugs, I was troubled and confused. Apologetically dogmatic, I could not cope theoretically with the idea of Crippsian wage restraint in large, privately owned, monopolistically inclined engineering plants. The whole concept seemed wrong.

In retrospect I believe that it was the wage freeze phase of the 1945–50 Labour government which damaged it deeply amongst working people and contributed to its eventual fatigue and disintegration. The steps taken to deal with profits and non-wage incomes such as those derived from the control of capital were obviously ineffective. The wage and salary earners took the brunt, the incomes the workers lost went for ever. The profits tended to stay locked up in the companies, helping to excite takeover bids a decade later, or were repatriated to other countries. This happened more than once before Labour's catalytic defeat in the General Election of 1979.

The ease with which the post-war unions accepted this situation, and their passivity, was quite remarkable. The formal deed was done at the Special TUC Conference of Executive Committees of Affiliated Organisations held at Central Hall on 24 March 1948. An interim report by the General Council on the economic situation was circulated at the end of December 1947 and the final version – a 5,500-word document entitled 'Prices, Wages and Exports', later published as 'A Policy for Real Wages' – was sent out only ten days or a fortnight before the Conference. The General Purposes Committee (which effectively administered such events) recommended absolutist procedures for the conduct of the day's business, which were to give the General Council a certain victory. Delegates would vote for or against the report and no finessing.

The conference opened at 10.00 am, adjourned for ninety minutes at lunch and voted at 4.45 pm. A decision which effectively restrained national wage moves for two years was taken after five and a quarter hours' discussion, of which an hour and ten minutes was absorbed by two General Council speeches and fifteen minutes was scheduled for consultation within the separate executive committee delegations. After this, as laid down in the procedures: 'The speaker replying to the debate on behalf of the General Council . . . should conclude by moving the acceptance of the Report, which will be formally seconded, and the vote will then be taken on the straight issue for or against acceptance of the Report.'

Amendments were not permitted, which was particularly unsatisfactory. When one delegate asked if it would be possible during the adjournment for the General Council to consider an amendment, the Chairman's response was: 'No. It has been made very clear that you vote either for or against the recommendations before you.'

There were 1,500 delegates; from the floor came ten critical speeches and only four speeches in support (two of which were made by General Council members and another by a member of the National Executive Committee of the Labour Party. But the vote in favour of the document was 5,421,000 to 2,032,000: classic self-inflicted defeat.

The tide of the argument ran hard against the General Council, and the question of profits was raised time and time again. In an effort to stem the flow, although the vote was never in doubt, Arthur Deakin, General Secretary of the Transport and General Worker's Union, stressed that the government could not be charged with failing to carry out a Socialist policy:

> Our friends representing the mining community, electricity supply, transport and other industries which have been brought, and will be brought, within the ambit of public services know that they have got a far better deal out of the recent transition than they could have got out of any other circumstances. . . But you say it is not wages that should come first, it is profits and prices. That is all right as far as it goes, but where do you start: which comes first? How can you practically deal with an issue of this character? You have heard reference to the effect of wage contents in cost of production, plus that of the production costs of raw materials, and I say you can do very little about it unless you are prepared to make an effort by way of stabilisation for a period of time that will enable the government to grapple in an effective manner with the question of prices and profits.

This emphasis on wage restraint *first* damaged union membership morale, but more amongst the full-time officials than the shop elites. Throughout the period, wages 'drifted' up by around 4 per cent annually. 'Drifted'? What really happened is that the shop stewards went in to their managements and said 'Let's adjust the prices' and they did. Power flowed to those actively doing something about wages and conditions, which is why most workers are in unions anyway. They did not join for abstract reasons.

At the fateful TUC Conference, Sam Watson, speaking for

the Executive Committee of the National Union of Mineworkers, drew horrifying parallels with the past, recalling the terrific slash in miners' wages afer the First World War and after the 1926 General Strike:

> As a result of that we went through two decades of bitterness and gall until they brought this Labour government into office, and you as our employers decided to give us a fair deal. I am therefore fully alive to all that is involved in this, and we are still prepared to accept our responsibility, because in our view this is the solution to the continuation of social democracy under the leadership of this Labour government . . .
>
> As far as the Mineworkers' Executive is concerned we feel that, realising all the difficulties involved, we must face up frankly to our responsibility and not blame the Labour government and not blame the General Council of the TUC, but as an organisation representing 700,000 men and boys be big enough and courageous enough to go to the men and tell them quite frankly . . . 'Gentlemen, the situation in this country at the moment is such that we are advising you not to press that claim, and we do that for this reason, that the events of the next few months are not on our side', because this crisis will deepen and get worse, and as it deepens we will be confronted with alternatives quite dissimilar from those which we have the opportunity to accept this afternoon.

He concluded emotionally:

> Rather than lose this Labour government, I would go to my own men in my own country and advocate the reduction of wages. But we are not confronted with that. We are confronted with the question of whether we are prepared, as individual unions comprising this great Trades Union Congress, to accept our own responsibility. We are prepared. We know the difficulties but we welcome the opportunity because this will, for the first time in our history, give the trade unions some opportunity to be practical in their approach to the economic problems concerning this Conference.

It seems hard to believe now that what was being advocated was wage and salary restraint in a situation where there was no real control of prices and profits. As Ian Mikardo pointed out for our tiny Association of Supervisory Staffs, Executives and Technicians (he was then Labour MP for Reading), the statement that the greatest pressure on prices was wages, made bluntly and without reservation, was extremely misleading. There was an idea that workers' wages were causing the greatest demand on goods in the shops:

Inflation has been defined as a condition in which too much money is chasing too few goods; but . . . whose money is chasing what goods? When I walk down Broad Street, Reading, on a Saturday afternoon and see the wives of the agricultural workers and railwaymen who are trying to run a home and sustain a family generally on less that £5 10s a week and sometimes on less that £5 a week, with present price levels, I do not think those women, as a lot of people would have us imagine, are walking with their handbags stuffed full of pound notes, looking desperately and in vain for some goods on which to spend those pound notes.

He criticised the General Council's report for not looking more at the relationship between wages and profits, and for its vague references to the stabilisation and control of profits. 'Nowhere in considering this question of profits is there any reference to profit margins – the percentages allowed to manufacturers, to wholesalers and retailers under the existing price control schemes.' The margins of profit in the price control orders announced by Harold Wilson – who had succeeded Cripps as President of the Board of Trade in 1947 – 'were fixed so widely that even the most inefficient could get by and if that is so, those who are more efficient with the same margins must make a hell of a lot of profit. It is out of that hell of a lot of profit that this inflationary pressure is coming.' Without an assurance that the government would fix profit margins at a lower level, rather than at the present percentage 'designed to subsidise inefficiency', he called for the General Council's report to be rejected.

Vincent Tewson, the TUC General Secretary, did not reply

directly to these points. He had a leaden delivery and was surely the weakest ever General Secretary. His deputy, the greatly over-rated George Woodcock, was contemptuous of him and sometimes would not talk to him for long periods. But his speech had some highly emotive passages:

> . . . this Labour government is our government. Think of the years of struggle we have had to achieve it . . . allegations are made that the people we have sent there, our own Cabinet, are fools, knaves and traitors. That is not the view of this Movement or of the electors or anyone in the solid basis of opinion upon which our Movement is based. You will notice that here we have no Ministers present at all. The General Council was determined that this thing [the wage freeze] should be fought out entirely by the General Council in an industrial conference on an industrial issue entirely upon its merits and it is as that that we intend to fight it out.

The only propositions that he could make on prices and profits were that:

> there is no authority in this country which could hope to restrain demands for wage increases within the limits proposed unless vigorous and successful efforts were made to put a limit to profit and price increases. We are agreed on that point. We state it in the Report . . . In the General Council's recommendations, we give the pledge that immediately after the Budget, the Special Committee will meet and also at regular intervals, to keep in touch with the position. We have gone further than that. It has already been determined that these matters shall be the subject of special consideration by our ordinary Economic Committee as a day to day matter.

History has shown just how unsuccessful were these efforts. The sacrifices were made by the workers, who were quite inadequately led. The Engineering and Allied Employers National Federation, now a shadow of its former authoritative presence, commented frankly on this situation in its much-neglected angry pamphlet, 'Looking at Industrial Relations':

Lend-lease was discontinued almost overnight with the end of the war and import prices began to rise faster than export prices. The first instalment of the Welfare State added to the government's embarrassment with its trade union supporters and chief financial backers. The policy of wage constraint outlined in the 1948 White Paper on Personal Incomes, Costs and Prices, was the inevitable sequel to the growing threat of an inflationary spiral . . .

The TUC listened to a lecture on economic restraint from the Chancellor of the Exchequer in its Margate Conference in September 1948 without outward resentment and for two years, the loyalty of the trade union movement to the Labour government was such that few major claims were pressed for more than a nominal amount . . .

From January 1948 to September 1950 retail prices rose twice as much as wage rates, but living standards were generally maintained by the incidence of overtime and the return of married women to work . . .

When a change of government came in the autumn of 1951, the country could look back on an enviable record of good industrial relations for the five and a half years since the end of the war.

This was published in 1959 as an obvious warning to a Conservative government to stay out of wage disputes and leave the employers unfettered. It shows vividly the inadequacy of the TUC's 'Prices, Wages and Exports' report, with its strong recommendation that trade unions 'exercise even more moderation and restraint than hitherto in the formulation and pursuit of claims for wage increases'. This could only come from 'a recognition by workpeople in general and by responsible Trade Union executives, in particular, of the economic and financial consequences of constant increases in wage rates unaccompanied by corresponding increases in output'.

The TUC Special Committee admitted to difficulty in accepting the government's policy on incomes, costs and prices but had been won over by a meeting with Attlee and various Cabinet ministers on 11 February 1948 when 'they were able to clarify some of the White Paper's rather ambiguous references to future wages increases and received greater assurances than we had hitherto had from the government about the steps the government proposed to take in the matter of prices and profits'. The committee concluded in its report that 'the principles of the White Paper relating to wage movements are acceptable to the Trade Union Movement'.

It is almost inconceivable that the trade union movement should ever have placed itself in such a clearly inferior position in a mixed economy where the rules of the market-place were so obviously potent and 'workpeople' (who were the other 'people'?) were so inferior and pliant. But the leadership did: and I have stressed this point because lightning kept striking in the same places over the years of several Labour governments.

The only period in which there has been a really effective wage freeze was when the unions co-operated with the Labour government up until 1950. Their helpful 'freezing' activity may well have contributed to Labour's subsequent General Election defeat in 1951 because it was really an unplanned loyalist reaction in an inherently unplanned economy. The union member, paying his money to get more, actually paid in order to get less in many cases. Is it any wonder, or any cause for criticism, that power flowed then to the local elected union committees?

The whole situation in 1948–50 made for great difficulty for a union organiser. What unique selling proposition did he have to offer? 'Join us and we'll all freeze together when we freeze?' It was particularly difficult in the almost virgin white-collar field, where all but a handful of the potential recruits had never been in unions and needed an inducement to join. Anyway, I wanted to negotiate something for them: they were not getting their share.

I was used in debate (and I negotiated this way, I knew no other) to use active words, to abrade the enemy's case. My verbs were meant to hammer or slice or, at least, to lend a sense of irresistibly logical forward movement to my own argument. But these tactics were useless, irrelevant in a situation where interruptions in production were thought anti-national.

Most of the trade union officials in the Labour Party felt this way; we felt a responsibility, too, for Stafford Cripps's 'Battle of Production'. My own union even organised meetings for Board of Trade efficiency experts to talk to workshop supervisors. I still remember the shock and resentment that many felt when the Communist Party undertook a major shift in its industrial line and raised the slogan in 1948 'Production for What?'. For this was only a short time after Arthur Horner, a lifelong Communist leader, had been in charge of raising the production of coal on behalf of the National Union of Mineworkers by meetings throught the country.

This classless, patriotic drive for increased production overlaid and muffled class antagonisms after the war, and many of the younger union officers had a difficult and confusing time. It was made even more complicated by the steadily degenerating financial condition of the country and the endorsement of restraints on wages from minor trade union leaders, often in office simply by seniority.

The wage-freeze meetings of 1948 were a watershed for me: they steered my economic thinking firmly to the left, and deeply influenced me in later opposing the 'income policies' of the Wilson and Callaghan governments. Income policy will be a central issue lying between the leadership of the unions and future Labour governments, but it could be on a quite false basis. The General Council of the TUC, in the post-war Labour governments, were quite wrong in persuading union executives to accept restraint in claims, with hints or promises that something would be done about incomes other than those obtained as wages, salaries and pensions. Bluntly, this did not come off.

The Conservative political centre agreed with my analysis here, for quite dissimilar reasons. As their pamphlet, 'More about the Trade Unions' by David Clarke, puts it:

Wage restraint was a necessary and practicable policy as a temporary expedient in the situation of 1948, and at other periods of crisis. It helped to control the situation until long-term remedies could become effective. Unfortunately, the government never produced effective long-term remedies. Instead, they cast upon the TUC the greater part of the burden of maintaining economic stability which should be one of the prime duties of government. The government at least had the power to achieve stability, if not the will. The TUC had not the same means. In the result the government has done far-reaching harm to the trade union movement and has held back their leaders' efforts for greater productivity. Nothing has so divided the leadership from the rank and file nor so created dissension between the craft and the general and industrial unions.

A future political initiative here – and it *will* be necessary – must take account, from the beginning, of incomes derived from rent, interest, dividends, speculation and the deployment of capital resources. The capital owner is in an entirely different and infinitely more privileged position than the wage earner in a steel mill. During the 1948–50 wage freeze period company shareholders not only had their dividends but the value of their shareholdings also went up because the money remained within the companies: the wage freeze restrained consumption only within the working class.

In a future central incomes policy it simply will not be enough either by persuasion or controls of some kind or another to deal with one sector of incomes and promise action on the others in a consecutive fashion. It will have to be simultaneous.

3

The First Major
Dispute and Early
Campaigns

It now seems extraordinary that foremen in the 1950s and early 1960s were thought to be special representatives of the employers. They were praised as part of an illusory 'middle management' group and yet were scandalously paid to a point where they commonly earned far less than the workers they supervised after incentive payments and overtime (which the foremen usually did not get). The workers were not very interested in such a job and only took promotion from time to time for the benefits of holidays and pension schemes.

The engineering union branches would often refuse their foremen members the right to attend meetings (unless they were 'branched' as a result of a complaint from workers they supervised). Consequently, foremen usually left the engineering union, which secretly tolerated some of them belonging to the anti-union Foremen and Staffs Mutual Benefit Society. But this was still the time of the song 'The working class can kiss my arse, I've got the foreman's job at larst'. All that meant was that he might get 'superannuation' and not be laid off during a strike.

The foremen (men – very few women) were socially aggrieved and ripe for organisation. But how to accomplish it? How to heighten an awareness that their worries were not unique – that they *could* band together. White-collar workers in general had no real organisation or representation outside local government and the civil service. The brilliant David Lloyd George had

27

instigated an enquiry under H.J. Whitley in 1919 to look into the representation of staffs employed by central and local government, as a result of which the Whitley Councils emerged as joint bodies of employers and employees. It became respectable for such staff to belong to a trade union, which led to deep organisation in Town Halls and in the civil service organisation, which was carried through, after some key nationalisation acts, into the new public corporations. But in private enterprise as a whole it was a desert.

Attempts to organise foremen in the Midlands met with quite hysterical responses from employers. I recall going to the old Standard Motor Company in Coventry in the early 1950s at a time when foremen were earning so much less than their chargehands and toolmakers that they decided to take a desperate step of joining a union. I organised a branch and went back to the first branch meeting a week later to be turned away by security guards and told that the meeting in the canteen had been cancelled by Sir James Black – who was in other ways an innovative director of the company. I later learned that he had called a meeting of all the supervisors, had given them a substantial increase in pay and enrolled them into the Foremen and Staffs Mutual Benefit Society, which prohibited its members from becoming members of a trade union, (and which we had to deal with by parliamentary action in the early 1970s).

So all the application forms were ripped up and my toe-hold in Standard Motors disappeared. I was stricken – and outraged. I resolved to reverse all this, and I did.

Over the years the same kind of thing happened from time to time in the automotive industry until it was possible to establish that people were more secure and better paid in our union. The manual workers' unions had almost a contempt for the foreman and clerical workers were treated as quite unimportant. Who had heard of computerisation then? It was an unhealthy attitude and it was only the political sense of some of the Communist shop-stewards' convenors, who in the old Communist Party tradition could fix almost anything, which helped me. I was thus able to go after the Austin Motors complex with the help of the shop-stewards and their canny longstanding Communist convenor, Dick Etheridge.

This was at a time when I was for four years in the British Communist Party. It was a Party rich in intellectuals, historians, doctors, professors and old-guard trade unionists who were held in awe by the otherwise middle-class members. The Secretary of the Birmingham District of the Communist Party, Bill Alexander, had been in the British battalion of the International Brigade in the Spanish Civil War and on his return to Britain had joined the British army to fight fascism, becoming an officer cadet and winning the Sword of Honour at Sandhurst. He sent me to a fellow brigadier who was the Secretary of the then powerful Coventry District Committee of the Confederation of Shipbuilding and Engineering Unions. This was Jack Jones, later to be the General Secretary of the Transport and General Workers' Union (and a Companion of Honour), who was building a base in Coventry by organising engineering workers who were not deemed to be skilled enough for the Engineering Workers' Union. He was one of the many leaders of trade unions who came through the heartland of British engineering in the Midlands, now a sorry and devastated area but in those days its automotive industry was looked upon as the engine for the whole of the British economy.

Jack Jones helped me and gave me contacts, although he did not really care about organising my 'fringe' groups (who were later to become 'core' groups). I reminded him of this forty years later when he had become the Chairman of the National Museum of Labour History and I was handing over my collection of printed General Strike material to it (collected by the boys of Bishop Snow's House at Eton and me). He said he thought it was one of his mistakes. I questioned him about his political responsibilities in the Major Attlee battalion and the stories that he had been a Commissar. He replied, 'A very modest little Commissar, I was really just a shop-steward for the lads.' He was an extraordinarily powerful trade union figure. His detractors say he supported the flawed Callaghan government's wage policies too long. He was humiliated at his own union's conference. But was he wrong? I doubt it now. In Tony Benn's *'Against the Tide'* diaries he notes a security report sent to him as a Secretary of State declaiming Jack to be a Communist. He did not tell Jack about the report, but Barbara Castle did.

In 1950, when I had built up some organisation in the East and West Midlands, there was an event which changed my and the union's life. There was a charming official called Sanders, known to everyone as Sandy, based at ASSET's Mayfair head office in Park Street (when I first saw it there was a hole in the top floor where an incendiary bomb had burned its way through). He was a long-time Communist Party member, as was quite common in white-collar unions – no one else was willing to do the work or believed in it – and he had a repertoire of anti-fascist jokes and little songs such as 'If short-sighted people wear glasses should fascists wear glass hats?' He had the responsibility of trying to organise the newly emerging airlines after the Labour government had created three separate airlines based upon pre-war patterns: British European Airways (BEA), which took into account such organisations as Railway Air Services in the thirties; British Overseas Airways Corporation (BOAC), which was essentially the old Imperial Airways and its rival British Airways; and British South American Airways (BSAA), which later collapsed after unexplained losses of its Tudor aircraft over the South Atlantic. Sandy's experience was virtually zero and he was rooted entirely in the 1930s. He collapsed under the strain.

I was summoned from Birmingham to pick up whatever threads there were and to begin my lifelong love affair with airlines. Heathrow in those days was tiny and some freight forwarding was still being done out of bell tents. ASSET had about 700 members throughout the British Airline Corporations, of whom most were at the engine-overhaul plant at Treforest in Glamorgan, which had been established during the war with a view to diversifying away from London and also to provide jobs for miners who had been disabled in the pits. We had an Airways National Advisory Council and the National Executive Committee appointed Ian Mikardo to be its Chairman, with me as its Secretary.

By 1951 ASSET had a large group of supervisory and technical workers well organised in BEA and BOC, though we had lost some of the BSAA personnel, who were scattered around the world. The problems of differentials were just as acute in this state-owned, relatively high-technology industry as they were elsewhere, and we were convinced that the workers were all underpaid. Our claims were resisted strongly by BEA and BOAC, their managements still conditioned by the political directives that they had received from successive Labour Chancellors. I still recall my surprise that when the spokesman for the employers was faced with our salary claim to put this right, he simply said 'No, we cannot do that' and sought to go on to the next item of business on the agenda. This was in 1951 after the TUC had finally given up on support for Sir Stafford Cripps's rigid wage restraints which had so harmed the Attlee government. Aneurin Bevan had been moved from Health to the Ministry of Labour at the start of the year, resigning four months later citing disagreements over health service charges and military expenditure, and Alfred Robens became Minister of Labour.

When our Airways Council met in June in a committee room of the House of Commons, we had to decide between three propositions: should we make another approach to the employers? Or refer the dispute to the Industrial Court? Or recommend our members to work strictly to the terms of their agreement and the regulations of the corporations? The last proposition meant dispute action with an incalculable result: we had never tested it. ASSET had never had a large-scale and highly public dispute action.

As we went around the table for opinions, the Chairman, Ian Mikardo (still Labour MP for Reading at the time), asked me for my view. I thought the situation completely deadlocked, and I was not satisfied that the Industrial Court would bring any result. The situation in the country was warming up on salaries, and I plumped for 'a policy of blood and fire'. He then went around the other members of the committee and each in turn said 'blood and fire' without any further comments.

This was our first major dispute and we approached it apprehensively and even with a certain nervous flippancy. We were anxious to avoid doing any gratuitous damage to the Airways Corporations, feeling very responsible for the newly nationalised industry, so we started the first 'adherence to the agreement' dispute at the Renfrew Maintenance Base in Scotland. This was following an emergency meeting of our representatives which had taken place during the annual conference of the union, held that year at the Butlin holiday camp at Filey. Counsels were divided. Executive staff, in particular, felt that following the rules as part of a battle was unfair and alien.

The Renfrew Branch accepted the instructions, but felt unhappy that we were seeking only a limited demonstration: they were uneasy and wanted everybody in. But by this time we had become convinced that BOAC and BEA management views on the situation (Sir Miles Thomas on one side and Lord Douglas on the other) diverged very considerably. We therefore decided not to take any action against BOAC and I informed all our branches on 3 July that folowing our letter of 13 June, which the employers had not acknowledged, a further letter had been sent informing them that the Airways Council of ASSET would seek the authority of the Executive Council to instruct our members to work to the strict definition of their duties. Discussions had subsequently taken place. Meanwhile, 'all engineering groups and branches are asked to progress their detailed plans for any contingency which may arise and despatch them at once to Head Office. If we are compelled to take this action we will start with one base first and extend, should this be necessary.' I stressed that bases would be informed individually of when they were required to implement the plans submitted to Head Office, which would be by cabled authority under my signature. And I concluded: 'Discipline is vital. The rules must be strictly observed and we shall win.'

The response of our members exceeded our estimate and they went to it with a will. An initial report from Renfrew said:

> The first day of our 'Work to Rule' has been encouraging. All members, with a few expected exceptions, have co-operated. Examples: a shop with a daily output of ten wheels released one wheel – Compass Bass has been snagged and is now awaiting Survey – Hydraulic Section clocked many hours against equipment. We will try to furnish statistics in later letters. We are meeting some obstructions by 'higher-ups' namely our Acting Inspector in Charge, who has granted a number of concessions . . . Aircraft on-ground overtime is being strictly adhered to.

It was said that they were so enthusiastic that the inspectors not only attached red 'reject' labels to all suspect parts, but one was seen tying them to telephones and it was rumoured that one had been pinned to the works manager's dustcoat as well as to strategic door knobs.

The other workers on the shop floor joined in the fun. After the work-to-rule had been running for several days and piles of components began to mass on the benches and aircraft began to acquire an uncared-for look, the ASSET members came in at 8.00 am, to find that there were flowers hanging from the propellers, 'weeds' were growing around the equipment and sprays of leaves could be seen poking out from between the components. This was a gay but gentle hint that the operative workers' bonus was being affected by our dispute and the time had come to intensify it. We did.

As BEA was still maintaining a much more rigid attitude than BOAC, we turned our attention to the BEA base at Northolt, following a tactic I had noted with interest: the 'rolling' strike which had been developed by certain Italian unions, giving the maximum effect with the minimum of strike payment. BOAC members were keen to join in and one branch wrote to me in a vexed way saying: 'BOAC orders are so numerous and many so petty that a conscientious "worker to rule" might well overlook a rule known to another member and this might throw doubts as to his zeal.' They wanted to stop the lot: we held them in reserve.

We moved the dispute to the BEA Northolt base to the great satisfaction of all the members there, and to the immense perturbation of the management, who became greatly excited and started issuing voluminous press statements which only the most tolerant copy taster on the national newspapers could have read. After all, it was the *first* airline dispute in history. Our friends on the newspapers read juicy bits to us and we drafted pithy counterpoints. Notice-board announcements at one stage were coming to us by union despatch riders.

BEA then committed the error of chartering aircraft from BOAC to handle eight services a week to Copenhagen, Nice and Zurich. Our members at London Airport responsible for these on the No. 1 line sharply protested and declined to handle the aircraft. This resulted in ASSET inspectors approaching a row of Argonauts, working busily on the first two and sitting on the wings of the third, discussing the merits of the dispute. In the end BOAC found it convenient to tell us exactly which aircraft were being chartered in order that we did not do this to all the aircraft at the same time. As we said to the lads, 'if you've picked them up, put 'em down'.

The dispute developed towards what Peter Masefield, then Chief Executive of BEA, called 'the lost weekend' (when forty-two services were cancelled after an earlier fifty had already been lost); it was nevertheless a record traffic month in BEA's history up to this point. On 24 July, the Corporations and ASSET were invited to meet the Minister of Labour, Alfred Robens (later Chairman of the Coal Board). In those days Ministers of Labour were expected to intervene and settle disputes, a role which various ministers persisted in until the early 1980s.

We found out some years later that BEA's embarrassment at the Ministry was because they had done their sums wrongly, and that in calculating their answer to our wage claim they had left one figure out of their estimates which, in fact, almost bridged the gap between us. Whether or not the Minister was aware of this, the post-mortem over the years has made it fairly obvious that he was sharply critical of the way the situation had been handled, and he urged direct negotiations that night, saying in open session that the Corporations should have known that the government's policy of wages was under review and there was no desire to penalise unions who had had their wages 'frozen' as a result of the economic difficulties of the years before. He strongly criticised a BEA statement that 'their adviser had said that there was no room for negotiations' and also a lame assertion by a BEA director that they had developed a policy of deliberately going to arbitration because only an industrial court could be 'up-to-date' on industrial figures and BEA preferred *them* to award. It was all very well thinking this, but fancy saying it there!

Alf Robens wanted the aircraft off the ground. He had the chance to make a reputation and in a quite fundamental statement he said that it was government policy that industry should reach its own settlements providing they took account of the quarterly economic surveys. He took the view that there was a leeway in the industry to reach the settlement. He said that if the parties had got to a stage where ASSET wanted 15 per cent and BEA were offering 12½ per cent, that was the sort of issue which might go to the industrial court, but a situation where the unions made a good case for 15 per cent and the employers were sticking on 5 per cent should clearly *not* go to arbitration. This represented a positive shift towards us. Sir Miles Thomas, the Chairman of BOAC, intervened decisively at this point and said that the area of disagreement could be narrowed still further and admitted that BOAC's attitude had been 'shaded' by BEA's insistence on going to the industrial court. He said he much preferred a situation where wage claims were settled domestically – he had always tried to do this when in management at Morris Motors – and that the industrial court would be entitled to send back references such as BEA were seeking to make to it. He stated that he did not consider the major part of the claim as 'unreasonable'.

We were home and almost dry. We looked at each other and decided to withdraw, when we argued in a heated way amongst ourselves about our tactical approach. We finally decided not to compromise at that stage but to seek an immediate meeting on the premises. As I was so junior, I had to rely on Ian Mikardo's support against my own General Secretary, a muddled Buddhist and Moral Re-armer, and our National Officer, an ILP and Communist Party member who was later to resign and go off to sell encyclopedias door-to-door. (The ministry pointedly declined to offer us any refreshment to help sharpen our wits; we had to make our own commercial arrangements with members of the ministry staff, i.e. we bribed them.)

We had our meeting and a complete settlement was reached very near to our original terms. It had been a new type of dispute for us: the first national high visibility battle for ASSET. The employers had been caught on one leg – and they had divergent interests. Government policy was changing. But that was too late for the autumn 1951 General Election.

Ian Mikardo drove me away from the ministry (in his open Morris Minor: he never locked it because he thought thieves would break the locks) and said, 'I hope we never have to do that again, but if we have to, at least we have learned a few lessons'. So we had, and they have come in immensely useful since. I was blooded and went back to my basement office in Park Street late at night to send all the telegrams announcing the victory and explaining that we could now go back to disobeying all the rules.

The employers later slightingly referred to the 'Robens folly' (though only while there seemed no immediate possibility of the return of a Labour Party member to the Ministry of Labour). During the course of the meeting, the Minister had underlined the need for adequate differentials for skill in a sensible and constructive way, and this dictum was constantly used from that day onwards. Most of the employers' leaders concerned are now dead but the union still administers some of the principles.

These were important discussions during which principles were laid down for almost two decades, yet all that the public knew about it was a brief press statement: 'British Overseas Airways Corporation, British European Airways Corporation and the Association of Supervisory Staffs, Executives and Technicians expressed their appreciation to the Minister of Labour for summoning them to a meeting today.' The statement went on:

> Following this meeting negotiations were resumed and agreement was reached on the working methods and remuneration of the members of ASSET employed by the Airways Corporations.
>
> During the course of the meeting reference was made to the statement issued by BEA on the 23rd July, and it was made clear that the statement was not intended to impute any improper motives to the Officers of ASSET.
>
> Normal working will be resumed in BEA tomorrow morning but it will be some days before all BEA services can be fully resumed. BOAC services, which have been unaffected during the dispute, will continue to run normally.

The whole exercise was an example of groping towards a pressure-group tactic which in the political circumstances of that time proved highly successful. It caused the cancellation by BEA of more than 800 fully booked services and cost BEA some £150,000 – a great deal of money in those days. Out of it grew a strong, well-integrated white-collar technicians' and supervisors' organisation with a very high visibility which rapidly extended into the administrative and executive grades in air transport.

The dispute was well timed and was followed, interestingly, by a statement by the Chancellor of the Exchequer, Hugh Gaitskell, on 26 July when he said: 'The trade union leaders made great efforts in difficult circumstances to pursue a policy of wage restraint which we all agree contributed very greatly to our national recovery: but they made it plain that they could not continue the policy of extreme restraint which followed devaluation, nor do I think this would have been possible or reasonable.'

This was my first major national dispute and gave me my first sense of real satisfaction as a collective bargainer. I was twenty-four years old. Deeply influenced by this set of events, I learned that it was possible to have disputes which were immensely interesting to the public as well as being attractive to potential members as long as they were in high technology industries. Over the next decades I attempted to pioneer all sorts of new advances for working men and women which were based upon my airline experience. Although this faded as computer technology became a new battleground, we were able to push the earnings of supervisors and technicians in civil air transport into British industry as a yardstick.

Airlines were so important as a component of our union that we gave annual dinners for the nationalised corporations' managements. I remember one in the Washington Hotel in Mayfair, which was attended by Whitney Straight, Deputy Chairman of BOAC and on the board of Rolls Royce, scion of a rich Anglo-American family with a distinguished World War Two flying record. Before the speeches, he was walking down a corridor alongside me when he suddenly spun me into a linen cupboard, saying his relative, Michael Straight, was locked into litigation with him in the United States. 'You used to be in the Communist Party. Can you get me his Communist Party card? That will settle him in America.' I knew nothing of Michael Straight's legal battles with Whitney, whom I had heard supported 'liberal' causes and publications which I believed to be anti-Communist. This was some twenty years before it emerged that Michael Straight had been recruited by Anthony Blunt at Cambridge when he was in the Communist student movement and that he was part of a Soviet underground which included Guy Burgess. I had no idea. I made my excuses and left the linen cupboard. It was also Whitney Straight who introduced me to pink gins. Never again.

In the Cold War climate of the fifties, Communist could be a dirty word and a friend of mine named Don McKernan, a taciturn Scotsman, was smeared by allegations that he was a secret Communist when he ran for election to the executive committee of ASSET in the mid-1950s – and consequently lost. I mentioned this in a discussion about unions with Aneurin Bevin, who said 'Go and see Arnold Goodman. Tell him I sent you.' Who? I had never heard of the celebrated solicitor, later Lord Goodman. He saw Don and me in his office above the *News of the World* in Bouverie Street and we retailed the story. He fitted a cartridge into his fountain pen, the first I had seen of that kind. 'Disgraceful,' he said. 'We shall not permit this.' Nor did he. The libellers were identified: they employed inquiry agents to try to find any link between Don and the Communist Party and failed because Don had never been party political in that sense. He obtained substantial damages. At the beginning, and all through the process, Arnold Goodman never inquired whether Don (or me as his sponsor) had the money to employ him as one of the leading libel lawyers in Britain. He simply was affronted and saw that some justice was done.

At this time I also ran for election to the St Pancras Borough Council, which had a fine history of councillors, among them Bernard Shaw, Krishna Menon (later India's Minister of Defence) and Barbara Betts (Castle). When I moved from Birmingham at the end of the forties, I had rented a flat in Regent's Park Road in north-west London, overlooking the delightful Primrose Hill, and I almost accidentally remained there, after a court case involving the landlady, a rabbi's daughter who traded on her father's honourable reputation to take deposits on flats from numerous duplicated would-be tenants. She went to gaol. I stayed on but without her fat white cat which she used to spray with Chanel No.5. Where I lived there were many architects and lawyers but it was a mixed ward, with nineteenth-century 'railway cottages' for workers (only later to become expensive mews with carriage lamps at the front doors) and a substantial Greek Cypriot community. (My election address was printed in Greek.)

These were the years when the struggle for Cyprus's independence was violent and I remember going down to Goodge Street into the Greek restaurant and patisserie area in an open car with a Greek girl married to a friend of mine. She took the microphone and electrified the streets. The kitchen workers, pants-pressers, pastry-makers – all turned out and cheered. After the tumult I asked her what she had said. 'Vote for Jenkins and hang the English hangmen.' I topped the poll.

I am told they still remember me in St Pancras for other reasons. As Chairman of the Council's Staff Committee I led the fight to get sanitary inspectors regraded. This was a serious point. London was out of step with surrounding local authorities, we were losing vital qualified people and in St Pancras we had a huge daytime population with three 'ports', Euston, St Pancras and Kings Cross, all receiving perishable cargoes.

In my term of office, from 1954 to 1960, we had fun and not just running the Red Flag up over the Town Hall on May Day but making every effort to keep down council rents. As a result we were surcharged and when many years later I heard Trotskyists in a Labour Party delegation meeting urging local councillors to break the law and take the consequences of surcharging, I was able to point out that I was probably the only person present who had done just that. It took years to pay off the debts and I don't recommend it – it deflects attention from those responsible for injustices and I recall the anguish of councillors who were also old age pensioners. But it seemed the right thing to do at the time.

More pleasurable was helping to organise a rally at St Pancras Town Hall to 'free Paul Robeson', who because of his left-wing associations was unable to obtain a passport to leave the United States to sing on concert platforms throughout the world and was effectively denied any opportunity to display his incredible talent in the United States itself. There was willing support from various artistes, although some actors took the reactionary view that because Paul Robeson was a Communist he should be refused a stage. One of the rudest replies I got to my letters asking for support was from Sir Donald Wolfit.

At the rally I had suggested that we lease some time on the transatlantic cable so that Paul could sing across the Atlantic to us, which he did, following some very emotional singing by a South Wales miners' choir, in their helmets, performing songs with which he had been associated. The response was so great that we took an immediate collection of money and pledges, and extended the cable lease time so that Paul could sing for a further period.

Eventually, in 1958, Paul got his visa and came to London, where a reception was given for him by Donald Ogden Stewart, the American screenwriter who had written *The Philadelphia Story* for Katherine Hepburn to star in, and his wife, who was the widow of the great 'muck-raking' journalist Lincoln Steffens, who wrote *Shame of the Cities*. Donald, a sweet and funny man, had himself been virtually exiled from America by McCarthyism after having been one of the most acclaimed and highest paid screenwriters in Hollywood, and he and his wife were particularly helpful to us. (Much later, when David Frost was interrogating Nixon on television after Watergate, they asked me to watch the interviews with them; being elderly and easily tired they wanted to watch it in bed, so I sat on the bed beside them and as the trauma of Watergate was re-investigated and their chief hounder and persecutor was wriggling under David's questioning, I looked at them. They had fallen asleep. So I crept out.) The Stewarts lived in Frognal, Hampstead, in what had been the home of the first Labour Prime Minister, Ramsay MacDonald, whose full-length photograph – presented to him in 1931 by Kodak as an example of their new technology, and found in the cellar – was brought out to show Paul at his reception. I later saw Paul playing Othello at Stratford-upon-Avon, where he had generously arranged front-row seats for us, and I can still hear the voice rumbling like a minor earthquake.

One could only be humble before this man of enormous talent – athlete, scholar, singer, actor, writer and political agitator.

A more solid monument to the period when I was on the Borough Council were The Nash Terraces in Regent's Park, which were, incredibly, threatened with redevelopment by the Crown. The Labour group hung their ornate silver-gilt badges of office around their necks (after seriously changing the blue silk ribbons for scarlet) and off we went, led by our Mayor, to parade around the threatened Palladian façades with their elegant white statues backed by a blue frieze. We won that one.

Years later I went to one of these hugely expensive mansions for the first time, to a reception for a foreign Communist Party leader. The host, who lived there, was Phil Piratin, only the second Communist Party MP (the first, Saklatvala, in the mid-1920s also had a Labour endorsement) elected to join the genial and courageous Willy Gallacher, who had sat in the Commons through the growing build-up of fascist aggression, rearmament and then World War Two. But when Willy came to address a small political seminar in my flat in Regent's Park Road, he devoted much of his opening to his regrets that he would never see 'a proper tunnel under the Clyde in my lifetime'. Also there that evening was the legendary Wal Hannington, then a national organiser of the engineering union but renowned as the leader of the national unemployed workers' movement in the 1930s. He had devised the 'tea-in' at the Ritz, attended by hundreds of long-term unemployed all supplied with sixpences to offer to pay for their tea. This guru had a fund of anecdotes and a formidable collection of bound press-cuttings of the 1930s struggles of the unemployed – a true social history of the Depression. I wonder where they are now.

Wal and I happily worked together in civil aviation. We were not competitive: he spurned foremen and I was not at that time after skilled blue-collar workers. So, in the late 1940s we had gone off together in the twilight of his political and trade union life to organise. We were photographed bemusedly among the lovely old BOAC Flying Boats at Hurn on Southampton Water (we even helped to organise a campaign to try to save them as they were such comfortable and delightful craft to fly in. I also felt safer: after all seven-eighths of the world's surface is water).

As a result of some of my union activities during the fifties and of ASSET's growing prestige in airlines, the Soviet Civil Aviation Workers' Union invited ASSET to send a delegation to the Soviet Union in June 1957. I was asked to lead it and as British European Airways were very interested, we added their Works Manager, in charge of maintenance, to our four-man delegation. At this time there was still no direct London to Moscow air link; since the war the journey had involved two airlines and two stops, one of them overnight in Stockholm and one a lunch in Riga. There had been a British government delegation to Moscow to negotiate reciprocal air services in 1955 but since then, simply, nothing had happened. Before leaving I went to see Air Marshal Lord Douglas, the Chairman of British European Airways, to talk about the archaic Cold War situation and agreed that, if possible, I would take a message to the Minister-General who presided over Aeroflot, expressing BEA's continued interest in setting up a direct Moscow-London air route.

Aeroflot, now familiar throughout the world's airports, was then mysterious and secretive. *Reynolds News*, the Co-operative Party newspaper for which I had recently begun to write, was interested in my writing anything that could be found out about the virtually unknown Soviet civil air effort and they funded me to buy a Rollei-flex camera – which in itself was a story. As I was buying film for the new camera, at Selfridges in Oxford Street, I noticed a *Daily Express* leaflet on the counter featuring a dramatic photograph sent in by a reader of a woman jumping from a burning building and asking for readers to send in any other such pictures. A few minutes later when I was driving by Oxford Circus on the way to the BBC, there was a bus up on the pavement on the other side of the road surrounded by pools of oil and bundles of rags. Because it looked interesting for a photograph, I walked back after parking my car at the BBC and with shock realised that there had been a disaster and that the bundles were all dead people – I had never seen any before – and the dark-coloured liquid was blood. Remembering the *Daily Express* leaflet, I started with trembling hands taking pictures until the police arrived on the scene.

After the BBC, I was due to go to *Reynolds News* and when I said to the features editor, 'Something remarkable I think has happened in Oxford Street', he replied, 'Yes, a number of people are dead and it is coming over the tapes now.' There was a great commotion when I mentioned my photographs and it was arranged for me to go immediately to the Blackstone Picture Agency, where they did a printing and enlargement in minutes – some of the photographs were out of focus because my hands had been shaking – and distributed them at once to the newspapers. All the horrific, exclusive press pictures were mine: the professional photographers had arrived too late. I refused a credit because it seemed ghoulish on reflection, but at least the fees provided some money for the Lord Mayor's Appeal Fund. It turned out that the driver had had some kind of seizure and had ploughed into a bus queue.

Armed with my camera, I went off to the Soviet Union and, remarkably, we found that a decision seemed to have been made somewhere to show us everything, possibly because we were the first delegation that had gone into the Soviet Union since the 1956 Hungarian uprising. I used all my trade union contacts. Victor Maximovitch Dinilych, the head of Aeroflot's international department, could not tell me what had happened about the British government approaches, but he did arrange for me to see Lieutenant General Nikita Alexeivitch Zaharov, the Deputy Head of Aeroflot, a huge man in Red Air Force uniform, responsible for Research, Supply and New Projects. He had headed the Aeroflot-USSR government team which had met the BEA-British government delegation.

Zaharov told me, 'When we heard that the British government wanted to establish an air link, we were glad and readily entered the talks at the British invitation. Our proposal was to establish a point of connection at a German airport. We suggested a point in East Germany. The British government did not want this. We suggested Templehof [Berlin]. The British government thought it over. So we then suggested any British RAF field in Western Germany. The British government thought it over again. We spent a long time in adjournments – although the question was as clear as the stars in the sky.' It seemed that there had been obstruction from the Adenauer government but Zaharov dismissed this by quoting the current treaty between the three western powers, Britain, France and the USA, and the West Germans which strictly reserved for the former occupying powers the previous rights in respect of USSR aircraft flying through West German airspace. 'So, what is the problem? A commission of Britain, France and America takes all the decisions on such questions, *not* the West German administration. We know this treaty clause pretty well. Although your Ambassador, Sir William Hayter, wanted to forget it existed.' He added, 'The British government promised to go into all of this for us and said we would hear within five or six days, but we never did.'

As longer-range jets were becoming available, it seemed that the Americans wanted to go on the route but only when they had competitive aircraft without any landings at intermediate airfields. Pan American had already sent a party to Moscow to negotiate a commercial agreement and the mutual honouring of tickets, and they hinted they would be back when they had a suitable aircraft.

It may well be that the Soviets decided to put more pressure on by letting our delegation see all the Aeroflot operations that we wanted to. We travelled throughout the Soviet Union, including central Asia where air travel was essential. They showed us all their impressive new aircraft and either allowed me to take pictures or gave me files. By the time I left Moscow, they asked me to bring the message back that they no longer wanted to have half-way houses; they were only interested in direct flights.

I returned with masses of material and went to see the editor of *Flight*, which, on 2 August 1957, as a trailer, published a sweaty bestubbled photograph of me alongside the 'mighty turbo jet which powers the TU 104'. Their 'most important series of articles on Soviet civil aviation' dominated the next three issues and were editorialised on 9 August:

Once in a while we experience a particular feeling of pleasure in printing an article which we know not just to be a scoop in our line of business, but a significant contribution to technical or industrial knowledge. And if the significance is international, we are not only pleased –

we are satisfied. This week then, we are satisfied because Clive Jenkins' account of Aeroflot is a solid nugget of information which we can be sure will become currency in every country of the world . . . the sheer immensity of Aeroflot is summed up by Mr Jenkins in a few, but weighty, words: 'everything *civil* that is done in the air by the Soviet Union is done by Aeroflot. It has the status of a Ministry and undertakes all those functions which would, in Great Britain, be shared between all the supervisory and ministerial bodies, airlines, the Air Transport Advisory Council and the contractors who build the airports. To this comparison may be added the aircraft purchasing and financing powers of the Ministry of Supply.'

I also brought back verbal and other messages from an Air Marshal who seemed to be the effective Chief Executive and political head of Aeroflot. Lord Douglas arranged for me to lecture his senior managers with my photographs and slides, and then took me aside after a debriefing and said he was going back to the British ministers concerned to seek to reopen the whole issue. Sholto Douglas, who was a Fabian and a compassionate man, (as Commander in Chief of the British zone in Germany he had refused to sign a single death warrant), hammered away at the British government and eighteen months after the first talks had aborted, an agreement was reached.

I was pleased about that. So were the Soviets. My mentor was the legendary Boris Averyanov, later head of the international department of the Soviet trades unions and always described by the *Daily Telegraph* as a 'full Colonel' in the KGB. 'I should be at least a Lieutenant General,' he riposted. *Time* magazine in the Cold War fifties called him one of the ten most dangerous men in the world. He was always a good, courteous, knowing friend. When I went back to have another look at Soviet civil aviation in 1963, General Shetchikov expressed appreciation. The Soviets have long memories and when a British airline wanted some help to over-fly Moscow to the Far East in 1986, I was able to call upon old friendships.

In the late fifties, this trip helped enhance and underpin ASSET's prestige in airlines and aerospace generally, and brought the members in. But the union had a long way to go. In September 1960, when I became acting General Secretary of ASSET, we had about 14,000 members and an income of £65,000 a year. My first task was to see what kind of resources we could bring to making trade unionism for private sector white-collar workers a possibility and then a reality. To overcome their fears we had to *seem* successful and we had to look respectable or even fashionable from the beginning: we had to ride the media waves. Narcissus had a muddy pool to reflect in. I aimed to use the cathode ray tube.

4

Lobbying, Reverses and a Few Victories

At the beginning of the sixties it seemed to me that the wave of mergers and takeovers, resulting in the abrupt and distressing decanting of managers and scientists from their jobs, needed to be addressed in a very new and different way. So I went to the ASSET Parliamentary Committee and raised the whole issue there as to whether we could have in the United Kingdom some kind of protection and compensation for women and men who lost their jobs as a result of national policies entirely beyond their control.

Our Parliamentary Committee had been invented in 1947 by Ian Mikardo, who was the MP for Reading seats from 1945 to 1959 (when he finally lost to Peter Emery, another ASSET member). Mik had recruited MPs to the committee, including Harold Wilson, on the grounds that he was eligible for ASSET membership as an executive advising the timber firm of Montague Meyer on 'trade questions'. Other unions had their own committees of sponsored Members and would meet with them quarterly or annually or sometimes never; while others paid retainers to back-bench MPs (from various parties) to represent their interests where necessary. But our ASSET Parlimentary Committee, due to Mik's initiative and the organisation abilities of him and his secretary, Jo Richardson (later to be come an MP and front-bench spokesperson), became a large and influential regular forum for ideas and discussion. In 1961 I became its secretary and remained so for the next twenty-eight

47

years, although the real engine for it, responsible for all the hard organising work, was Muriel Turner, later a TUC General Council member and an Equal Opportunities Commissioner of distinction, who as Baroness Turner of Camden has become a front-bench Opposition spokesperson on employment in the House of Lords.

When I raised the redundancy issue at our Parliamentary Committee, it was sympathetic and we decided to raise a Ten-Minute Rule Bill from the back benches to test out opinion in the House of Commons. Julius Silverman, then the MP for Erdington in Birmingham, took the lead in it. The initiative received a lot of attention in the media; the Conservatives hated it, and some Labour MPs were doubtful and the Bill did not progress. I asked our Parliamentary Committee to launch more Private Members' Bills on the subject and Harold Wilson, after his election as Leader of the Party in 1963, rang me one day and said he would be willing to give general front-bench support if we had a 'senior member' of our Committee to lead. He suggested Jack Diamond, in his time a Member for the Manchester (Blackley) Constituency and for the City of Gloucester, a Treasury minister and later a defector to the Social Democratic Party, finally in the House of Lords.

Jack Diamond had introduced a Bill in one of the last Parliamentary sessions in 1962, calling for severance pay on the basis of one fifty-second of total earnings in a lump sum for workers dismissed for reasons other than misconduct. Again, the Bill was blocked but the issue was at least being aired and I talked to anyone who would listen and ran press conferences about it.

The TUC was also tinkering with the idea, although really far too late. I can recall my suggestions that we should look into the issue of redundancy and compensation being greeted with horror and cries of 'sell out!'. At the 1962 Trades Union Congress a motion on severance pay had to be withdrawn because we were going to lose it but after much manoeuvring and useless compositing of motions, I was given a chance of seconding a motion from Frank Cousins which instructed the General Council to initiate an enquiry into the whole range of 'fringe benefits', with some exphasis on redundancy procedures and compensation for displaced workers.

The unions were beginning to discuss the issue and the Confederation of Shipbuilding and Engineering Unions had a major clash in June 1963 between those who wanted to have agreements about redundancy and those, backed by the British Communist Party and the traditionalists in the Amalgamated Engineering Union, who felt that 'apart from any matter of principle, a motion that dealt only with compensation was no treatment of the problem and its acceptance would weaken the fight in the workshops'. These were the words of the veteran Communist Claude Berridge; he was supported by Danny McGarvey of the Boilermakers who feared that three million workers would get the impression that the Confederation had accepted the principle of redundancy if it adopted a motion from the Plumbers' Union that there ought to be compensatory payments for redundant workers of a minimum of one month's wages for each year of service. The motion was remitted to the Executive and effectively made no progress whatsoever. McGarvey said, 'Such a policy with its code of rules would give the employers the green light to chop and change when they liked.' This was clearly reactionary nonsense. When we finally got a law about redundancy compensation it was clear that this was not a ceiling but a floor and over the decades ahead ordinary workers did have some protection which ran into many millions of pounds they would not otherwise have had.

I passionately believed that protective labour legislation was either weak or missing in the United Kingdom and when in 1963 the opportunity arose of standing for selection as the Labour party candidate for Shoreditch and Finsbury, I was very interested. It fitted in well with my belief that I could be the General Secretary of a medium-sized union but also initiate legislation on the back-benches. The sitting member for the safe Labour Shoreditch and Finsbury constituency had died and I was approached by a number of trade unions and ward Labour parties to stand for selection. This idea, however, clearly proved unpalatable to some forces and I believe I was the target of a dirty tricks operation.

I was at the 1963 Trades Union Congress in Blackpool when

a journalist came to me and asked whether I had seen a letter about me that was being distributed to the general management committee of the Shoreditch and Finsbury Labour party. At the back of the hall I was then shown a foolscap duplicated document which was utterly defamatory and untrue. It characterised me as the chief Trotskyist in Great Britain, alleged that I had a yacht (actually a small craft moored at the bottom of my garden on the Regent's Canal) and that I was planning the violent overthrow of all the institutions one could numerate in the United Kingdom.

I found out that this letter had widespread circulation, and I went down to the front of the hall to find Ray Gunter, then Chairman of the Organisation Committee of the Labour Party. He expressed horror at this unprecedented event and said, 'I will get you a longer time than the other candidates to speak to the Management Committee.' I declined this on the basis that it would do me harm rather than help me. I then left the hall surrounded by journalists, from whom I learned that the scurrilous document had been handed to them in a bar by Jim Matthews, a national industrial officer of the Municipal and General Workers' Union. He was then a member of the National Executive of the Labour Party and renowned for issuing statements attacking his fellow Executive members and in generally being a nuisance. I suspect he was on retainers from some newspapers. I know that he certainly regularly leaked to the Press private and confidential memoranda from the Labour Party to its Executive members.

I consulted my lawyers and we issued a writ for libel against Matthews. However, not one of the journalists to whom he had handed the document was willing to give a statement to that effect, pleading that he had so much power they were worried about their jobs. I subsequently told them that we would subpoena all of them. In the end the libel action, because of difficulties in getting witnesses, made no progress. Matthews, or his supporters, paid money into court and I took the damages and costs. In the course of this a firm of private investigators had been employed, who finally gave up the job and declined a charge or fee, saying they were up against other agencies with which they could not deal. They were warned off.

One of the likely lines of investigation was a small private news agency in Fleet Street which apparently produced the document, but, again, it was difficult to pin down a named man. Fleet Street had at least two CIA-funded agencies (or was it three?), and I was told by reliable friends that the anonymous letter which had been mailed to every member of the selection committee came from a man who was seemingly a member of the CIA and operating under the cover of a petty news agency. I still wonder how the dirty job was engineered: who provided the up-to-date list of addresses of the General Management Committee? And why was I so dangerous?

On the selection night, when I looked at the righteous delegates, the General Management Committee, some of whom were knitting away, I realised that they thought that at least some of the letter must be true. Anyway, by a few votes I lost to Ron Brown, the brother of George Brown, who also wore a dark-red tie and matching handkerchief and defected to be a Social Democratic Party MP (briefly). I turned my energies back into the union movement.

During this period up to the 1964 General Election, the Labour Party's programme 'Signpost for the Sixties' suggested: 'Trade Unions have been able to reach satisfactory redundancy agreements with some progressive firms. It is high time that what is now the exception became the rule.' Meantime, the Conservative government had been exhuming and re-interring Rab Butler's 'Industrial Charter', which had argued in favour of individual contracts for workers ever since 1947. A Tory MP, John Rodgers, supported by a number of other back-bench MPs, including Edward Heath, Reginald Maudling and Iain Macleod, also suggested that there should be more protection, arguing that the period of notice should be one week for each year of service. With the 1964 General Election in mind, the Conservative Party ended up working on the principle of one week's basic pay for every year of service and a qualifying period of five years of twenty-six weeks and over, with a multiplication factor of a half week for service between the ages of forty-five and sixty but no benefits after the age of sixty.

By 1964 we had promoted three Private Members' Bills sponsored by different groupings of ASSET MPs. We did our own whipping and briefed MPs in a multi-faceted way, but all the Bills were blocked. I was made more infuriated by the case in Scotland of Mechans Limited, where five foremen and one inspector with service ranging from thirty-seven to forty-one years and aged from fifty-six to sixty-three years were sacked on the spot, in breach of an agreement to consult with us, with only four weeks' salary in lieu of notice. Younger workers were upgraded to charge-hands to fill the vacant posts and while the case was going through the Engineering Employers' procedure, the firm found a job for one foreman and made an ex gratia payment of £25 to the other four and £20 to the inspector. This was outrageous even for a backward Scottish engineering employer. The Engineering Employers were deeply embarrassed by the whole affair and subsequently our members received more reasonable sums of money. This was another milestone on the way to protecting working people and we made the most of it. Who could defend it?

One complication in any proposed legislation on redundancy was the issue of alleged misconduct by a dismissed worker; in 1960, 140,000 workers had been dismissed for alleged industrial misconduct. Someone suggested Industrial Tribunals (now it seems as though they have been there for ever) to deal with this issue, which was also complicated by the question of what a contract for a worker was.

The National Coal Board had, I found, been suing miners for breach of contract for a number of years. The current legal inadequacy to deal with the question was highlighted by an exotic case at Guildford County Court, where an aircraft engineering firm sued two employees, a toolmaker and a capstan operator, who had taken four days off without permission to run a 'book' at the Royal Ascot Race Meeting. The firm had sacked the two men, who sued for the wages they claimed were due to them for the several days' work before the race meeting started. The firm counter-claimed damages for lost production and the judge decided that the men had been guilty of 'gross misconduct' since they well knew that their absence would create great difficulty and financial loss for the company. The judge ordered that the money due to them be deducted from the firm's loss and he also held the men to have been properly dismissed, so found in favour of the company's claim too. The company did not ask for costs. The toolmaker explained that he had been with the firm for more than seven years and that he was a 'spare time bookmaker'. The judge queried, 'Did you boys do well?' The toolmaker replied, 'We lost a lot of money.' The judge said, 'I thought that bookies never lost.'

The whole question of compensation for redundant workers had become live. I went to see Harold Wilson and secured an undertaking from him that the question would be put into the Labour Party Manifesto for the 1964 General Election.

At this meeting one of our few genuine misunderstandings occurred. Discussing the forthcoming General Election, he said, apropos foreign policy, 'I'll send Foot to the United Nations as Ambassador.' I commented, 'That will be a *remarkably* imaginative appointment.' His face glazed, 'No, not Michael, Hugh.'

After the Labour Party victory that October, the government eventually legislated for redundancy compensation, something which is now assumed to have existed almost for ever. But at some union conferences I had been losing my motions on this issue on a scale that has since prompted me to say, 'I used to lose by eight million to two. Not two million. Just me and my seconder.'

Ian Mikardo returned to Parliament in 1964, as MP for Poplar, but he was not given a ministerial position by Harold Wilson, which I thought a loss to government. Mik had great intellectual and organisational powers, as well as being a generous personality with many interests – he was a ballroom dancer, a Talmudic analyst and an excellent management consultant. In his management consultancy days, he related going to advise a clothing factory on efficiency. They offered to make him a suit so that he could follow the garments through the process and when he saw his unsewn trousers on the assembly belt they were chalked 'LDH'. 'What does that mean?' 'It's just a code.' He persisted, 'I need to know.' 'All right – LDH means Large Dance Hall.' Perplexed, he pressed the point. 'It's actually a guide to the cutter – "Big Ball Room"!'

It was typical of him that when in the early 1960s nasty anonymous letters were being circulated about me and I asked whether he had received his, he replied: 'I don't remember. I can't be bothered to read anonymous letters. Straight into the waste-paper-basket.' He loved a wager and bet almost every day of his life. He said he made a steady income, though he always lost when he took me to the races with him, whether that meant the white-robed bookmakers under their umbrellas in Karachi or the very last night at Alexandra Palace where a constituent's wife introduced herself by telling him that her husband hated him. She gave me tips on each race, explaining that her distant husband had 'special information'. So he did. I won and Mik lost. He was cross, but she made her husband buy us all champagne in the wake surrounding the closure of Ally Pally. Mik certainly made money on his 'book' over political elections and would reopen it immediately after each polling day. He said he never gave his wife housekeeping money but told her to keep all she found in his pockets.

Mik was no one's acolyte, though he was very fond of Michael Foot and respected Aneurin Bevan. The Bevanite movement of the fifties owed much to his skills. It used cricketing terms: the First Eleven was made up of Bevanite MPs and the Second Eleven those adopted for or likely to get adopted for constituencies. I don't think there was a category for trade union officials (there were not too many Bevanites among them), but there were loners like the brilliant individualist Sydney Silverman, who spearheaded the drive to abolish hanging but was impossible as a team player. When we formed 'Victory for Socialism' – which did not have a very long effective life – Sydney almost at once walked out. Somehow, he and I nevertheless found ourselves in Varna, Bulgaria, together, where the sea was full of seaweed and he entranced the swimming children by draping it through his white moustache and beard and then giving them tiny tortoises which gypsies brought down in buckets to sell to the tourists. His fair skin became badly sunburnt and I covered him with yoghurt as the local remedy.

It was under Mik's chairmanship that the ASSET Parliamentary Committee became such a large and effective force, until he finally proposed that he step down and The Chair be elected annually. Many ideas were tried out there.

After a discussion on the problems of university technicians and funding, Harold Wilson said that he had been thinking of a

'University of the Air', teaching and awarding degrees by television. What did the Committee think of this? That was the first public mention of what finally emerged as the very successful Open University.

On another occasion Basil de Ferranti came to talk of his work at International Computers. He told a good computer joke, alleging that in Vietnam a commanding general had all the logistics and variables programmed into his HQ computer. He asked the question, 'Do we advance or retreat?' It replied 'Yes.' 'What do you mean – "yes"?' 'Sorry, yes, *Sir.*' Then he went on to make a sharp procurement point, explaining that the Hungarian Academy of Sciences had purchased more ICL equipment than all the British government agencies put together. This was at the height of the influence of the Hungarian-born economists Tommy Balogh and Nikky Kaldor. Julius Silverman interjected, 'You mean *their* Hungarians are better than *our* Hungarians?'

There were many and significant victories in our Parliamentary Committee. I recall receiving a 'round robin' from technicians and scientific researchers working in Glasgow University (I later investigated and think some of them were at the prestigious Beatson Institute). The text of this classic round robin (which does not have a list of signatures but a circle with the names at a tangent to it, so there is no beginning and no end, no ringleaders and no followers) raised fears that our members were being asked to undertake work at the frontiers of science in the field of genetic manipulation and that there were no adequate standards or controls. I asked MPs who, like me, had no concept at that time of the benefits and dangers of this work to raise questions with ministers.

As the issue was gradually ripening in the public and scientific consciousness, the government set up a Working Party chaired by Sir Robert Williams to review the field. Out of it came a supervisory agency, the Genetic Manipulation Advisory Group, which oversees key areas of scientific and commercial activity. This has been very effective and must be the only one of its kind in the world with direct trade union representation. It again showed the unique value of a professionally organised trade union forum in Parliament.

Our agendas over the decades covered all the issues we could not deal with in collective bargaining, moving through industry, education, defence procurement, blood laboratories, everything. The membership was all Labour. Conservatives pleaded they should be allowed to join, but were refused because being rooted in one of the Parliamentary parties beats all-party campaigns. Dr David Owen was dropped from our invitation list when he left the Party. In the eighties, at the time of the ballots to retain union political funds, I encountered him outside the Strangers Bar: he wanted to know why he had not received his ballot paper. I reminded him he had been lapsed for arrears of contribution to the union.

Meanwhile, ASSET was facing hard challenges. In the steel industry we were rolled over by the decrepit institutionalised might of blue-collar union leaders and we had a special problem in ICI where the management did not want to recognise us as the representative of our large membership. We were extremely cross that they were sponsoring an internal staff association and that, as a rather desperate ploy, they had decided to commission a survey of staff 'attitudes' by the Tavistock Institute. We asked the Tavistock not to enter into a dispute situation, but it did and we subsequently blacked them for years because we thought that their attitude had not been responsible.

But there were other features which helped ICI delay giving us recognition. A bundle of correspondence was sent anonymously to a national newspaper correspondent from someone in the office of an International Labour Organisation. It slowly came out that an international civil servant had been accepting fees from ICI in respect of the staff attitude survey, and the documents had been stolen from his office. There had been a clear breach of the principle of tripartitism in the ILO, which demanded a neutral position, and also the independence of the ILO itself was being threatened by this official's action. It appeared the survey results had been misinterpreted against our case. So what to do?

I protested very strongly to ICI on the basis that a great corporation should not lend itself to subterfuge or seek to influence persons in what seemed to be a clearly improper way. We also decided to complain to M. Blanchard, the Secretary

General of the ILO. Ian Mikardo and I went to meet him in Geneva and laid specific charges before him and his legal advisors with all the damaging correspondence and expense claims. It took months before our reminders took effect but eventually this extremely reputable Secretary General telephoned me from New York and said that he had taken steps to deal with the matter as tripartitism had been thought to have been imperilled. The hitherto distinguished international civil servant left the ILO service.

We eventually got our recognition and persuaded people who had been in the ICI Staff Association to join us. But it was a very colourful and difficult story. Whatever did the managers think they were doing – and running such risks? Were we so dangerous, so threatening, to their corporative imperatives?

We had another problem with a major British insurance company when they employed a prominent polling agency which seemed to report after a staff survey that we were unrepresentative. We took it into the courts and the executive responsible admitted some data 'had been adjusted'. His very reputable and now even more influential organisation suffered greatly, particularly as judged by its peer organisations, who took disciplinary action.

The underlying forces creating a climate in which you could appeal to people were now quite clear. The repeated interventions of governments, Labour and Conservative, into collective bargaining, the ineffectiveness of the prices policy and the dampening effect of wages policy – because it was not an incomes policy – made lower middle class people feel that they were being discriminated against. The continued initiatives in the field of legislation, and the threatened penalties for unions and their representatives, enhanced this perception.

At the same time great companies were merging without regard to the interests of their employees. So we pursued every grievance with the utmost zeal. If we wanted to deal with a piratical independent airline and we did not have the muscle to stop them on the ground, I usually objected to the Air Transport Licensing Board. That, however, failed because unions and their members had no such right to be heard, although airlines and aerodrome owners did have rights. We discussed this on our Parliamentary Committee and the bright idea came up that we should buy an airline or an aerodrome – on paper. Jack Diamond said he would look for a shell company and he found one called Trailblaze, which I think he bought off a shelf from a shop in the Strand for £20. It had taken powers in its Articles of Association to operate aircraft for hire and reward, so it suited us precisely. We were corporately in business. This caused immense press interest, and the companies which had given us difficulties, aware that we could now confront them before the licensing authorities, came to terms.

Other companies, where our members were being treated unjustly and where we were lightly organised, also felt us at their annual general meetings. We bought small numbers of shares in all of the companies where we had large numbers of members but also in those companies which had been giving us trouble. In the course of one dispute there were more of our shareholders at a meeting (all holding one share) than the directors and other shareholders. We voted down everything except the date of the meeting. When the proxies were counted we had of course lost but it was another example of doing everything we could, with journalists and photographers there. For a while we used to put somebody up at the annual general meetings of great companies to second the vote of thanks to the staff. This palled after a while, but managements always knew that we were, or could be, there.

We paid special attention to women, as for the first time we had a substantial number of them, especially young women coming from the insurance companies. We had a dispute over a London allowance in Romford, which was very brief because the chain of young women around the building, stopping the computers, cost Lloyds a great deal of money hour on hour.

At the Liverpool Victoria Insurance Company, the extremely vigorous young women marched around and around with posters saying 'Liver Birds Out for Chicken Feed'. They also complained about the cost of cleaning the main building when the company was pleading poverty. When we raised this with the management, they said, 'We regret it, too, some of that soot was from the Titanic.' The young women were very confident and got a good settlement. (I only heard years later that the strike had been prolonged so that I could personally go and settle it.) This was a first, before many of the judgements on equal pay and before the trade union movement so wholeheartedly took the lead. Shamefully I recall one union officer arranging a meeting with another, 'My girl will talk to your girl.'

This was the background to Muriel Turner and me being provoked on a visit to a Japanese motorcycle assembly line where there were teams of six young women. The manager showed us a board with six nude outlines of the team, alongside each of which was a bunch of pink 'suggestion slips' for improving efficiency. The more slips, the more an artist would paint in apparel on the nude silhouettes – shoes, stockings, knickers, bras. I did not see one with a hat. We were amazed – so were our hosts. 'They *like* it.'

In terms of my own learning curve, the longish strike of our field service computer engineers against International Computers in 1964 was seminal for many of the things we did later. When the dispute started over pay, we were still not sensitive enough to the immense importance of the computer banks and the cross connections – formidable even in those days. After the first few weeks, we found that we had not just stopped the company servicing operations but that we had also affected everything from banking, insurance and retail trading to newspapers and even the Ministry of Labour's industrial statistics. The Labour Minister, Ray Gunter, complained to me and brought in another firm, so for the first time ever the Ministry of Labour was picketed as well. It was a close-run thing. We were under pressure from all of the other employers with whom we did not have a quarrel and I learnt from that how pervasive and influential the new technologies were.

We gained a partial victory, which we settled in the Cora Hotel, with thunder and lightning outside. Both sides had become tired by the dispute and it was as much as we could do (but it was enough) to show that we had made some gains as a result of all of the suffering. We came out of it in debt but some friendly unions were willing to help us with money and in particular Richard Briginshaw of SOGAT said he would ask his Executive to make us a loan. We were running out of cash,

at a Labour Party Conference, to which he simply said, 'Well, it seemed to be the right thing to do, so I did it.' I liked that.

My next encounter with him was much later when he was Social Democratic Party candidate at the Warrington by-election and almost won against our ASTMS candidate, Doug Hoyle, in this previously rock-solid Labour seat. Warrington was in many ways a proving ground for the Labour Party when it came to the SDP assault. What we had not appreciated was that the mass media was able to exercise an influence which led to a last-minute surge against us which did not show in any of our canvassing. We were driving people to the polls who had said they were for us but had decided they were going to go against us. I think of Warrington as Labour's Stalingrad where the SDP was turned back.

Back in the sixties, however, the Concorde project had gone ahead and in December 1967 I went out to Toulouse to see the first roll out of the French Concorde. I went because I had championed the aircraft, although at the time I was campaigning against the Common Market. Tony Benn, then Minister of Technology, gave a speech explaining that the 'e' of the French-spelt Concorde stood for excellence, entente and entry into the European Common Market. He was then for entry but not a marketeer. I have mentioned this position to him since and he does not recall the speech.

I came back with Julian Amery, the determined Conservative Minister for Aviation in the early sixties who had signed the contract to build Concorde with the French. It was water-tight, so that if the UK had withdrawn, the government would still have had to put up its share of the money. He wickedly said to me, 'If you and I had only been together on the same side we could have saved the TSR2 as well.' But I had not wanted to do that. Concorde was a civil, not military aircraft. When aircraft workers had rallied in London shortly after the review of all aviation projects by the incoming Labour government, I had seen Harold Wilson at 10 Downing Street and told him: 'I will make sure that the banner at the front of this great parade will say "Let's build it Big and Civil".' Harold liked that, and it looked good.

By this time I was writing fairly regularly in the national press, one of the uncovenanted bonuses of which was the brains trust in the corner of the Red Lion pub just off Fleet Street – now burnt down, the genial landlord, Wally, dead and his upstairs Chinese restaurant with a regular turnover of pretty Hong Kong Chinese girls gone for ever. There were a group of us who either worked or freelanced for Sunday newspapers – we became known as the Sunday Newspaper Industrial Group (or SNIGGERS) – and from this was born the tactic of thwarting the Wilson government's diktat on pay increases, which countermanded all agreements reached by unions and employees.

One of our members was 'Curly' Manning (called Curly because he was very bald indeed), who must surely be the only Communist engineering shop stewards convenor ever to become a managing clerk for a major firm of solicitors, then W. H. Thompson, the leading firm of union lawyers, now so big it is divided into two. He was an immensely attractive personality and deeply concerned about the cases that he had to allocate. He kept a collection of photographs of young women who had been scalped by machines in order to keep up his red flame of resentment against careless employers. But Curly always enjoyed himself and was fun to be with. At a conference of shipbuilding and engineering unions on the Isle of Man he reproached me for being the only person he knew to actually fall off a one-horse-power vehicle into a puddle: the horse had stopped before I did when jumping off the tram. While there too, he became involved with the late-night cabaret turn at the Casino. We had been told that the previous night the comedian had said that I was in the hotel and commented, 'Clive Jenkins does dress very well', to which his scantily clad assistant replied, 'And so quickly too'. The crowd had loved it. The next night I was in the audience and a rather nervous comic said, 'Oh. Clive Jenkins is here now'. He went along the front row and said to the man with the bald head, 'I expect you are his lawyer' at which Curly said, 'As a matter of fact I am', and handed him his card! Very sadly, Curly was killed in a motor accident one icy Christmas.

He certainly brightened our Red Lion group discussion of the phenomenal decision of the Wilson government to breach everyone's contract. I was pursuing the thought that so much of British commercial law enshrined the sanctity of the contract – so how could a government without some specific legislative basis simply issue a virtual decree? To which Curly commented, 'That's a good one, how can they?' We decided amongst ourselves that they couldn't and they shouldn't, and I went back to my Office to talk to my senior colleague on these questions, Muriel Turner. She agreed and went to talk with the unsung brilliant solicitor David Phillips, and we were away.

We were clear that the union *as such* could not sue for outstanding monies that had not been paid because of a government edict. The contract must be between the employer and employee, and as long as the employee kept turning up for work he could sue for the agreements which had been reached in his name. We found a foreman in Thorn Electric as a test case and went off to the Edmonton County Court. To the amazement of the Press – although not to us – we won the payment of the increase which had been withheld. This was deplored by George Woodcock, and I cannot think why he called it a black day for trade unionism.

We then brought more than forty other cases in the United Kingdom and won them all. We were also able to establish that the legislation did not apply to our members in the Channel Islands, although the agreement to pay the Jersey engineers had been reached in London. We then pursued the cause of airline engineers throughout the world, on the basis that they were not covered by United Kingdom legislation, and we won them all. As a result of this, more precise repressive legislation was introduced, aimed at giving the government power to block increases. The first order was served on me to halt some modest increases for the limb-fitters at Roehampton Hospital. We resented it and had it 'prayed against' in the House of Commons.

I believe that the government's policy did immense damage to the Labour Party over the years ahead; a Conservative government would not have dared to do it at that point in history. But from our union's point of view it showed that we were willing to take whatever unprecedented action was necessary to protect our members' interests in any quarter whatsoever.

5

Unions and Intrigue
in the USA

The Intelligence services of the world have seen the trade union movements as crucially important in economic and political terms and for gossip about policy formation and leaders. During World War Two the remnants of the pre-war international trade union secretariats were vital networks for information and sabotage in Nazi-occupied Europe. With the first frosts of the Cold War in the late forties came intelligence money. The World Federation of Trade Unions, founded in party post-war amity, was split from the outside (the British Trades Union Congress played a sorry, junior partner's role in this). Some of the international trade union secretariats, by declining to have some of their functions integrated into the new World Federation, helped to precipitate the crisis and fissure. Decades later it became clear that some of them were infiltrated by the CIA; scandals erupted and people left office.

The main French trade union centre had a breakaway financed by the Americans in the late 1970s. When I asked an official of the US national centre if the rumour was true that he had personally carried £500,000 into France, in a suitcase, for this specific purpose, he did not even smile. I wonder where the money came from. Some unions were used as conduits for money and men. I recall Jerry Wurf, President of the American Federation of State, County and Municipal Employees, telling me that after his electoral victory as a reform candidate for the Presidency, a whole group of staff in the union's international department departed overnight – forever – with their files. 'So what did you do, Jerry?' 'Changed the locks, what else?' Jerry was a fascinating, Jewish working-class organiser-intellectual from New York who became a firm argumentative friend on my second and third visits in the early 1960s to America.

On my first trip the US government, allegedly because of my brief membership of the Communist Party in the late forties/ early fifties kept me waiting for a visa until three hours before the plane was due to depart. (I can still only get a visa for eighteen months at a time.) I went Icelandic Airways because they were outside the airline cartel of those days. They were also the cheapest and slowest, and after a stop in Reykjavik and a cold boxed meal for the long piston-engined crossing of the North Atlantic, I arrived to my first experiences of jetlag. The trip arose from invitations to address an exotic range of socialist, labour and student organisations. I went to Berkeley where the student body was fizzing, met the leaders of the seminal Students for a Democratic Society and financed my air fares for three weeks with over seven meetings in a week from the east to west coasts.

There were some odd encounters. For a Thanksgiving dinner I was invited through a long-forgotten friend to an immensely luxurious hotel, with huge candles lighting up the driveway, in the desert outside Cathedral City in California. The host turned out to be a wealthy manufacturer of plumbing appliances. Another guest was the fabled J. P. Cannon, one of the founders of the world Trotskyist movement. He was going blind but swam in the multi-millionaire's pool the next day and it was fascinating to listen to him as he deciphered for me the passionate minutiae of the fissiparous Trotskyist sects and their influence on some American unions – in particular the Dobbs Brothers, famous in Labour history for being prosecuted for leading a strike in Minneapolis condemned by the Roosevelt administration for being against the war effort, and later renowned for helping design part of the enduring internal structure of the Teamsters Union.

I kept encountering Trotskyists among my organisers and contacts, and saw the shadowy shape of the genial Gerry Healey, then General Secretary and all round guru of the British

Workers' Revolutionary Party. His Party effectively owned Plough Press, at that time the cheapest printers around and where we had our ASSET publications printed. My friend Jim Mortimer, whom I had first met in the early 1950s soon after he had been elected as editor of the Draughtsmen's Union newspaper, helped edit and lay out the ASSET publications and he would spend hours at Gerry's press because the Trotskyite compositors would engage him in long ideological debates. Gerry would later be supported faithfully by Vanessa Redgrave through all the Party's factional splits and Gerry's personal problems; and he had wealthy American and Canadian supporters who funded him. He amused me in later years when he said, 'You are the only general secretary who will talk to me.' It was not much of a bond that we had but it led me to the aged Earl Browder, the legendary former General Secretary of the US Communist Party.

A frail old man, he saw me in his book-lined study, the snow lightly falling outside, and complained that he was still under surveillance and that his son was being victimised because of him. I listened entranced as he told me his side of the argument which convulsed the world Communist movement as he led the post-war move to reconstruct or dissolve the American Communist Party and replace it with an educational League of Communists. 'Why?' 'Because Joseph Stalin told me to . . .' Students of this period, and Marshal Tito's apostasy, will recall the famous open letter from the French Communist leader, Jacques Duclos, 'exposing' Browderism. I queried how he managed to survive that period and he said he was given a salary and rights in the distribution of books from Eastern Europe (particularly Yugoslavia). 'How did *that* come about?' 'Oh, that was Joe Stalin, again.' It was all engaging, fascinating and hallucinatory.

What was curious was that the largest union in the United States, the Teamsters, had always had Trotskyist influences and had been condemned for these before it was later arraigned for its Mafia connections. Jimmy Hoffa had been its President since 1957, when his predecessor, Dave Beck, left under the shadow of charges of income tax evasion and of grand larceny. Since then he had been the target of more investigation and publicity than any other man in American public life ('They've had 133 agents working on me at once – and I'm still walking the streets').

My contact in the Teamsters was Harold Gibbons, a St Louis trade union official and now chief ally of Hoffa's who had apparently been an acquaintance of Aneurin Bevan (he kept a photograph of them together on the wall of his plush office on Washington's Capitol Hill). He had once been called the 'White Hope' of 'progressive' American unionism because in Detroit he had pioneered low-cost housing and medical services. He had taken his local union into the Teamsters and been rewarded. 'You can call me an ex-socialist now,' he said to me. An interesting, articulate man with, as he told me in a softly lit 'Happy Hour' bar, on enormous salary(ies) and expenses, he replied to my questions about the charges of corruption and violence levelled against the Teamsters:

They have tried to make us the scapegoats. They threw us to the wolves at the union convention in 1957. I went to Atlantic City and said, 'If you're dissatisfied with us, appoint a committee of the AFLO-CIO [American Federation of Labour-Congress of Industrial Organisation] vice-presidents but don't throw us out.' But they had done a deal. Now their friends in Congress have turned on them and we've got the worst Labour Bill we've ever had – after electing a Congress of friends of labour! Then, they made us get out of the International Transport Workers' Federation. Meany [then President of the AFL-CIO] told them that if they didn't throw us out, he would get the railroad unions to disaffiliate. So we've stayed away. They didn't do this to John L. Lewis. He's still in the Miners International and he's not in the AFL-CIO. Why doesn't the AFL-CIO do some organising, instead of fucking around? Look at Reuther. He hasn't organised a plant since he became President of the Autoworkers.

It is possible that the honest Walter Reuther, like Hoffa and some of his associates was later murdered; he survived one assassination attempt only to die later in a mysterious light aircraft crash. Not like that guy in there. [Gibbons waved towards Hoffa's office, connected to his by an office suite with open doors.] That boy in there is the hope of American labour. He's on the picket lines all the time.

Sure, there is violence. But remember this, violence is not a phenomenon of the Teamsters alone. It's a phenomenon of American labour and American society. I was in Detroit at the time of the big Ford strike. They had 100,000 around Ford's. Automobiles were strung across the streets to stop the scabs. They had action squads too. I saw an autoworker sweep his arm right across a counterful of cosmetic bottles. Others had sharp knives and razors and slashed clothing in the shops. In Lansing, they held up a whole community – banks, stores, state offices – they all closed down. Governor Murphy had to fly back to mediate. I was for them. This is how we built our labour movement here. Why are they all complaining now?

Look at Jimmy. He was on every picket line. They beat him. They wrecked his office. Once he was arrested eighteen times in twenty-four hours. They killed his people. All this had an effect upon the development of our union.

At this point I asked about the dozens of charges made before the McClellan Committee on Improper Activities in the Labour or Management Field, about the employment of ex-convicts as union organisers and contacts between the Teamsters and the organised criminal elements in American society. Gibbons produced a list of names. 'These are all the persons mentioned before the McClellan Committee who were said to be criminals,' he said. He scored two names: 'Those are out.' Alongside another he scribbled 'found innocent' and lower down the page he noted 'jailed for perjury'. 'Sixteen of these people we couldn't trace at all. Nine are ordinary members we had to take in under our contracts. Seven had been prosecuted but acquitted. Twenty-six were convicted before they came to work for us. Fourteen have been convicted because of what they did for us in official labour disputes – we're examining their cases now. Thirty-seven are no longer in the union.' This was, of course, all deception.

He called for an assistant to bring in a recording of a Jesuit, the Rev. C. D. Clark (known as the 'Hoodlum Priest' for his rehabilitation work among ex-convicts), addressing a Teamsters' local meeting in St Louis. In the recording the Rev. Clark referred in glowing terms to the help given him by Gibbons in finding work for the Teamsters men, protesting that these 'good men' in the Teamsters' leadership were now being pilloried for their social welfare policies.

One of the names on the list described as 'not now and never were members, officers, agents or representatives of the Teamsters' Union' was John Dio Guardi, better known as 'Johnny Dio', who was imprisoned in 1958 for extortion. Robert Kennedy, when US Attorney General, said of him in the McClellan Committee hearings that he was 'a well-known gangster in New York . . . convicted of extortion, who brought all these hoodlums into the labour-union movement in 1952 and 1953.' The Committee had heard a recording of a tapped telephone conversation between Hoffa and Dio in 1953 which implied a deal involving Hoffa's payment to one of Dio's men. Hoffa was repeatedly questioned about this conversation but insisted that he could not recall its purpose beyond that it was 'apparently something I was having done'.

From all the evidence before the committee it seemed clear that some Teamster leaders had links and liaisons with the criminal syndicates. In this situation, the Teamsters pointed out that many American unions have had such connections – as have the two major political parties. Gibbons said:

> Eisenhower maintains relationships with Ibn Saud. He doesn't have to approve of him. Remember we have 12,000 paid officers. There are 900 locals with seven officers each. Yet only four of them have to resign as a result of the new law which says that they are ineligible if they have committed certain offences in the last five years. Is this so terrible? Shouldn't people be rehabilitated? Do you know why they are really after Hoffa? He presents a threat to the status quo. This is an attack on the labour movement and on the Teamsters because we are the only people organising. We're going in for political action too. You should have

heard Jimmy in Detroit last week. He's talking the class war. He wants to elect workers to Congress.

An aide of Gibbons who had come into the room interjected at this point: 'A sort of indigenous American Marxism.'

(This aide was Sidney Zagri, who, after Hoffa had been indicted and there was a long-drawn-out trial, came to London to meet British union officials because he said that Hoffa was being 'framed'. Typically, he stayed at the Savoy and untypically he had not brought his many credit cards, so I had to vouch for his financial standing at the Savoy. He later died in a 'flash fire' in a rooftop restaurant in a southern State and his widow told me that she was having trouble over his insurance payments as there was a doubt whether it was an accident or murder, and whether it was his fault.)

Gibbons took me through to meet Hoffa in his adjoining office suite, where his desk carries the gilt and black slogan '*Nil Bastardi Carborundum*' (Don't let the bastards grind you down). He was short and burly, working in his shirtsleeves: both shirt and tie were monogrammed 'J. H'. The sweet, ironed-out music that played in the other offices was absent. 'Let's get this straight', he said:

We're a controlled union. We want the members to respect the officers. No-one steals in the Teamsters. There have been some problems but we've cleaned them up. We've got difficulties they don't get in other unions. Because of our reputation new members expect us to deliver. They used to be satisfied with 5 per cent or 10 per cent increases, but if *we* don't get them 25 they beef about it. But we expect them to be militant. If they won't fight we don't want them. Do you know how big we'll be? Our natural rate of growth should be 12½ per cent. Why? Everyone is moving out to the suburbs. There aren't any railroads there. Everything will have to be carried by truck – and driven by a teamster. In October, we had 103,000 membership applications: that is 10,000 more than at any time in our history. Can you see why they are worried about us? We're a challenge.

He reeled off a list of plants that he had organised personally and challenged Walter Reuther – with whom he had a sharp personal rivalry – to do the same.

They have not seen anything yet. We have contracts in freight covering twenty-eight states all in identical language. We are planning for a period of ninety days when all our contracts will fall in. Then we are going for nationwide collective bargaining. We made Montgomery Ward bargain nationally: now, for everybody else. We are in for a tough time. They'll never let you print this. The State Department will go crazy. But it is going to be tougher than it was in the thirties.

Do you know what I did last Saturday? I had some young business agents into my home in Detroit and showed them three movies about the strikes. The sit-down strike at General Motors, and the shootings at US Steel. They were all shot in the back. There was a guy in a gas mask with a sub-machine gun. [Hoffa rose from his desk as if he were holding a sub-machine gun in his hands.]

He was just shooting – like rabbits. [He sprayed the room with gunfire in pantomime.] That's the way it's going to be again. Gas and shootings and violence. This is what the employers are preparing for. But we'll be ready. Who else fought against those laws except us? Last week in Detroit I talked to 900 delegates and then to 1,800 stewards. I told them to run for office and we'll back them. Don't believe what you hear about the Teamsters. Come to our Central States Conference in Chicago. We deal with all the grievances: four full days. Come and sit by me and you'll see real democracy. I'll give you a room in my suite.

Gibbons added, 'He'll cook you breakfast. He's a good cook. He does it for the people who come and see him. He works all the time'. (I wish I had gone: I didn't because a Democratic rising star had offered to see me – I went off to meet John F. Kennedy.)

In the UK I reported on my meetings with Hoffa and Gibbons in *Trade Union Affairs*, a quarterly journal I founded in 1961 and edited with the help of Jim Mortimer. In retrospect, it was over-ambitious, decades ahead of its time, and it ran for only six issues. We still have nothing which resembles it. During its life we addressed everything from radiation to reforming the TUC, reviewed the case for compulsory arbitration and looked at trade union tactics throughout the world. We analysed the key disputes in the UK and also the issues facing British unions if the UK ever joined the Common Market. So why did it fail? It was not so much the financing of it, because employers bought it as well as Labour movement aficionados, but that we simply ran out of people who could write cogently and interpretatively – and on time – within the trade union movement. There were not enough of them. This was in spite of the fact that we, for the first time, looked at the dynamic of public service pay claims and their impact upon the private sector and whether there was such a thing as a 'pay round'. It was a gallant but doomed enterprise. Most trade union officers do not write, and I did not want pieces from academics.

However, my account of Hoffa and the Teamsters in *Trade Union Affairs* attracted attention. I quoted the cab driver who had said, 'I sure wish he'd come and organise us', and the AFL-CIO lobbyist who had shaken with anger in talking about the same man: 'Hoffa? He's a crook. He cost us the Landrum-Griffin Bill [a bitterly restrictive anti-union piece of legislation]. But they'll get him and I hope it's soon.' He added, 'and that goes for Gibbons too'.

I reported, rather innocently:

Since December 1957, when the Teamsters were expelled from the AFL-CIO, the American trade union leadership and Congress have done all in their power to grind down the top echelon of the Teamsters. But in spite of this, there has been little change in the Teamsters' power elite, while the overall membership and revenue has continued to grow spectacularly at a time when membership of other unions is stagnant or declining . . .

The Presidency of the Teamsters is in a position of immense power and responsibility and of a nature which cannot be imagined in terms of British union structure. Hoffa's history would also be thought strange and disturbing in Britain. But he *does* run the fastest-growing union in

America – and the pressure of the State on him seems to be converting a proletarian militancy into something else . . .

The Teamsters are an American phenomenon: their methods are alien to us. British governments have never appreciated the uncorrupted non-violent nature of British trade unionism.

Hoffa at this time had been hauled into court, though never convicted, on numerous charges which he alleged were simply meant to harass him and the Teamsters. It is now clear that Hoffa was part of the powerful Mafia-dominated underworld of the United States. His disappearance in July 1975 was obviously murder and so too have been the deaths of his associates linked with the enormous pension funds that the Teamsters influenced. When I went to see Hoffa in Washington, the ante-room was crowded with businessmen holding briefcases on their knees. I apologised for breaking into his work. 'They only want to borrow money,' he said. 'They'll be back tomorrow, or they'll wait.' They did, and they did because the truly colossal pension funds were honey-pots for every developer, every would-be casino owner in America – and all the insurance companies who wanted a share of the action. I wonder how many were privileged to have chunky gold cigarette-lighters – one inscribed from Jimmy and another from John English, the venerable Teamster Secretary-Treasurer who seemed to provide a respectable front? Alas, these formidable flint-wheeled artifacts – only for display – were burgled from my home in St Marks Crescent. Does another criminal have them, or are they safely melted down?

The miasma of the Mafia was detectable after a while. In my involvement in the airline industry and American airline unions, I was constantly being offered hospitality, menus without prices, gambling chips. Why? They wanted to do anything to keep aircraft flying, moving people between their hotels and casinos: and the casinos were the key. When Jimmy Hoffa was in the Lewisburg Penitentiary, a convicted top Mafia thief, a mobster and brutal enforcer, Vincent Theresa, who was also an informer, wrote that they discussed Theresa's financial future. Hoffa had told him:

'If you have any money you want cleaned . . . legitimised . . . you go see Lou Poller at the Miami National Bank and show him this letter . . . Whatever money you put with him he'll take 10 per cent. It might take him a year or two years, but if you give him ten million or one million that money will be invested for you in something that's legitimate. You'll be able to pay taxes on it . . .' Poller, I found out later, was one of Meyer Lansky's men and he washed the mob's money through the bank . . . The government could trace all day and never find anything illegal.

Hoffa was released, went to a lunch meeting and disappeared from a restaurant car park in Detroit on 30 July 1975. The last glimpse I had of Gibbons was on a press photograph: he had grown a patriarchal beard and was standing, very uncomfortably and very much offside, as President Richard Nixon entertained the Teamsters' Executive Board. A labour affairs specialist said of him before his earlyish death, 'The booze and the broads have got to him.'

Of course, he was corrupted. He provided a rationale for Jimmy Hoffa's activities. Presidents of the Teamsters were regularly indicted: some went to gaol. But almost all the members tolerated them because they delivered the 'meat and potatoes', and weaker groups joined because of Teamster 'muscle'.

In 1987, the International Chemical Workers asked me to receive the then hugely corpulent President of the Teamsters, Jackie Presser. So I did, wanting to do them a service and also to be fraternal to one of the largest affiliates. He came with his photographers and I told them to cap their lenses. He gave me a bronze American eagle and went home to die of cancer under indictment and also saying he was an FBI agent on the side. The next year the Teamsters rejoined the AFL-CIO, and the American House of Labour was reunited; the pressures of the US government and its attempts to crack down on racketeering by threatening to 'take over' the Teamsters were obviously too great.

Besides my encounter with the Teamsters organisation, I had two other dramatic insights into American union moves. I was taken to one of the 'pistol locals' on the waterfront to meet a rising young president ('his father is a long-time mob family head but he's educated, left-wing and determined to change things'). All the meeting rooms seemed dedicated to Catholic orders. He was fluent and attractive, and took me to a 'family' Italian restaurant where I was surprised to see a substantial figure (mainly by seniority) in world trade union Councils.

My host had earlier explained a new longshore contract, which seemed to me to be worse than I had seen on the West Coast. The dockers had, he said, approved it at a local meeting: 'I asked – all in favour say "aye". So they did.' I queried, 'What about the "noes"?' His response was, 'When I want the "noes" I'll ask for them separately.' He ended up in gaol for extortion. I was not surprised. His colleagues carried guns and replied to my naive questions about the Mafia, 'It doesn't exist. We only have a cultural organisation – the Sons of Italy.'

I was later told that this section of the waterfront was dominated by Albert Anastasia (allegedly the High Executioner of Murder Incorporated), who was shot in the back of the head by two men in the barber shop of the Park Sheraton Hotel because he was too ambitious. Perhaps he should have paid his bodyguard more?

In national legislative affairs (where they did not have to pay in the end), the underworld clearly had links with elected officials, particularly in New Jersey where legislators of high standing and respect in the field of industrial relations succumbed. One told me at a soirée at the British Embassy when I had a Fellowship at the Woodrow Wilson Center, 'I'm from the state where the bodies are buried.'

In New York a rag trade union organiser had told me of recent problems:

We were met with violence and run-away employers who moved their shops to the South to beat us. I finally caught up with one. We waited until he came out of his factory. 'You've stopped running,' I said. 'Who's stopping me?' So I called S---i. He was my personal goon. He got out of the car, all ten foot of him, came over, took the guy by the lapels gently and said, 'You try running. I'll pluck your eyes out and eat 'em like grapes.' We got a contract.

Unions and Intrigue in the USA

The hatred shown towards British unions by Conservative Ministers here could not start to envisage such confrontations. Our unions are relatively bourgeois and incorruptible.

6

Promoting the Cause

It was my piece on Jimmy Hoffa that started off my television appearances. The American writer Clancy Sigal, who had been both a Hollywood agent and for a short time an organising official of an American union (he gave it up after his room-mate was seen to be wearing a gun), suggested to a researcher on the BBC 'Tonight' programme that this might be an interesting item. As a result I was invited to be interviewed by Cliff Michelmore. The presiding genius of the 'Tonight' show was Donald Baverstock, whose ideas were to influence so many programmes from then on, not least the brilliant 'That Was the Week that Was'. After the 'Tonight' programme, Donald – a fellow Welshman – took me to the bar at the BBC in Lime Grove and said, 'I would have fried you in that interview.' I replied 'Oh no, you couldn't have. I was simply being sincere and trying to explain things.' We proceeded to shout at each other in our relative Welsh languages for an hour, interrupted every so often by someone coming into the bar and announcing, 'Mr Baverstock, the taxi is still waiting for Mr Jenkins', to which Donald responded, 'Put it on the budget, put on the budget, boyo.' He was a charming, talented man and much envied by his peers. In any event, that programme led to me going on television about every couple of weeks for the next twenty-five years. As Lord Beaverbrook said to the Royal Commission on the Press about his newspapers: 'I used them all as engines of propaganda.'

I experimented with advertising ASSET on two smallish

television stations, Tyne-Tees and Ulster TV, but it simply proved not worth the expense because we were buying too many useless heads, that is, people who could not have joined us anyway. The message, I soon found, could be made in other ways and I used my regular column in the *Tribune*, for which I wrote for ten years, as well as writing for other journals and national newspapers. And I made myself available as necessary for anyone who wanted to write a feature or have me on radio or television – and there were many.

The great advantage I had was that no other trade union official was writing regularly in mass circulation publications. Through the late fifties and sixties, at a time when the union did not have resources, I used words as weapons. Following the Latin line, *Oderint Dum Metuant* ('Let them hate me as long as they fear me'), I advanced the concept that collective bargaining was the human face of some of the market forces. We lifted our game at ASSET, producing some of the most attractive union material around. Our metallic gold-coloured executive policy paper entitled 'The Gold Plate Handshake' stressed security for white-collar workers and the raising of redundancy payments, while our metallic silver-coloured pamphlet featuring a rocket sitting on its base and entitled 'All Systems Go' argued for British high-tech industries. All the time we relentlessly publicised what we were doing.

I became a regular guest on the 'Any Questions' programme, first appearing with Freddy Grisewood at the time of the 1961 Cuban missile crisis, just after President Kennedy's quarantine speech. This was of course discussed and I took a very clear line, stating that I did not believe there were Soviet missiles in Cuba. Someone challenged me, saying that there were pictures of them. I retorted 'forgeries' and there was general pandemonium. Of course, I was wrong. I had not appreciated that a large proportion of the Soviet first strike capacity was already in Cuba. At this time I presided over a mass rally in Trafalgar Square and was making a speech condemning the aggression of the United States when a man from the *Daily Worker* rushed up to me and whispered in my ear, 'The Soviets have announced they have turned the ships around and are sending the missiles back.' Try and handle that at a mass meeting! However, I did and there was enormous relief from the audience. But I really did get the Cuban situation wrong.

As the Chairman of the British Cuba Committee, I had visited Cuba, which wanted spares for their ageing Bristol Britannia aircraft. I arrived at Havana airport at a humid 7.00 am. It had been raining overnight and the mist was lifting from the palm trees. No one was there to meet me so I followed the pattern of behaviour I had adopted in Warsaw in a freezing dawn arrival: 'Please take me to your leading hotel.' It worked. A suite was waiting for me at the Havana Libre (formerly the Hilton), where I was greeted as Lord Sir Clive Jenkins and given a fiercely air-conditioned room which gave me a sore throat and influenza. Ian Mikardo was able to find the needed aircraft spares, but the Cubans could not deliver the necessary bankers' drafts in time, although I saw Fidel Castro in the early hours of one morning with his influential brother Raul, the minister responsible for industry and the old General Secretary of the Cuban Communist Party. The bureaucratic procurement agencies simply did not respond.

When in Havana, I went to stay with Cedric Belfrage, one of history's leftist reformers. In the 1930s, as the *Daily Express* critic on the entertainment scene, his sharp pen had attracted threats from showbiz advertisers that they would withdraw the advertisements which surrounded his reviews and columns. 'Lord Beaverbrook defied them to do their worst,' Cedric told me. 'And they came back.' Senator Joseph McCarthy secured his expulsion from the United States and the paper, the *National Guardian*, which he had founded with other prominent witch-hunted journalists, suffered from his absence; its editorial mast head read 'Cedric Belfrage – Editor in Exile'. This was the foremost (and almost only) publication to publicise, illuminate and condemn the trial and execution of Ethel and Julius Rosenberg on specious charges.

I had first met Cedric at a Labour Party conference in Margate after he had been deported from the States, and we became firm friends over the decades. He left London for Havana and was there when the disgraceful American invasion of the Bay of Pigs aborted. He was the only journalist capable of sending out stories, but right-wing papers in Britain would not publish him.

As a friend of the Cuban revolution, Cedric was allocated a villa belonging to a rich business man who had fled, leaving behind a refrigerator of rotted food (we washed it out), a (purchased) signed photograph of the Pope and a closet of suits (unwearable: he must have been even shorter and fatter than me), some nice silk ties all made in Miami and, oddly, mink fur tippets. I wore two of the ties for years. We went to listen to Fidel speaking at the Chaplin Theatre, arriving at eight o'clock in the evening and leaving after a while to have our dinner, which was a rarely obtained chicken which Cedric's wife Mary had boiled. When we returned three hours later, Fidel was still speaking. In the tradition of oral history, he was expounding to his audience; he had the distracting habit of tapping the microphone to check if it was working.

Cedric eventually went to live in Cuernavaca outside Mexico City on the rim of an ancient volcano crater where, it is said, it is springtime all round the year and rain comes at four o'clock in the afternoon and lasts for thirty minutes. His villa, with a distant view of the dormant Popocatepetl volcano, attracted exotic political friends, from the radical Jessica Mitford – one of the fascinating five Mitford girls – to the first woman to be elected to the US House of Representatives. When I stayed with him there, he took to the nearby kitchen of David Alfaro Sequeiros, the towering Communist muralist who ranked with Diego Rivera and who was working on a heroic mural of revolutionary peasants and soldiers (for a luxury hotel!). He reminisced of his involvement with other romantics in the machine-gun attack on Trotsky's fortress home after his exile to Mexico City. When I was in New York I met George Novak, a contact of the ubiquitous Gerry Healey, who said that he helped to raise the money to build machine-gun towers around Trotsky's fortress. Trotsky of course survived the painter-poet's murderous assault to expire from a Stalinist agent's ice-pick. Years later in the 1980s, at the Labour Party's Conference which expelled the intrusive 'Militant' Trotskyist faction leaders – who would have appalled Trotsky by their petty assumptions – their supporters picketed with freshly painted placards that referred satirically to the trade union vote: 'Six million ice-picks can't be wrong'.

As a result of my union and media activities, there were many personalities, attractive and otherwise, I met in the early sixties. Another 'Any Questions' regular was (Lord) Dick Marsh, who as a back-bencher did some pioneering work in extending health and safety legislation via a Private Members Bill to a number of areas of British industry not previously covered by it. His fall from grace was spectacular. He had become Minister of Power under Wilson and I remember a dinner party at a Labour Party Conference given by Will Camp, a public relations adviser to the British Steel Corporation, where Dick couldn't resist joking: 'I enjoy going to see the Prime Minister in his office at Number 10. It is furnished so simply: just a throne and a prayer mat.' I noticed a Labour Whip wincing. Dick was invited to leave the Cabinet very shortly afterwards and he gradually took up an anti-Labour role which I think does him no credit – to come from our loins and end up chairing the Newspaper Proprietors' Association?

He is rivalled by (Lord) Frank Chapple as one of the least attractive persons I have met in our fraternal movement. He was not unique in building a career upon a disaster, in his case by exposing the ballot rigging scandal in the Electrical Trades Union which led to the union's expulsion from the TUC after a much publicised trial in 1960. He later became General Secretary of the reinstated union, and the darling of the right-wing media – which perhaps accounts for the lack of detailed notice taken of his past in his autobiography *Sparks Fly*. From it I take the following excerpts:

> I do not pretend that I had a blinding flash of light that turned me overnight from a committed Communist to a fierce anti-Communist. Like most political decisions involving a fundamental shift of allegiance this one evolved over a period. But once I fully realised the sick and squalid past in which I had shared and the gross injustice our members suffered as a consequence, I had no choice. There should have been no choice for anyone who held a similar view . . .
>
> It was not just paper that went missing; there were union members who could have backed us with telling details.

Some of them quit the Communist Party in disgust, but, when it came to first hand racket-busting, they simply lacked the guts to see it through. Yes, there was intimidation. These men had wives and families, and there was no certainty of ending up on the winning side. Some of them doubtless considered they would be throwing in their lot with surefire losers, or perhaps they just could not face the ugly prospect of standing in the witness box and confessing to their own past misdeeds. None of us relished that. Many of them had dirty hands. I know that I did. [Chapter 1, pp. 10, 12]

Further on, he writes:

My faith and belief that the members would benefit from Communist rule was steadily disappearing. It was not just politics. Pay rates slipped by comparison with other groups of workers. The electricians, regarded among the aristocrats of labour, dropped from eighth to thirtieth on the industrial pay ladder during this period, even though electronics was increasing in importance. There was less and less consultation with the members, even those who, like me helped the leadership by rigging meetings and ballots. For much of my time as LSE No. 10 Assistant Branch Secretary, our Secretary was unwell and left balloting arrangements to me to deal with, and there were several occasions when I fiddled branch votes by one or other of the methods later disclosed in the high court. It was simple enough to do with the slapdash voting arrangements we had – arrangements which most unions irresponsibly still permit . . . [Chapter 5, p. 48]

My apparent deviations brought me trouble inside the Communist Party. My predominantly Jewish Stamford Hill Branch were mostly with me and the majority of them ultimately quit the Party, but it was different in the Earls Court Industrial Branch, a multi-union set-up covering London Transport. The comrades there used to get up to the usual conspiratorial tricks. One Prominent Communist shop steward once got me to fill in spare ballot papers for union elections – and he was in the National Union of Railwaymen. [Chapter 6, p. 56]

I simply do not understand that last sentence – how could Frank have been 'got' to do this? The truth is that I found this amateur pigeon fancier and sheep-keeper personally and politically unattractive. When on a TUC Economic Committee visit to the United States, I tried to establish a momentary rapport, a brief lubrication of our relationship, by inquiring in the Golden Gate Park in San Francisco after his flock of Jacob sheep. 'How many do you have, Frank?' 'Oh, about 400,000 – and if you repeat that I will sue you,' he joked. (At that time he was claiming the electricians' union had 400,000 members.) I took it as a considered quotable aside: what else could you do if your source was wearing incredibly broad-checked trousers (and proudly claiming he had two pairs)?

As the ballot-rigging trial was going on, I recall Jim Mortimer and me questioning George Sinfield, then the highly respected industrial correspondent of the *Daily Worker*. George insisted that it was a conspiracy against the capable and mostly well-liked Communist collective bargainers in the union. It was not: most of them were corrupt and had corrupted, and we were disturbed by the evidence that there was a route established for the posting of forged ballots. I was uneasy that the innocents had no money for their defence and I helped with George Elvin of the cine technicians and Harold Poole of the coppersmiths to establish a fund for their legal costs at the request of Jack Hendy, an official of the electricians' union with whom I had worked happily for years in air transport bargaining. He was ostracised for a while but changed careers, became a lecturer and eventually president of the teachers in further and higher education. The fund was called 'The Light and Liberty Fund' from the electricians' own logo and when the trial was over we had a surplus which we divided between Arnold Wesker's Centre 42 cultural project and the excellent Manor House trade union hospital at Golders Green (shop stewards for every ward and very concerned surgeons). But the careful Fleet Street electricians, then at their peak (and rich), asked for the £5,000 back. Frank Chapple never forgave me for helping set up that

1a *left* In school uniform in 1938 **1b** *right* On Banbury station in 1947
on my way to the local aluminium factory in the hope of
organising the workers to join the union

1c With colleagues from the laboratory where I worked in 1943.
We spent a week on a scheme near Haverford West, living in
chalets and picking flax for a small sum of money

2a At Moscow airport, speaking on Moscow Radio, in June 1957.
I led a delegation to the Soviet Union which resulted in a series of
articles in *Flight* magazine and, eventually, in the London–Moscow
air route

2b After my speech to aircraft maintenance engineers at Kiev
in the Ukraine in July 1957

3a At Transport House, headquarters of the Labour Party, on General Election night in 1964 after the Labour victory (Barry Evans)

3b Talking to aircraft workers at Speakers Corner in 1965 after a demonstration in favour of major civil aircraft building project. Following Labour's election, many military projects had been cancelled (Hulton Picture Company)

4a After three nights without sleep, a celebration drink after agreement had been reached for ending the BOAC pilots' strike, 5 April 1969. With Captain Laurie Taylor, Chairman of BALPA, Keith Granville, Managing Director of BOAC and Captain Max Reveler, Chairman of BALPA BOAC council
(Hulton Picture Company)

4b Talking to demonstrators against legislation to restrict the trades unions at a special TUC conference in 1969
(Hulton Picture Company)

5a Frank Chapple, General Secretary to the
Electricians Union, 1964 (Hulton Picture Company)

5b Vic Feather, General Secretary of the TUC (with
Jack Jones behind him on his right), at a
demonstration by trades unionists against the
Industrial Relations Bill, February 1971 (Popperfoto)

6a Len Murray, General Secretary of the TUC, with Vic Feather
at the TUC conference in 1973 (Hulton Picture Company)

6b Taking part in an ASTMS demonstration at Imperial College,
London, May 1969. This was the first ever dispute involving
university technicians after the creation of ASTMS. On my left is
Ian Mikardo, with John Dutton, joint General Secretary of the Union,
on his left, and Russell Kerr MP next to him (Hulton Picture
Company)

" You say you are Prime Minister? There must be a mistake! Mr Clive Jenkins is perfectly convinced HE is Prime Minister "

7a Cummings cartoon from the *Daily Express*, March 1970, at the time of the campaign for a single national airline (*Daily Express*)

7b Emmwood cartoon from the *Daily Mail* in 1972 depicting Edward Heath, Hugh Scanlon, Denis Healey and me at the time of the campaign against the Heath Government's wage and price policy (*Daily Mail*)

8 Demonstration in 1973 at the headquarters of the
National Union of Mineworkers, Euston Road, in support of a pay
claim (Srdja Djukanovic)

fund, although his titular leader, Leslie Cannon, certainly did
before his tragically early death in 1970.

It seems to me that in this complicated, sordid affair Frank
Chapple does not give adequate credit in his book to Mark
Young, who first raised the ballot rigging issue in a long detailed
letter to the *New Statesman*. Mark, a highly proficient national
officer, was later ousted from the electricians' union under its
new 'democratic' leadership. He and I collaborated in the civil
aviation industry, becoming firm friends, and Frank Chapple
accused me of leaving him in office as a 'ticking time-bomb' to
undermine him. After some celebrated airline diplomatic activity, Mark went on to great success as the General Secretary of
the British Airline Pilots Association and we had a great deal of
robust fun together in our international work.

I was also having fun laying about me with zest on all sorts of
topics in my *Tribune* column. Sometimes my pieces caused
unexpected controversy, which all helped the union cause
indirectly. After I had attacked the BBC's 'Black and White
Minstrel Show' as 'a revolting disgrace . . . a cultural obscenity.
Its black-faced singers recall the stereotypes of the Ku-Klux-
Klan', the *Evening News* was not alone in its reaction. Under
the heading 'A Pearl of Prejudice', its editorial began:

> We have a great respect for the Trade Union movement –
> at least for the responsible thinking faction which sticks to
> its brief and its last. But from time to time we wonder at
> the mental processes of certain Trade Union officials who
> seem to regard themselves as *ex officio* oracles on subjects
> quite outside their professional ambit. Such as Mr Clive
> Jenkins, General Secretary of the Association of Super-
> visory Staff Executives and Technicians (more commonly
> known as the foreman's union).

My attack, it went on,

> must have surprised 17,000,000 viewers – or at least those
> of them who read *Tribune*, for this brilliant programme has
> warmed their hearts and tickled their fancy for more than
> three years without – so far as we have been able to discover
> – ever once, until now, evoking a single word of contro-
> versy on the colour question. Blacked-up entertainers stem

from the plantations, Uncle Tom, the Swannee River and the Old Folks at Home – and the Black and White Minstrels are the best ever. They present the most lovable and endearing characteristics of the coloured races.

It is quite remarkable that this kind of racialist nonsense could have been written in 1964. No one would ever write such an editorial now and the Black and White Minstrel show is long gone. I had almost as sharp a reaction to my criticism of 'Curry and Chips', which had the sympathetic Spike Milligan impersonating a Pakistani. It was excruciatingly embarrassing and I wrote so. I later learnt that Spike, to my regret, was deeply upset by it and retired to his bed for a couple of days. But, once again, it was the kind of television programme which I think, now, could not be transmitted. At least I hope so.

Not all the comments about me were derogatory. By the mid-seventies, the *Daily Telegraph* magazine could write this gushing piece in a feature on graphology that showed my signature writ large on the front:

> Clive Jenkins thrives on prominence without being pretentious, his large and pleasing initial capital letters bear this out. Through his comfortable, relaxed and natural manner he is easy to get along with. Endowed with cool judgement he knows how to present complicated affairs in a simplified way and is co-operative and constructive in negotiations. Well organised, reasonable, literate and, although not particularly dynamic, he has a feeling for tone and colour. Sensuous, yet controlled, he is a man of warmth and human understanding, liked and respected by friend and adversary.

Yes, well . . . it was all good for trade, and helped show people that we white-collar workers were there for good.

I had some soft official targets in the years of Harold Wilson's first government, following the Labour General Election victory of 1964. I had been programmed early on to be against 'incomes' policies in a multi-national-influenced society and competed with my friend Jim Mortimer to make or move the setpiece oppositionist speeches on economic policy and the Common

Market at Labour conferences. I recall tossing a coin and losing to him while lying on the grass at Beachy Head, so he put the critical motion.

After Harold Wilson and Barbara Castle, as Secretary of State for Employment, set up the National Board for Prices and Incomes, I debated the Board's report on salaries for executives, managers and special staffs with the Board's chairman, Aubrey Jones, on a BBC Radio news programme. John Tusa, the questioner, asked me whether I agreed that there was no system in managerial pay. I replied, 'Not only do I say there is no system, I say that the present situation is chaotic, unfair, discriminatory and nepotic, and I would like to have some comment upon that. I see in the summary before me the incredible statement: "The Board found the assumption that people worked only or mainly for money widespread." Well, that's the discovery of the century, isn't it?' Aubrey Jones rejoined, 'I think this is a quite unfair description of that part of the report.' I simply retorted, 'I am reading it from the summary.' And I went back to the attack, because it really was a poor report. Aubrey Jones himself was a man of quality, but he had not been backed up well enough and had to say, 'I don't have a copy of the report in front of me so I can't quote a sentence, but I am not against collective bargaining for things other than wages.' This was a marvellous provocative situation for me, so that when Tusa called on me to make my final comments I could say: 'I am anxious to revolutionise the status of the British manager, under-rewarded, under-regarded, with a low status and a basic insecurity in employment.' Tusa asked if I could think of nothing good about this report – 'Isn't it going to be useful to your union in any way?' I responded, 'The only useful purpose from our point of view is that it will adequately provoke and make indignant and inform people that they can't rely upon the Board to act for them, nor the State, nor their employers. They are going to have to rely on ASSET.' I fear that I was so ferocious that Aubrey Jones ended by saying: 'My view is that Clive is exaggerating some of the features of this report. I doubt really whether he has read the report and, leaving aside the exaggeration, I don't think I fundamentally disagree with him.' That again was not a bad advertisement for us!

Aubrey Jones, a former Conservative Cabinet minister, was an attractive, feline personality. I remember that at one of our discussions in his office, Bernard Ingham, who worked for him – and was later to become Mrs Thatcher's press secretary, repeatedly interrupted to protect him. Unnecessary, for Aubrey was on the side of the angels: me. He had wanted a currently active trade union officer to be a full-time member of his Board, to make it respectably representative. He had acquired a veteran, the formidable and acerbic Robert Willis of the small, powerful London Compositors (surely the only TUC General Council member ever to go to gaol allegedly for stabbing his lady) and a Co-operative peer, Lord Peddie. Aubrey took me to lunch and asked if I would be interested. An inveterate, anti-corporate state, free collective bargainer like me? No, but I knew someone quite like me who I thought was looking for another challenge – Jim Mortimer. Aubrey asked me to sound him out.

I asked Jim to my home in St Mark's Crescent on the Regent's Canal and put the proposition to him. He was greatly surprised at the possibility, but interested. He was, as I had thought, jaded in the narrow draughtsmens' union. I arranged for him to talk to Aubrey and he was then asked to see Barbara Castle, who appointed him in her capacity as Secretary of State for Employment. The appointment was greeted with amazement and horror on the 'Left'. I was at a reception in the Banqueting Hall in Whitehall on the evening of the announcement and some people would have repeated the execution which had been the fate of Charles I on one of the balconies there. After Jim had shown himself to be both good and innovative in chairing Board inquiries, that all faded. The Board was the first public body to criticise the anti-union Foremen and Staffs' Benefit Society for its obstruction of normal industrial relations.

After an incoming Conservative government dismantled the Board, Jim went on to be the director of industrial relations for London Transport, where he helped to make them smooth and constructive. He was plucked from there to become the first Chairman of the Advisory, Conciliation and Arbitration Service. This was when ACAS had powers effectively to decide on claims for union recognition. There we had our only quarrel. I thought he could have given a casting vote on my union's application for recognition at the General Accident Insurance Company based in Perth. He did not, and the dispute and inter-union rivalry raged and then smouldered for years until we established an overwhelming superiority. After his retirement from ACAS, he became General Secretary of the Labour Party; the field was open and I was at my cottage in Essex when Dame Judith Hart, then Chairman of the Labour Party, telephoned. She thought Jim would be an excellent candidate; what did I think? I heartily agreed, and added intuitively, 'I think he is with you now?' He was. She passed the phone to him and I urged him to run. He did, and was selected. I let out a whoop of pleasure on hearing the telephoned news in a director's dining room of an incandescent lamp factory in South Wales.

I discussed many of my ideas about trade unionism and economic policies with Jim, who, like me, had been pro-grammed early against incomes policies. Jim was also against petty officialdom, quoting his Bradford father: 'Always distrust the man in the peaked hat.' We discussed reforming the TUC General Council, something which is still going on. In my fourteen years on the General Council (I should probably have been elected ten years earlier but for prejudice from blue-collar manual unions fearing competition) I only secured minor reforms: the major changes in structure were all reactionary and suited factioneering.

We wrote pamphlets and articles together and attacked the TUC for its document on incomes in *Tribune* in February 1968, prior to the ill-fated conference of trade union executive com-mittees. The government's policy, and the TUC's acquiescence to it, was a nonsense. There were signals of merit, such as a minimum wage, but also absurdities, such as a wealth tax – what of those UK residents whose assets were overseas? Jim and I agreed that almost all governmental incomes policies were wrong. At one Labour conference, I called the incomes policy 'as relevant as a blush on a dead man's cheek' – a phrase the BBC wanted to include on an LP of quotes of the year. When I asked about payment, they said, 'This is such an honour, we don't pay fees. But we could put you next to the Pope . . .' I accepted.

Although I then agreed with Jim's view, I now think that an incoming Labour government would have to decide the incomes of pensioners, the sick and disabled, those on Social Security, the unemployed and the young people in training or education, just after it takes office (the Party having made this clear in a General Election campaign), besides having to guide or influence pay negotiations in public-owned industries, the NHS, the Civil Service and local government. This is a huge task and probably cannot be attempted in Opposition. And where are the guide-lines and touchstones? What will the comparators be for public service employers: a shrunken but highly profitable, globally orientated private sector with financial institutions as the lodestone? Even though I am *now* for a policy for incomes earned and unearned, and wealth, I recognise that there are obviously colossal difficulties in providing fair shares for everybody in the UK given the 'liberalisation' in Europe (and the world) of capital movements. But while people like Jim Mortimer remain sceptical of such policies, there will at least be a healthy debate.

It was with Jim in the sixties that I co-wrote two of my books. I wanted to propagate ideas. Journalism, television and press conferences were not enough; one needed books to give an ideological basis. I had published *Power at the Top* in 1959 and *Power Behind the Screen* in 1961, and when I found that there was no textbook for schools about trade unions, wrote *British Trade Unions Today*, published in 1965. My union activities had pointed up the lack of an agenda for trade union law reform, and Jim and I therefore attempted to give a theoretical basis to security of employment, protection against arbitrary dismissal and the need for an arrangement whereby pensions could be transferred from company to company. We called this approach *The Kind of Laws the Unions Ought to Want* (as opposed to the kind that they had thrust upon them). It appeared in 1968.

Barbara Castle later claimed that *The Kind of Laws the Unions Ought to Want* influenced her very controversial White Paper 'In Place of Strife'. I doubt that, although we raised all sorts of new demands for workers, demands which now look faded because they have been won, such as a compensatory cushion for readjustment if made redundant, industrial tribunals which would be cheap and accessible for people feeling they had been unfairly dismissed (300,000 *a year*), the right to have a voice in company policy at board level and a tender regard for citizens entering a labour market pool as small fish when the supra-national sharks had discarded them. The European Community's Social Charter is now insisting on this.

The publisher of our book, and other later books, was Pergamon Press, owned by Robert Maxwell, a long-standing member of ASSET and then a Labour MP for Buckingham, having run one of the classiest election campaigns the country had ever seen. When I was talking with him in the House of Commons Tea Room about wanting to do a few campaigning books, he said, 'I'll publish for you.' Later I went to his office to negotiate with him over the contract. This was my task because Jim was embarrassed talking about money; (he always said that he left the commercial bargaining and 'purple passages' to me.) I asked Bob, 'What about royalties?', alleging that Jim was a hard man: 'It really isn't me, but Jim can be difficult.' All untrue of course. I was playing the scene from Shaw's *Major Barbara* where the gentile Undershaft blames his partner, Lazarus in a commercial transaction. Bob came to terms, alleging that he had only ever given such a large advance before to Peter Goldman (the unlucky Conservative loser of the Orpington by-election to Liberal Eric Lubbock).

Bob is a man of quite remarkable energy and imagination, as well as generous personal qualities. He had told me that his door was always open, saying that his mother had always welcomed people who knocked on her door in Czechoslovakia and would never turn them away at night. I soon had an opportunity to test his word.

During the oppressive regime of the fascist colonels in Greece in the early seventies, some of our trade union friends in Olympic Airways either were incarcerated or threatened with gaol in the course of an industrial dispute with Aristotle Onassis, owner of Olympic Airways. Mark Young and I went to Athens to show solidarity, a memorable trip in itself. I had prudently advised the Foreign Office that we were going and on arrival at the airport I could see an Embassy official obviously hovering to meet us. There seemed, however, to be some reception party on the tarmac and I was instead greeted by an elegantly tailored gentleman with an entourage and an outstretched hand. I asked who he was. 'He is the Minister of Tourism'. I replied agreeably, 'So, he is one of the torturing fascist bastards. Tell him to f . . . off. Can he speak English?' 'Yes . . .' So I raised my voice and repeated my greeting. We got out of the airport guarded by our British attaché, a splendid man with a vigorous, anti-fascist Scandinavian wife, and went to one of the best hotels in Athens, where we later had the most primitive difficulties on the telephone in trying to reach the British Embassy.

As we bustled around, trying to get our trades unionists out of gaol, we were obviously shadowed by a man and woman, both with moustaches, so we spoke loudly, colourfully and misleadingly. One day we went off to the Port of Piraeus, where the tables were under umbrellas on the sands on one side of the road and the restaurant was on the other, with agile waiters bobbing in and out of the traffic with lobsters. A yacht heaved in and down the gangplank came Leslie Blakeman, head of industrial relations at the Ford Motor Company, with whom Mark had been having a major battle on behalf of the skilled workers there. My own union for foremen was refused recognition at Fords for many years, although Leslie made friendly protestations to me about it – 'They don't have a foreman's union in Detroit but we'll get to it here eventually.' It would all, he said, change for the better in due course. (It did, but only after he had left.) On Leslie's arm was his wife Joan, a professor in managerial studies at Imperial College, and Mark and I walked over to the jetty to greet them – to their great surprise. We asked the tame or accommodating Greek unions to add the Blakemans to a dinner party planned that night in a luxurious restaurant just across from the floodlit Acropolis, where Joan lectured the silent and unhappy passive trade union leaders on the virtues of democracy and trade union independence.

Back in London, Mark and I found ourselves at 11.30 one evening in Holborn Circus and, recalling Bob Maxwell's open invitation, I suggested we call on him for help. We were seeking publicity in the cause of the imprisoned Greek pilots. We told a surprised security guard at the *Daily Mirror* building that we had no appointment but would he tell Mr Maxwell that we would like to see him. Bob came down in the executive lift from his penthouse office and asked us up. On hearing our case, he contacted the Greek Prime Minister, the Greek Minister for Transport and the Greek Foreign Secretary. The pilots were eventually released. When I later mentioned to Bob the help he had given, he did not recall it; it was Joe Haines, Harold Wilson's press secretary who was then working for the *Daily Mirror*, who remembered the episode.

Equally characteristic of Bob was his behaviour later when Ray Buckton, the leader of the engine drivers, was dangerously ill. Bob phoned to ask me what he could do to help 'our mutual friend'. Ray had spoken in support of Bob in his 1959 Buckingham election campaign, when Bob had lost, and again in 1964 when Bob got in. The hospital where Ray was being treated was hot and dusty – there were building works in progress outside – and it also seemed to be under-staffed. I had the unfortunate experience when visiting him of being asked by a junior nurse to hold a catheter which had come adrift while she went into the corridor and called for help. I left with spots of Ray's blood on my white suit. I also didn't care for the diet he was being offered – fish and chips? So I sent my driver to Harrods to buy baby food and other soft prepared material.

When I told Bob of the situation, he arranged for Ray to be moved to an air-conditioned room in another hospital. He also, on hearing of the lack of a suitable piece of equipment to help Ray out of bed, had an electrically operated chair manufactured, and arranged for a second specialist opinion, involving one of our most distinguished surgeons. Ray, I know, believes that his life was saved by the special care that was provided.

Another unusual experience with Bob was when he was anxious to buy the helicopter operation from British Airways and the workers were uneasy because of his unwarranted reputation as a hard employer. The management had, I think, floated a false hope that there could be a staff buy-out of the helicopter operations but it was not real. Mark Young, as General Secretary of the British Airline Pilots Association, the

Secretary for all the unions and I, together with Lew Britz of the electricians union, went and bargained a deal in Bob's elegant drawing room high in the *Daily Mirror* building at Holborn Circus. We said that we could recommend the workers to collaborate provided he gave them some representation on the Board and a share of the equity in the company. He agreed this and I wrote out the agreement, which was then typed and initialled. It was witnessed by Joe Haines and Peter Jay, formerly British ambassador in Washington, who was operating as Bob's Chief of Staff.

Bob was always under attack from the Trotskyists in our union who wanted him expelled because they said he had been anti-trade union or had behaved badly to the unions and workers. The truth was that if some printing union leaders had taken his advice, or had found it possible to persuade their people to take his advice, many of the Murdoch excesses could never have taken place.

One of the newspapers for which I occasionally wrote was the *News of the World*, whose editor, the wise and extremely experienced Stafford Summerfield, used to take me to the Savoy and I returned the favour by advising him about his conditions of service when Rupert Murdoch seemed about to defeat Bob Maxwell in the struggle for the paper. My advice was to get a new service contract, for five years. There was indeed an attempt to buy him out and according to a perhaps apocryphal story, a Murdoch manager later asked Lord Goodman how to break Stafford's contract. Reply: 'You can't.' – 'Why?' – 'I wrote it.' The only time I met Murdoch was at the bar in El Vinos when Stafford was uncomfortably introducing his new proprietor into Fleet Street. Stafford once reminded me that the page for which I was writing used to be occupied from time to time by Winston Churchill, whose driver would wait outside for the fee. Aneurin Bevan wrote there as well.

It was, however, the books I wrote, either alone or with co-authors, which gave the ideological underpinning. In all, over the years, they numbered nine. One critic jibed: 'He has written more books than the General Council has read.' This may have helped cost me millions of votes, for the deeply entrenched old blue-collar unions were determined to keep me off the General

Council of the TUC. They thought I would try to change things. They were right. I did and it helped my union to be seen to be influential in the power structure and to articulate demands our members did not know they had.

7

Amalgamations: Creating a Critical Mass

Early in 1967 a rumbling concern about union amalgamations in the white-collar field came to a head because we were obviously absurdly fragmented. The most important union in the area of engineering, metalworking and shipbuilding generally was the Association of Engineering and Shipbuilding Draughtsmen (AESD). This quite narrowly based design draughtsmen's union had carried on a courtship off and on with the Association of Scientific Workers and the Association of Supervisory Staffs, Executives and Technicians; we had co-operated on the De Havilland strike for a third week's holiday in 1964. But the AESD had a major ideological hang-up. The Draughtsmen believed that the engineering and metalworking industries were absolutely essential to the health and prosperity of the country; anybody not working in engineering was seen as of no real significance.

Jim Mortimer, who had been immensely influential in the De Havilland dispute and who was a life-long student and aficionado of the trends of the Labour movement and its trade union core, was the architect of the theoretical concept of One Great Engineering Union. That meant the merger of the AESD with the Amalgamated Engineering Union – and all the craft unions. The AESD told the AScW that they would be quite willing to take their engineering members. But only the engineering members. Those parts of the AScW which were not in engineering were not considered as very significant; indeed they might even hold up the process of having a great proletarian engine for advance. The AESD's proposition was clearly outrageous: an invitation to the AScW's self-dismemberment.

One Saturday evening in the middle of 1967 John Dutton, the General Secretary of the AScW, telephoned me at home, in despair because there was no possible way that they could divest themselves of their non-engineering membership and carry on. Their members there would not, could not, go. He had telephoned me as a friend: it had been a long acquaintanceship going back to the time when I was a lay member of the AScW in South Wales (at sixteen years of age) and John had the odd responsibility of looking after the Welsh and Scottish members. He was a Communist Party cadre product – in and out several times.

Without any authority whatsoever, I said that I would write him a letter on the spot from ASSET proposing an amalgamation, one with a special twist. I told him: 'This could be such an interesting marriage that I will recommend that we do it on a 50-50 basis down the line in spite of the difference between the unions sizes.' (They were claiming around 22,000 members, which we subsequently found to number about 15,000, and I was claiming about 75,000, a figure that was roughly right.) He gasped and said, 'Can you get away with that?' I wrote it all down and my wife typed the letter up on ASSET notepaper which I had at home at 16 St Marks Crescent, and I drove around to the County Hotel in Kingsway to meet a worried and relieved John Dutton. He took it in, as a godsend, to his Executive Committee on the next day. He rang me and said, 'We've done it.'

This was my first amalgamation campaign. We did not know what to call the new creation and before we went into the Registrar of Friendly Societies, John Dutton and I and Muriel Turner sat in a coffee bar near Grosvenor Square where I invented the title of the Association of Scientific, Technical and Managerial Staffs. It was meant to be a catch-all to bring everybody in. Muriel Turner wrote a new rule book in York between union meetings, which made it all feel very real, and the brilliant designer and water-colourist David Gentleman, a neighbour in NW1, drew four logos, of which we picked one.

Lo and behold we carried through the merger and ASTMS came into existence officially at the end of January 1968.

We had a critical mass and it reacted upon the whole trade union movement. It gave us a major network of offices and an income of about £355,000, and we promised in the recruitment literature that we would aim at 100,000 members. We would be, as we put it, 'among the largest unions in the country and the largest technicians' union in the world . . . a union capable of wielding immense influence both inside the TUC, where pressure could quite legitimately then be exerted to secure more adequate representation, and with employers' organisations, ministries and other policy-forming institutions'. This was, however, by no means the end; what was very much in the back of my mind was, as we said, that 'Neither of the merging associations see this as a final exercise in the rationalisation of the technical unions. They would, in fact, consider a successful and integrated amalgamated union to be only a preclude to further advances.' Indeed it was, and when the time came in 1986 to try to bring together ASTMS and the draughtsmen's union, retitled the Draughtsmen and Allied Technicians Association and later retitled TASS – the Technical and Supervisory Staff Section of the Engineering Union, the same 50-50 basis tactic was followed, although ASTMS had become much larger than the draughtsmen's union over the period. We also used the same techniques, that is, one union was called Division 1 and the other Division A, and these were run in tandem until it was possible to bring them together at a Rules Conference. So some very important lessons had been learned. Who cares about previous minor structures once you have merged?

In the creation of ASTMS, I got the theory right and opened the way for all of the twenty-six amalgamations and mergers that came about over the next twenty years. As I wrote in *Tribune* in 1968:

The merger of ASSET and the AScW to form the Association of Scientific, Technical and Managerial Staffs created the largest white-collar technicians' union in the World – a pipeline bulging with new members. But more than that, it *might* create a new pattern. Voices are still raised in favour of Victorian 'industrial' unionism. But the British trade union movement now has less than half a dozen one-industry unions which aim at organising everyone within the boundaries of a given industry and there is not a single union which has accomplished it in real terms.

This is because the boundaries of the productive or extractive processes fade as the end-result becomes less primitive. An advanced piece of apparatus owes much to several 'industries'. And who is to determine where metals and plastics demarcate from each other?

The new fact is that a common technology (based upon common training) is coming into existence. The new union (ASTMS) seeks to organise within that technology regardless of where the member is temporarily located. For he is more and more mobile – and he often has aims which can be expressed within an occupational or professional community that spans all industry.

After all, what characteristics should a union possess? I think these are essential: an accessibility, an openness to its members, so that they can feel genuinely involved – and capable of lever-pulling; a shape designed to protect and improve the membership's interests; and a sense for the 'forward move'.

We are going to aim for this in a spectrum of eligibility which runs from the factory floor to the university. This is not a union based on the varied but simplistic nineteenth-century formulae in an industry, craft or geographical way. It is a conscious attempt to create a bargaining profile that matches that of the new industrial giants; that seeks a settlement pattern which is not distant from the mass of the membership but linked with them – and inspired by them.

We are also out to bring fresh and better fuelled energies to the classic task of organising the unorganised. Both the founding unions had good records here (with almost all new recruits never having been in a union before). But there are tens of thousands left to be brought in from the enormous reservoirs of non-unionists who are now becoming aware that the great new companies will need special arguments if radical revisions of personal status and pay are to come – as they should and must.

So wish us well – we are going to essay the traditional union task, but with a new weapon and a new strategy.

I was writing about technicians and scientists without yet having a precise realisation that a common technology was emerging which embraced all white-collar workers, whether in health, education, banking, finance, airlines, automobile assembly or medicine. But the concept I had of a new kind of union dates, I believe, from then. It was late but we did it.

The new union started to recruit marvellously as a result of a lot of attention being paid by me to the mass media and also because the employers wanted to come to terms with us. However, in the first year of ASTMS' existence, we were involved in one of the worst media exposures I have ever had over the collapse of British Eagle, one of the privately owned airlines which had mushroomed in this period and with which we were constantly running into difficulties. On 2 August 1968, when in fact the company was in dire difficulties, we reached a three-year agreement at British Eagle. On that day I dictated a letter to them in their own offices in Conduit Street (which they typed for me): 'On behalf of the trade union side of the National Joint Council for Civil Air Transport I want to extend to you a warm welcome to join the National Joint Council. We are glad to have reached agreement with you and look forward to a constructive relationship.' They rejoined on the spot with much expression of mutual good-will and then went spectacularly bust on 6 November.

I had a very noisy exchange with British Eagle's staff on a television programme for which John Cousins, then the Airway's Officer of the Transport Workers, and I had left a trade union celebration (all I recall is that Engelbert Humperdinck sang) at the Hippodrome in London's West End to attend. We were subjected to impassioned pleas from representatives of the British Eagle staff to let them (even if they had no right to do so) pledge the £1.25 million in their pension fund to 'save' the company. I explained that this was absurd: that they were throwing money into a drain. As tempers rose I went so far as to say that if they attempted such a thing I would have lawyers in at once with injunctions to stop them, and at one point I angrily told the stewardesses, 'You can get stuffed'. It was injudicious, yes. But it was clear to me that £1.25 million was an absurdly small sum in relation to the liabilities of British Eagle and that they would need this money in the future.

The reaction in the media was violent and editorial writers round the country attacked me for interfering with the workers' rights to dispose of their own money. The outcry continued for weeks, so much so that there was a 'recall' television programme – which was understandable given that a group of obviously responsible pilots and attractive stewardesses were stating their willingness to work, as they put it, 'on doles wages' to keep the airline in existence. I held to the view that this was an extension of British Eagle's undercutting of other airlines and would deeply damage the interests of all the other people working in the air transport industry. On the subsequent television programmes there were dozens of cartoons depicting me as either a lustful pig or a jack-booted dominant union boss. What became clear was that the British Eagle debts were very large indeed. I thought that they might be between £6 and £9 million, which would make the sacrifice of the workers quite immaterial to saving the company; in fact the losses turned out to be much larger. We also subsequently found that for five weeks prior to the collapse, pension fund contributions had been taken out of the employees' pay and the company had not made any contributions to the fund.

We consequently opposed in every way we could the phoenix-like revival of the company and, again, we were subjected to all sorts of abuse. I was angry and showed it. Conservative MPs around the country quoted what I said on the 'Twenty-four Hours' television programme: 'You bloody well need rescuing from yourselves. To put your pennies into any company's begging box is a misunderstanding.' I was particularly angry because when the company collapsed there was no reference whatsoever to the fact that they had just decided they would have to come to terms with us (that is, all the unions) and lift their pay rates to a common sensible level, joining with the other employers in the National Joint Council for Civil Air Transport.

I went off, on behalf of all the unions, to see F. S. McWhirter, the liquidator, who commented that 'the financial resources of British Eagle have been strained for some time prior to liquidation. During the period January 1st 1966 to October 31st 1967, long-term indebtedness increased from about £2.7 million to over £5.5 million and there was a bank overdraft on October 31st 1967 of over £400,000, compared with a balance in hand as at January 1st 1966 of about £400,000. During this period net profits amounted to only £326,000 . . . the company had clearly become severely "undercapitalised".' He also commented on the overall managerial efficiency of the company writing: 'In this connection it is clear that Mr Bamberg [the effective controller of British Eagle] himself carried a very heavy burden of responsibility. The reasons for the loss of many of the principal executives in 1966 and 1967 have not been examined but this disturbance in the management team cannot have helped the company's fortunes in the succeeding two years. It may well be that lately Mr Bamberg had been forced to become too involved in the day-to-day management of the company.'

When I went to the Air Transport Licensing Board I argued that 'a management that behaves as badly as this company ought not in the future to be allowed to operate in any part of the British civil aviation effort which is subject to licensing by British governmental agencies. *They ought never to be allowed to operate in the future any aircraft that is not powered by an elastic band.*'

Over the years since I have had letters from individual employees, including stewardesses who were thrown out of their employment as a result of this reckless venture, thanking me for looking after their pension entitlements which they might otherwise, naïvely, have lost. From my union's point of view, while we had a great deal of malicious publicity, it became clear, in the end, that all we (and I) cared about was the interest of the employees. I was, however, stung by motions of censure such as that from the Wellcome Research Laboratories Branch of ASTMS on 15 November 1968, which declared that they 'deplored and disassociated themselves from the impression created by Mr Clive Jenkins, Joint General Secretary of ASTMS, in the BBC interviews of Friday the 8th and Sunday the 10th November regarding the liquidation of British Eagle and the spontaneous show of loyalty by the company staffs. We consider that loyalty and trust which must be mutual between management and staff does have an important role in modern industrial relations.' Well, yes.

The last formal word was perhaps said by the National Joint Council for Civil Air Transport, representing almost all the employers in the civil aviation industry and all the unions, which declared that they unanimously deplored the 'lack of consultation and breaching of agreements by Eagle International Airline. In particular, the Council regrets that the company failed to inform its employees of the state of its affairs and has created a situation where they are exposed to the potential loss of employment at the most difficult time of the year for the industry.'

Out of it all, however, came the realisation that workers do need to have an independent, collective bargaining agent who can say the unpopular things and can also see through some of the smoke screens.

This unfortunate dispute reinforced the resentment and anger at the report of the Edwards' Committee appointed by the Labour government to look into British air transport in the 1970s. It was an absurd report and looking back to June 1969 the desire to have another second or third force, privately owned airline competing with BEA and BOAC seems odd. I wrote in *Tribune* at the time:

> There is a historical cycle in which private airlines get into trouble and demand public assistance. They receive public money and then proceed to lose it. This sequence of events is then followed by a committee which suggests they should get some more. This cycle must be broken because it represents a plundering of public funds for private purposes. Even the Gaskellite Ministers at the Board of Trade must surely see this?

Nevertheless, the ministers concerned went ahead and another dispute erupted in August 1970 when a new Conservative government intervened in a situation where BOAC wished to take over British United Airways. In the late sixties at the height of the conroversy as to who should control BUA, I had led a delegation to Anthony Crosland, who was then President of the Board of Trade and responsible for airline policy. He was one of the most arrogant men I ever met, quite unwilling to admit to error or fallacy. He met us in his Victoria Street office puffing away at tiny cigars – which were eventually to kill him? (He had written a cruel review of my first book *Power at the Top* but that may have been due to jealousy based on a personal relationship.)

We were into the headlines again. I was depicted in the *Daily Express* as a king on a throne holding an image of Britannia and saying: 'We are conscious of the people bidding for BUA and entirely disapprove of these free-booting mercantile endeavours.' I said that the unions would resist any take-over by any political or industrial means; 'let them bloody well try' I commented. Adam Thompson, chairman of Caledonian Airways which was also bidding for BUA, said, 'If intemperate statements of Mr Clive Jenkins are to be believed and his threats implemented, the result will be anarchy. No country can run in this manner.'

The roguish Freddie Laker of Laker Airways, which decided to bid for BUA, was also rejected. I said, 'He is a professional full-time millionaire and we don't want him back.' Freddie characteristically joked: 'It is nice to know you can go away for a few days knowing that Clive Jenkins is running the aviation industry. It is unbelievable, the government's going to have a busy weekend deciding whether Harold Wilson is running things or Clive Jenkins.' The former Labour minister Ray Gunter said that I was 'intoxicated with transient power'. Every side seemed to get it all wrong. The *Daily Telegraph* of 19 March 1970 commented: 'Labour Presidents of the Board of Trade, whether allegedly centrists like Crosland or right-wing like Mason, were really quite terrified of private capital. Only the workers who were starting from the basis of their own self-interests got it right.'

At the end of the day, the British United workers *wanted* to be taken over by BOAC, and they were right, although it would be almost two decades before it came about. At the time, after much trauma, BOAC were not allowed to buy BUA and it went to British Caledonian Airways. I always thought that the political weight of the British and Commonwealth Shipping group was responsible for this.

Adam Thompson, who became the chairman and managing director of the new group, told the staffs at Gatwick Airport: 'The new airline will provide an alternative source of stable employment in the airline industry and will contribute significantly to the national economy. It fell to us to attempt to form the second force recommended by the Edwards Committee. I am delighted we have been able to bring this project to fruition. The unions did their best to stop it: they were frustrated.' And it took great losses and harm to the British aviation effort before, seventeen years later, a privatised British Airways was able to take control of Caledonian Airways. There had been much prejudice and profit-taking in the meantime. I had tried hard to shape something different. The best I could show was that I had helped to establish terms and conditions of employment in British Caledonian which were not worse than in the state corporations.

In the sixties the airline industry had been full of horrors. BOAC had gone into an agreement with Cunard in 1962 to have a joint company on the most profitable of the BOAC routes covering the eastern seaboard of the United States, the American Midwest, together with Central America and the northern part of South America. I bitterly attacked this and by 1966 Cunard was ready to divest itself of its interests in the company. Its chairman, Sir Basil Smallpiece – a thoroughly ethical if mistaken man – had been the managing director of BOAC when the agreement was negotiated. He had appointed the quite extraordinary Dr Kenneth Bergin as his head of medical services at BOAC and later took him into Cunard with him. I was with him at Dr Bergin's farmhouse near Heathrow when Sir Basil said, 'We have got to have a change. I think our personnel policies need a little "doctoring".' I thought that was right, but it is also true that people have soft spots for their doctors.

Colourful entrepreneurs regularly emerged in the private sector of British civil aviation. In a lunch with the arctic explorer Sir Alexander Glen (the honorary President of the British

Airline Pilots' Association – and a charming, generous benefactor), Mark Young topped my stories by recalling, during a dispute, going to a central London flat where the wheeler-dealer concerned greeted him with, 'I haven't got any money but I've got lots of whiskies.' Mark replied, 'I don't drink whisky.' 'Well, just look at them.' A door opened and in was wheeled a trolley with a range of Scotch, pushed by a smiling girl – quite nude.

The airline industry was anyway fascinating because of the struggle between the private and public sectors, and the large sums of money involved. Union competition was fierce and many of the individual union leaders concerned in civil aviation went on to make their names. Frank Cousins was active for the Transport and General Workers Union, of which he became General Secretary in 1964 and was appointed Minister for Technology in Harold Wilson's first government. There was also Bill Carron, later Lord Carron, President of the Engineering Workers Union and Papal Knight. I had some fun watching people's faces when I told them that Bill Carron and I once slept together: we had been on an inspection trip, by courtesy of British European Airways, to try to settle some issues in the Highlands and islands route of Scotland and in the Orkneys, when we were trapped by the weather and had to share a double bed.

Another figure was Sir Peter Masefield, the chief executive of BEA, who went on to be managing director of the Bristol Aeroplane Company. I vividly recall him recounting at a dinner in the Charing Cross Hotel a North Atlantic telephone conversation with Howard Hughes about the sale of his aircraft to Hughes' airline when Howard Hughes said 'I've got to take a leak now' and left Sir Peter hanging on – could it have been for half-an-hour?

An astonishingly reactionary and I think venal Jim Matthews of the National Union of General and Municipal Workers was also involved in civil aviation. When we disputed over workers' rights at Heathrow, his most argumentative response to me was 'Shut your cake hole, you'. He was also a member of the Labour Party Executive and I had successfully sued him for libel over the defamatory anonymous letter circulated about me in 1963 just before the selection conference for a prospective parliamentary candidate in Shoreditch and Finsbury. He was, I believe, somebody's tool and regularly issued press releases which were damaging to the Labour Party and trade union movement. He was tolerated for some years by the leadership of his union but eventually even they found that his excesses gave them a bad reputation, and the union distanced itself from him.

Over the years in civil aviation I was privy to all sorts of secret information and confidential memoranda, which ended up on the press front pages. Some of this information I found later, was the work of one man, even though it purported to come from a group of 'senior pilots'. I gave one piece to the journalist Peregrine Worsthorne, who printed it. It was a fake; I had been used. My source was high up in the management of BOAC and, I learned later, was an avid anti-Semite determined to expose various senior executives who had changed their Jewish surnames into Scottish-sounding ones. He was finally tumbled from his perch over some minor personal indiscretions about other directors. He went to see the chief executive and was asked to leave when it was found that he was wired for sound. But this elegant and slightly demented man gave me access to information for the furtherance of our members' interests and established me as a man of authority on the inner workings of the airlines, including key issues like aircraft procurement. We met in his Pall Mall club with his scarlet silk-lined bowler hat on the table and his secret files in an elegant black briefcase on his lap. He gave me my first pair of black silk socks after he had been on a New York visit.

His successor, John Gorman, a former senior police officer and head of security for BOAC, became a personal friend, after initially locking me in his office and expecting me to tell him all the confidential material to which I was privy. I didn't. In a period when airline managements were trying to explain their complicated tasks to trade union officials, we went round the world at least twice together, and had a lot of fun. I still recall an off duty evening in the Town and Country Club in Seattle when a representative of the employers went to a woman sitting in a corner and said, 'I will give you $5 to come and dance on the table.' She said, 'All right. Just wait until I put my teeth back in.' But these trips to study international airline comparisons were not all flippancies – although they helped. I still have a picture of myself in the plywood mock-up version of the Boeing 747 in Seattle. The plane was so big we did not expect it to ever leave the ground, but we warned our members in aerospace that it was on its way.

Our difficulties with privately owned airlines, epitomised by the collapse of British Eagle in 1968, were not the only ones in that period. Another dispute of considerable interest arose with the take-over of Associated Electrical Industries by the General Electric Company led by Arnold Weinstock. In February 1968 we faced a situation where Woolwich Arsenal was already closed down and Norton Villiers was in the process of shutting down their motorcycle industry. The prospect of substantial London unemployment, for the first time for generations, became real. I said at the time: 'We feel that this is just the start of tens of thousands of jobs that will disappear through mergers in the engineering industry alone. We see the creation of a pool of middle-aged qualified and skilled managers and scientists without any alternative employment where they live. Large firms should not be allowed to switch their operations without regard for the social cuts involved.' (Interestingly, this was the line being taken by Jacques Delors in 1988 as part of the social engineering in the European Economic Community so detested by Mrs Thatcher.)

When I talked to Arnold Weinstock about the GEC take-over, his line was, 'If you don't deal with me you will have to deal with Nippon Electric.' He was correct in his estimate: it was him or the Japanese. His personnel director was Sir Jack Scamp, the Labour government's favourite trouble-shooter on industrial disputes enquiries and a man of estimable worth. The pickets outside the GEC head office, however, had a nasty element within them carrying an anti-Semitic placard. I found this so detestable that I seized it and broke it over my knee.

In the end, we came to a deal which provided for a number of important safeguards for redundant workers, including a safety net whereby those who proved to be out of a job for some time and failed to get another job would be entitled to payments from GEC even though they had been off the firm's payroll for months. This was at a time when I used to go to the fortnightly Wednesday lunches at *Private Eye*, which, it became quite clear, was an upper-middle-class, anti-Semitic journal where some very odd people came, including, I think, at least one British intelligence officer. When I went to the lunch after the GEC deal was done, I was surprised to see Arnold Weinstock sitting there. He pointed his finger at me and said, 'Stop that man – he has got £2 million of my money.' The truth is that there *might* have been a quarter of a million pounds committed but in fact in the end GEC had to pay out to hardly anyone. We got severance pay provided by the law which I had helped to invent and we had a retention bonus paid to people who were required to stay in the factory to close it up.

Decades later I went to see Arnold at a time when he was seeking a new chairman for GEC. Our early evening meeting was possibly following a small but excruciating incident of prejudice in which a GEC employee had undergone a sex-change and 'his' old workmates, our members, declined to have 'her' back amongst them – supported by the local management. There was every objection, from 'nameless dreads' to there not being a suitable lavatory on the site. Arnold came out of his office (in his braces – years ahead of Wall Street) into his waiting room, where I was; in his own office, he often had an apprentice politician and would-be minister sitting and learning. As we were chatting in came Sara Morrison, evening-gowned, and sat on the arm of a chair. The last time I had seen her she had come to my office in an anorak wearing green wellies and apologising for the smell of the manure. 'I am a farmer's wife.' She was then married to Charles Morrison, MP. A charmingly forth-right, mid-stream Conservative, she was a GEC main board director as well as on the board of the Abbey National Building Society and the Imperial Group. She announced, 'Arnold is looking for a new chairman. Any suggestions?' My reply was that it probably had to be an anti-Thatcher prominent Tory (although Arnold told me he had donated money to the once renascent Liberals – and later to the proportional representation campaign). 'It seems to me that Jim Prior is your man.' I was due to see him a few days later about a trade union issue in Northern Ireland, for which he was still Secretary of State, and said I would mention it. We met in a very insecurely guarded office in Old Admiralty House and after doing our trade union business, I said, 'Do you know you are being considered for the Chairmanship of GEC?' 'No-one has told me,' he replied. I suggested he should ask around. He became Chairman.

I always trusted Arnold. Only at the time of the Westland Helicopters affair did I think he behaved in an unsatisfactory way by not fully informing me about a key meeting. He did not mislead me over GEC's role but he did not over-inform me. When I later reproached him he said, 'I'm not proud of that.' I left it there. During the time I was involved in trying to keep the Westlands plant afloat, Alan Bristow (an old antagonist) rang me on my unlisted desk line to talk. 'How did you get this number?' 'I have my ways; anything is possible.' I believed him. After all, as a self-described mercenary soldier for the French in Vietnam, he said he had hunted behind the enemy lines. I had against him the excessive length of his pink shirt-sleeves and his involvement in developing an explosive-headed harpoon for hunting whales. I asked him to lunch with Muriel Turner and Bob McCusker, then our union's national link to the metalworking industries. 'If you help me,' he said, 'I will keep Westlands afloat. I *know* there is a shortfall of work because of engine problems. But I can put in a major metal door contract. They can beat out metal doors until the high-tech is ready.' He reminded us that he had been a test pilot at Westlands in 1946–49 and left after a fiery confrontation with a senior manager. He really wanted his own back.

This was the time when I first started a campaign for very special protection for workers in mergers and take-overs. If only we had some of the protections that would have existed by having worker-directors as recommended by Lord Bullock's Report, some of the worst excesses of the Thatcher government might have been deflated or blunted.

Back in the early period of ASTMS' creation, we were already making headway in providing such protections, as in the case of the GEC take-over of Associated Electrical Industries. Our only major setback in achieving union recognition was in the steel industry in 1970, where we were crucified by the old blue-collar unions. The British Steel Corporation decided to refuse national recognition to ASTMS and the clerical and Administrative Workers Union (CAWU) on the advice of the TUC's steel industry trade union consultative committee. The Corporation's action was understandable, if inexcusable. It was between the devil and the deep blue sea because the trade union movement showed itself incapable of settling reasonably fairly its own internal problems. To offend the TUC Steel Committee comprising the predominant unions in the industry was to risk even greater trouble than that to be expected from the white-collar workers.

Exhibitions of power politics within the trade union movement are every bit as ugly as power politics in any other sphere. The struggle by manual workers' unions to prevent two white-collar unions from being given national recognition by the British Steel Corporation was particularly unedifying, though only too enlightening. Both the TUC and the Steel Corporation were in one way or another implicated in the injustice done to the CAWU and ASTMS.

A court of inquiry, headed by Lord Pearson, was held at which I sought persuasively to put our union's case. The employer adviser to Lord Pearson was Dan Flunder, a sophisticated manager from the Dunlop Rubber Company, who years later told me that Lord Pearson had said of me, 'What a loss to my profession.' I *was* good on the day, I *had* researched, Rumpoled, but I had a magical advantage: to my amazement the chamber had an echo-carrying quality so the whispers of the employers resounded in my ears.

The court accepted the view of the two white-collar unions that the consultative committee, consisting of members of the manual workers' unions in the steel industry, should not have the exclusive right to represent clerical and technical workers. And it recommended that we be given national recognition by the Corporation which, along with the TUC and the objecting manual unions, was criticised. The court's findings powerfully reinforced the case made by the Donovan Commission that we needed recognition procedures. It also spelt out the qualifications a union ought to possess to do its job:

> The factors to be taken into account in assessing any union's claim to recognition should include (a) the competence of the union to represent its members effectively; (b)

its general standing, total membership, resources, experience and, in a word, viability; (c) several aspects of its present membership in the industry, and grades concerned, e.g. the size of the membership, the proportion which it bears to the membership of other unions and to the number of workers in the relevant sphere, and whether the union's membership is increasing or stationary or declining; (d) any evidence of a demand from persons in the industry and grades concerned who are not yet trade unionists for membership of the union; (e) the union's 'roots' in the industry – the history of its previous activities, membership recognition, etc. in the industry; (f) any evidence of the union's capacity, or incapacity for working together with the other unions who have been or are to be recognised.

I wrote at the time that these looked like valuable guidelines for any future labour court that might be set up. In this case their application has led to the Court concluding that the decision of the British Steel Corporation to exclude CAWU and ASTMS from national recognition in respect of white-collar workers in the industry was mistaken and recommending that CAWU and ASTMS should have recognition.

The Court made the special point that the position of the Iron and Steel Trades Federation as the predominant union in the industry must be acknowledged. That is entirely reasonable and appropriate. In these changing times respect for each other's positions and a need to co-operate are quite vital if our member's aspirations are to be met.

In conclusion, I repeat that the case for some statutory-based authority for dealing with recognition issues gets stronger every day.

Although the recognition dispute in the steel industry was a setback, even that, in its way, was a signal to middle-class people that unless they were willing to be organised by themselves and on their own account, they would be trampled over by elderly forces of reaction. The message was certainly not lost on the workers in insurance companies.

In 1970 one of my assistant General Secretary colleagues, Bob McCusker, addressed a meeting for the Industrial Society on the changing shape of industrial relations law. He came back to ASTMS head office in Half Moon Street with the slightly surprising news that there had been a group of representatives there from the Prudential Assurance Male Staff Association and they wanted to know whether they could bring their Staff Association into ASTMS in some way, or perhaps pay us a fee for representing them. At the time it was quite difficult for Staff Associations, particularly in the finance sector, to keep abreast of all the changes in the law and incomes policies.

The request presented me with a problem because of my own background. I had always seen my task as organising the vanguard of the working class of the future, made up of managers, scientists and technicians: this was my Marxist error. But clerical workers? Were they not a somewhat lesser group within the community of manufacturing and engineering. I brooded. I knew that our somewhat antiquated Rule Book contained definitions of eligibility for membership which would barely include within them clerical staff.

I asked the leadership of the Staff Association to arrange a meeting for me to talk to them. It now seems remarkable that trade unionism in a large company could have been divided by gender as well as class, but the Prudential Male Staff Association in 1970 was separated off from the Ladies' Welfare Association; there was a separate association for the (manual) support staff (who were amazed when I went down into the Boiler Room to talk to them: no one had ever been down there in such a capacity), and there were other organisations for middle-level administrators and senior management.

I construed part of our Rules which referred to managers and administrators as covering clerical workers as well, so that the Prudential's Male Staff Association (and later other insurance workers) were eligible to join us. This interpretation was to cause a bitter debate at one of our ASTMS conferences, and there were vicious references to 'pen pushers' by our own bigoted office holders who did not want a bigger electorate. These were often Trotskyists, who courted the new masses quite unscrupulously once they were in. It took me back to the time when ASSET as the foremen's union were hostile to the Association of Scientific Workers on the basis that they were laboratory 'bottle washers'. We really have had some primitive demarcations inside the British trade union movement.

It was also necessary to go through the details of bringing about a merger or in legal jargon a 'Transfer of Engagements', and before a ballot took place we needed to hold a rally, which was set up to happen in the theatre at the top of the red-brick Prudential Assurance Company in High Holborn. News of our intentions deeply affronted other insurance unions. The National Union of Insurance Workers, which was a federation of a number of small unions – mainly insurance agents, and including the powerful Prudential Agents Section – complained to the TUC General Secretary, Vic Feather, as in a muted way did the Union of Insurance Staffs, which had perhaps 15,000 members who struggled for fifty years against great odds in this industry (if it can now be called an industry because the services offered are so widespread and sophisticated.)

Vic Feather convened a meeting under his own chairmanship, at which I explained that we had not sought this opening but we would like to go ahead. When I had spoken to Vic the day before, he had said without committing himself to me that the insurance unions were 'an amoeba facing a goliath'.

The Union of Insurance Staffs were of course strongly protective of their role in the industry but they had no important agreements apart from the relatively friendly Co-operative Insurance Society (which we were later to strike together). Their General Secretary was Maurice Reynolds, a man of great integrity who was to become a valued colleague. When faced with Victor's question, 'Can Clive go ahead with his rally next Wednesday or are you asking me to stop it on the grounds of inter-union competition being unhelpful to everybody?' Maurice replied, 'We have been attempting to organise Prudential Assurance Staffs for so many years that if someone now has the possibility of doing it I simply can't try and stop it.' So, not entirely under the rules of the Trades Union Congress, and without us having actually recruited a single member, Vic Feather summed up by saying, 'I think we should allow Clive to go ahead.'

Since I knew the rally was of historical importance, I invited Dorothy Wedderburn, then a senior lecturer at Imperial College, who was later to become Principal of Bedford College and, later still, of the merged Bedford and Royal Holloway Colleges, to watch it happening. A distinguished analyst of such issues, she came and sat on the platform with us. After a crowded rally the Female Association said they would like to come in as well and we had another enormous meeting. Some of the older career women were very unhappy about going into a reportedly militant union, though they were in a small minority. I can still see one of them with steel-grey cropped hair going into the centre of the hall, taking a roving microphone and saying, with her finger pointing up at me, 'Would you want to be led by that man?' There were massed hissings against her, and so we were away. Then came the Royal Insurance Company's Guild, and many other of the smaller staff associations.

However, before the ballot at the Prudential, the management unexpectedly announced an across-the-board ten per cent increase in salaries. There was amazement and consternation about this amongst our supporters. It later became known as 'the Welshman's ten per cent'. The leadership of the Staff Association were worried that the desire to join the union would diminish, but the city workers were very quick to appreciate that if they were to be given ten per cent for contemplating joining an effective union, then there might be even more money offered when they actually joined. A huge majority voted for the merger. In the room set aside for the leadership of the Male Staff Association they placed a plaque on the wall declaring 'Liberation Day' and the date of the successful ballot to merge with ASTMS.

The perception of the Prudential's workers turned out to be true and some of the best paid members in ASTMS became women working in insurance companies, who were on flexitime, which meant they were effectively doing a four-day week, and with an agreement that provided for a sharing with the management of gains made as a result of the introduction of computerised operations. There was a formal understanding that there would be no compulsory redundancies, and persons who no longer had a job to do moved to another area, protected by the 'red ring' around them, while those who wanted to leave through a 'cash-shaped exit' were also compensated and looked after until their retirement.

The line I took in addressing meetings of insurance staffs around the country was: 'The bad news is that you are poorly paid and under-represented, but the incredibly good news is that you have a very, very rich employer and I'm sure we can adjust these two ends of the equation.' I talked with Muriel Turner, who had been representing thousands of our members in the engineering and shipbuilding industries, about the new financial sector membership and we agreed that she would also take this on. She did it brilliantly. Over the years, we brought 80,000 members in all sorts of financial institutions into ASTMS, with Maurice Reynolds helping to bring in his own Union of Insurance Staffs. It created a situation where a white-collar union was spreading out from manufacturing, laboratories and transport into the whole field of services.

8

'We Don't Like the Colour of Your Eyes'

In the ten years from 1968 and the merger of ASSET into ASTMS, we sextupled our membership from 75,000 to 450,000 members. Crucial to this was advertising, getting through to the banks, the insurance companies, the down-trodden bureaucracies – the 'ant heaps' in which white-collar workers were as yet unmobilised. The television chat shows on which I was appearing helped enormously but in the early years I needed another major push and it came fortuitously. I was aided by a stroke of good fortune which came like so many of the lightning strikes around me over the years.

A member of ours named Barry Silverman, who was a buyer for the Co-operative Wholesale Society and therefore knew advertising agencies, came to talk to me in Half Moon Street about parliamentary candidacies and mentioned that John Pringle, the chairman of the American-owned Doyle Dane Bernbach agency wanted to meet me simply for a chat. He was a wealthy Jamaican who later became the Jamaican Deputy High Commissioner for Trade in London. (He once asked me if I could help black Jamaican workers by getting some kind of dispensation for ripening bananas to come through a London dock workers' strike but, alas, it was not possible, although I owed him a favour, and still do.)

He took us to the Connaught for lunch because he said they had the best pâtés and terrines in London. True. (The next time I went there was with a French general sent by his

117

government who was seeking my support in the Concorde controversy, knowing that I wanted the project to go ahead; they were so determined to have the Anglo-French treaty honoured that they briefed me to orchestrate British public support although against a Labour government.) I was told that Doyle Dane Bernbach in the USA had helped run Lyndon Johnson's campaign against Barry Goldwater. It was alleged that the telling phrase, after the Goldwaterites sloganised 'In your heart you know he's right', was the agency's, 'In your guts you know he's nuts.' Be that as it may, their copy-writers were scalpel-sharp. I was happy to explain what I was doing and trying to do amongst the lower-middle-classes. The agency was working in this field and at that time was developing a new style of razor for them which I happened to have bought. On learning this, John Pringle said to my buyer friend, 'I knew I was going to like this man!'

Out of that lunch came the idea that I should try to raise the money to buy advertising space for my union message where no one had ever bought it before. Where? In the, then, august and magisterial *Times*. John Pringle told me that his agency did social and charitable work and that, in classic advertising parlance, they had a situation where 'All our capital goes down in the lift every night' – making the point that their inventive, ingenious staff was all they had and he liked to keep them happy. He offered to get a full-page advertisement written and mocked up for nothing.

I was asked to brief David Abbott, an elegant, prematurely silver-haired man, who went on to become the doyen of advertisements which relied almost entirely upon text. So I sat with him, and others, wrote briefing memoranda and tried to illuminate for them how I believed technical, managerial and scientific workers felt, particularly when they worked together in large numbers. The merger mania wave was rolling over them. They had no control of their destinies. Their salary differentials had disappeared. The blue-collar workers were doing relatively much better, certainly had more industrial and political influence, and it was obvious that there were going to be all sorts of new labour and incomes laws and restraints which would bear adversely upon them if they did not have some kind of representative voice –

preferably powerful and respected. But the issue that concerned them most was the loss of jobs, which was to become a major and blinding passion among them over the next twenty years: careers were threatened, mortgages were at risk.

David Abbott, himself the son of a carpenter, went away with his colleagues to consider, while I meanwhile persuaded my cautious and apprehensive National Executive Council that it was worth us putting up £4,000 for a *Times* full-page ad to make a critical breakthrough. A meeting was set up and Ian Mikardo, the President of the union, and I, went off to the Doyle Dane Bernbach office in Baker Street, where we were slightly surprised to find Michael Manley, the former- and future- Prime Minister of Jamaica; he had just dropped in for fun. Abbott unveiled an ad which later won many prizes and which he says fuelled his rocket-like rise. It was all text, and brilliant. The heading ran: 'The Board and I have decided we don't like the colour of your eyes.' It was obvious that this was a winner, and the following text was crisp and succinct, and clearly marched down and off the page. We almost clapped. I said 'Will you book the space?'

The final version ran:

THE BOARD AND I HAVE DECIDED WE DON'T LIKE THE COLOUR OF YOUR EYES

It's not usually as brutal as that. Usually, there's a polite phrase about a 'clash of personalities'. But the end result is the same. A man gets the push because his face doesn't fit.

It could only happen at one level in British industry – the top.

Managers and executives in Britain today are working under conditions the workers wouldn't tolerate. Most of them don't have any kind of service agreement. They work long hours without overtime. Their pension schemes restrict their movement from job to job. Taxation blunts their initiative. Mergers can leave them in middle age out of a job. With a past, but no future. Thrombosis claims more of them than it does of any other working sector.

And as if that wasn't enough, they've now got Mr Aubrey Jones to worry about.

You may not know it, but the Prices and Incomes Board is shortly going to review executive and managerial salaries. Your salary. Your future. When it's done, it'll pass its recommendations on to the Government for action.

Before that happens, we think somebody ought to speak on your behalf. And that somebody is going to be us. The Association of Scientific, Technical and Managerial Staffs will be presenting evidence to the Board, arguing for a revaluation of your status and salary. Amongst our 100,000 members, we have more than 8,000 managers in British industry. But we know we'll be speaking for a lot more people than that.

Some of the problems we want to discuss will be sickeningly familiar to you:

Salaries. Should you get increases on a regular basis? Should there be a minimum amount? Or must how well you do always depend on how well your firm does?
Extra duties. Should you get extra money? Extra leave? Is there a difference between the odd occasion and systematic overtime, like weekend work?
Holidays. Considering the responsibilities of your job, do you get enough time away from it?
Contracts. Is an agreement necessary? Need it be in writing?
Inventions. Do they belong to you or the company?
Publications. Should companies stop you publishing the results of original work?
Dismissal. What's fair compensation for loss of your job? If 'misconduct' is alleged, who should judge whether it's true or not?
Restrictive covenants. Should an executive leaving a job be prevented from working for a competitor?

Until these, and many more questions are answered, we can't see how anyone can make a fair assessment of your position. And it's vital that the assessment is fair.

The manager is a key part of British industry. It's not simply a pun to say we can't manage without him. Yet to work with imagination and drive, he needs more security. More money.

He doesn't need the conditions which drove one of our members to write us this letter:

'. . . following the merger, I found myself at fifty, with less and less to do. I didn't really have a job. My secretary read books all day. I stretched answering two letters into a day's work. Finally, I became ill and had to leave. Though I know the real reason for leaving was redundancy, I, of course, had no redundancy pay . . .'

Fortunately we were able to help him. We could help more people if there were more of us.

But this isn't a recruitment drive. If you think you might like to join us we'd be glad to send you some literature. But right now we'd be happy if you'd do one simple thing for us. We'd like to send you a summary of the report we'll be making to the Prices and Incomes Board. Tell us what you think of it. Where you feel we're overstating the case. Or understating it. If you've had some bad experiences, pass them on. Your name and your company's name will be completely confidential. They'll not appear in the report.

We think it important that we speak up for all executives and managers. Not just our members. Because if we don't, who will?

The remit of the National Board for Prices and Incomes to analyse the problems and remuneration of managers gave us a peg on which to hang our message. The Board, under the chairmanship of Aubrey Jones, did not have as critical role in terms of the national economy but it provided us with the opportunity to publicise our view. We had prepared a submission to the Board and after seeing Abbott's text I edited and shortened our report, printed 10,000 copies and held the type just in case we had to reprint in response to enquiries.

The ad in *The Times* ran at the end of April 1971 and attracted immense media interest. There were countless stories in all the other newspapers about it and, of course, we had the interest of television and radio. We ran press conferences and put the ad in the provincial press. In the following week we had 4,000 separate approaches from people who had never been in unions before and we had rapidly to put in telephone enquiry lines. I loved it. This was a colossal response to a union that only had going on 100,000 members.

Even more significant than individual enquiries was the reaction from many staff associations and groups of office workers who approached us even though they had previously been anti-union. Some were employer-financed to the point where unions found that staff associations with tiny member-ships had a chief officer whose remuneration package was perhaps two or three times that of a General Secretary of a large union (try to beat that in a merger). We decided that we would further explore the psyche of the insecure administrator and also the fears of staff association leaderships that they would not be able to cope with all the new legislation and in particular the fears of their memberships, far from their pliant leaders, that they would fall further behind in terms of pay and conditions. This was more marked in the South-East and South of England because most of the staff associations were in the finance sector located there.

I did another detailed briefing and David Abbott and his associates came up with another full page *Times* ad: 'My Boss was very fond of saying that if I had a problem, the door was always open. I didn't know at the time he meant the front-door.' The text explained: 'It is a long-standing tradition that the white-collar worker does not need a trade union. Why have a contract when a handshake will do? Why spoil the atmosphere with talks of negotiations and agreements? Hasn't the company always looked after its staff? At ASTMS we understand how you feel. We think you are wrong for a couple of reasons.' We then went on to develop the idea that if the better-off in society all had contracts, why shouldn't the worse-off in society have contracts as well? An illustration was the American union leaflet which pointed out that if Barbra Streisand and Robert Redford were trade union members and needed an agent, 'Why not you, too?'

We were able to use the classic argument that more people were joining us all the time – at the rate of a thousand every week – and getting 'theirs': we had negotiated redundancy agreements which were much better than the legal minimum (which we had also invented). We capitalised on the fact that the first major insurance workers' staff association at the Prudential had received bargained increases, led by Muriel Turner, of up to twenty-five per cent in nine months. We had also negotiated the, for those days, breathtaking salary of £4,000 per year for senior Ford Motor Company supervisors (the manual workers on one assembly line at Halewood had chalked up the joke headline 'Ford Foreman Marries Commoner'). This too went quite well into our arsenal to win over the staff associations.

Doyle, Dane Bernbach did two more full-page ads which were also very successful. The headline of the first ran, 'My tragedy was that I picked up a pen instead of a shovel', which certainly hit home. For good socialists like Ian Mikardo and I, however, this was a difficult ad to approve because we wanted unskilled manual workers, who were relatively poorly paid, to have more money, although our appeal was to the better qualified and certainly poorly paid salariat. We were *based* upon differential payments then. So approve it we did and again it brought a large increment of members, although we had criticisms from the leftists and Trotskyists that we were appealing to the 'wrong kind of people'; this we disregarded as totally self-defeating rubbish. When the new unionists joined us they were liberated and inventive, and socially conscious; I was quickly transformed in their eyes from being a horned Bolshevik to a reactionary bureaucratic General Secretary.

The last full-page ad read, 'I'd rather be on the dole than join Clive Jenkins', with a picture of me. It ended with the poignant words, 'I didn't and I am'. Again the intention was to attack prejudice against unions and people like me who articulated the union's policy, and again it was very effective.

We had not overcome prejudice in the press and one of the London newspapers ran a critical editorial about the page we had bought from them. So out the ad came and went into other newspapers. This was when we had a purely London campaign with another agency, which targeted shipping company head offices and which was moderately successful.

So we rode the media. And as journalists are so imitative, the message fed on itself. Our news clipping service has probably become rich on our account over the years. I personally marked for our archives every interesting clipping from 1960 to 1988. These were regularly pinned up in our head office foyer so that our staff could read what was being said about us everywhere from *The Scotsman* to the *South China Morning Post*. After being taken down the clippings were put into books and were later deposited in the modern records centre in Warwick University, along with all my personal engagement diaries. I wonder what some aspiring PhD will make of those – and of all my personal codes.

As the seventies progressed, it was my estimate that there would be a huge job loss in offices where they were into the second wave of computerisation. The Research Director of ASTMS, Barry Sherman, and I explored this in a book *Computers and the Unions* in 1977, which stimulated us to write the seminal *Collapse of Work* in 1979 and to have a stab at what was likely to happen in the labour market in *The Leisure Shock* in 1981. All these books, the press conferences around them, and the subsequent reviews and radio and television programmes were creating a situation which made it seem fashionable, attractive and socially acceptable to join with us. So I put another plan to my Executive Council that we should run a further advertising campaign. By now David Abbott had long gone off into the stratosphere of the advertising world, so we used another agency. They were excellent but we did not have the same impact when we went on warning people that they were at risk from technology that we probably could not negotiate away. We could get them money but absolute protection of their jobs and careers we could not. There was a point at which people did not want to be told that they were on the equivalent of the World Wild Life Fund list of endangered species.

The advertising slogans were good, like 'Had your chips yet?' underneath a dustbin of discarded white collars and the comment 'Fact. One chip can replace 800 white-collar workers.' (I never knew where they got that statistic from.) Others were, 'You can get your cards when your employer gets his chips . . .',

'Any job you can do chips can do better' and 'How long before you are replaced by a silicon chip?'

Peter Parker, then Chairman of British Railways' Board, refused to let us show them on railway stations on the grounds that it would seem that we were recruiting at the expense of 'his' railway unions, and we had an extremely acrimonious before-breakfast meeting at his Marylebone headquarters. I suspect that he did not want his workforce worried either. We were prohibited from buying space on tube trains or buses, although due to local quirks we got them on buses in Manchester and the local trams and tubes in Glasgow. I still do not know Parker's motives. When he was in the glass container manufacturing industry, we got along, although he seemed bored with it and said he wanted to launch a Thames Bateau enterprise as well. Whatever happened to that?

We recruited as a result of the campaign and it showed that we were looking forward into the future, trying to protect our existing members and our potential clientele. But the revolutionary ploy of using full-page ads had clearly run its time. This was virtually the last of the paid advertising which ASTMS ever undertook.

In painfully building ASTMS, there were spectacular problems which I sought to turn to our advantage. In 1971 when I was holidaying in the weak sunlight of Marrakesh's orange-tree-lined streets, I opened the *Financial Times* which I had bought at the railway station and found that Rolls-Royce had collapsed. Only a few weeks earlier the unions had been given an upbeat presentation by senior managers, whose only criticism of their own performance was that 'we keep detailed records of *every* engine every built but it is expensive!'

I cut my holiday short, turned back to London and found a disastrous situation where highly qualified engineers were being sacked and where the 'workers' shares' were at risk. Was this the end of a British share in the world market for aero-engines? It seemed that the Rolls management had got the pricing of the RB211 wrong in the contract. There were crucial personality failures here.

Lockheed's (then untainted by scandal) desperately needed

the engine for its new civil aircraft and because of Lockheed's importance to US defence, the US administration was disposed to help by way of loans and support. But it did not have enough votes in the Senate (although Edward Heath had successfully (overnight) nationalised Rolls-Royce). What to do? Our members at Derby urgently prepared an appraisal of the delayed RB211 engine project and the action moved to Capitol Hill. I wrote a letter to every Congressman, every chairman of any committee who might be involved or consulted and, importantly and of immense significance, to every Senator.

I then ran into the difficulty that we had a long-running postal strike in the United Kingdom and the letters could not go. So I had them all packed into two large suitcases and I went on an over-the-pole flight – coincidentally with the chairman of the Lockheed Aircraft Corporation, Dan Haughton. We were filmed boarding together and the television news programmes reported 'a rescue mission'. He travelled first class and came back to sit with me in tourist class, wearing a small American flag in his lapel. He demanded 'labour peace' at Derby. How could I promise that? I told him that if we could rescue the RB211, Rolls-Royce and his great company, I did not see any industrial relations problems in Derby or any other of the Rolls-Royce plants. He said he would take it back to his directors.

My friends in the International Association of Machinists in Los Angeles set up an emergency operation to mail out all of my letters. I still wonder what effect they had. The Bill to authorise loans to Lockheed went through the Senate by only one vote. Senator Jacob Javits (Republican of New York) wrote to me that my letters and documents had changed his view and his vote. So, who knows? I think that my initiative really did work, although it was a close-run thing, particularly when I arrived in Los Angeles to find that there had been a small earthquake and some of the facilities I was relying on were not functioning adequately. But we were seen to be doing more than any union in helping to shape events.

In a post mortem, this horrendous event that obliterated so many careers had to be analysed. I asked the distinguished industrial sociologist, Dorothy Wedderburn, to set up a study of what actually happened to the people decanted from their jobs. Some of them would not speak to her researchers: the shock had been so great. She had earlier published a study of white-collar sackings in 1962 after the cancellation of the English Electric weapon, Blue Water. I had titled our union version of this: 'I am young, I am skilled. I am unemployed and I live in Stevenage.' I later had to abandon a book of taped reminiscences of the unexpectedly unemployed, 'No work, no hope?', because I found it, vicariously, too painful.

These caring initiatives attracted the media and had a quite remarkable, but calculated effect upon our collective bargaining, where our credibility was being tested every day. The local leaders were still unsure and unexperienced. I recall a crowded meeting at Heathrow where I was advocating a new deal. The money was good but it meant *change*. The debate ran for almost two hours when a specialist in compass adjustment rose: 'Our Secretary is a crafty bastard. But remember this, he is *our* crafty bastard.' So I was: we had a good agreement. Elsewhere, people were being chastened and learning all the time in a hostile atmosphere.

Educating our union officials was all the more important to me in such an atmosphere. Training was a special interest of mine and we had created a college of our own for training ASTMS representatives, based in the old Gilbey (gin) family mansion at Bishops Stortford. Inside the union there was resistance to that: 'training for what?' But we built a cadre of activists. As we grew and bought adjoining land, I treasured the words of a neighbouring landowner, Colonel Venn, a disaffected Tory and long-time local Conservative councillor: 'I'll be a good neighbour. I don't know much about unions but can I shoot over your land?' He could. When he died we bought his land.

The college was called Whitehall, the name by which the area had been known for hundred of years. My detractors murmured, 'He always wanted to *buy* Whitehall.' Shirley Williams, as Secretary of State for Education, was invited to open part of the college in the late seventies, but she was delayed by parliamentary business. She was always being delayed by something. I remember that around this time I appeared with her and Selwyn Gummer on a talk programme for Anglia Television and in the run-up to transmission, with still no sign of Shirley,

Selwyn Gummer got up and did a little twirl, saying 'I'll do Shirley in drag.' Pity it didn't prove necessary. For the college opening, a Minister of State deputised for her; I cannot remember his grey name but he too defected to the Social Democratic Party. The stainless steel plaque commemorating Shirley Williams' presence had another strip added to it: 'But she didn't come.' In the only act of vandalism at Whitehall College both were stolen. Pity.

The Labour Party leadership held summits at the college and the undergrowth got used to Special Branch and other marksmen. One of the pleasures of having a green and delightful resource of this kind was that we could also indulge in international work – which had its pitfalls. On one occasion, a group of twenty-five Egyptians came in response to our invitation to the Egyptian trade union centre. One of my colleagues, a formidable black lady named Allyson Lewis, took them sightseeing to Cambridge and, ushering them on to the bus for return to Whitehall, scooped up three too many unsuspecting foreigners from the streets of Cambridge.

I also encouraged a major health and safety office and the most effective (and largest) research department in the unions. This published a 'Quarterly Economic Review' because I became jaded with the Trade Union Congresses and Labour Party Conferences where my opponents would ask W.I.Y.A. (what is your alternative?). Our analyses and forecasts were better than those of institutions in the economic prediction field: the Treasury, the CBI and the Bank of England. Not that this was anything *really* to be proud of!

Meanwhile, I continued to plug our message in the ASTMS journals. They were designed by the late great typographer, Allen Hutt, a lifelong left-winger, who was brought to my office by his friend Frank Gullet, then news editor of the *Daily Worker*. When I felt I needed a relief in my pages from my endless campaigning I asked the admirable American cartoonist Jules Feiffer how much it would cost to reproduce his brilliant strips. His reply was generously sympathetic: 'Take what you want!'

I found cartoonists in general odd people. When I spoke at their association's annual dinner, I was struck by how glum or disenchanted so many of them appeared and how so many had moved rapidly from left to right politically. Giles was a loss: from sharp observation (in a left-wing framework) to grand-motherly pictures of family life for Beaverbrook, and Christmas stocking-fillers. The most brilliant (and worrying) cartoonist was Vicky, apart from the glancing illumination of Abu and Peter Fluck, later to have more fame through 'Spitting Image', who portrayed our members poring over skilled work at London Airport for my union journal. Vicky, one of the earliest Aneurin Bevan adorers, was deeply pessimistic, stimulated by working in a hostile newspaper format but unhappy, and we lost his insight sadly and soon. He once told me in the Scarborough Hotel, owned by Charles Laughton's brother, that he regretted conceiving the Supermac image for Harold Macmillan as it bestowed a panache upon Macmillan which was deserved but which was electorially unhelpful to Labour. As a quite passion-ate anti-Tory this nagged him.

Light relief, whether from cartoons or not, was certainly needed in the relentless fight for our workers' interests. Occasionally it came unexpectedly. One day the charming Barbara Kelly (partner of Bernard Braden), who ran a booking agency called 'Prime Performers', rang to ask me if I would do a television advertisement in a selected region. 'It's for frozen waffles.' 'Frozen waffles?' I conjured up satirical chants in conference halls as I strode purposively to the rostrum. 'Waffles, Waffles, Frozen Waffles.' She mentioned a substantial fee – £10,000 – and when I rejected the whole idea she responded, 'I told them it would not be good enough!'

This was long after the task of making the union *look* credible had been undertaken, and achieved. When I had become General Secretary of ASSET we had had about 14,000 members and an income of £65,000 a year. By 1988, when I was Joint General Secretary of Manufacturing, Science and Finance – the organisation superseding ASTMS and brought together by straightforward recruitment and amalgamations – there were more than 650,000 members in the union and the annual income was about £18 million a year with real estate assets of more than £40 millions.

9

The Common Market

'When the man wants it, he wants it.' The speaker was a *Daily Express* feature writer referring to Lord Beaverbrook as he took my dictation of an anti-Common Market piece in the main newsroom of the black-glassed building in Fleet Street in June 1961. It was a busy frothing room with an elegant Osbert Lancaster drawing – one of his Maudie Littlehampton cartoons – on an easel in the middle of the floor.

I had asked why page after page was being whisked away out of the manual typewriter before I had the chance to look at the finished article as a whole. Allegedly, Lord Beaverbrook wanted to see it as it was composed and typed. But he was not in the building. So page by page by despatch rider? It was my first national press article in the campaign I waged from 1960 right up to the 1975 Referendum against British entry into the European Common Market. Along with Lord Beaverbrook, General de Gaulle, Enoch Powell and Tony Benn, I got it wrong then, and got it right over twenty years later.

Most of the Left was against entry, but some idealists and a few Trotskyist groupings saw the prospect of an United Socialist States of Europe. In the Labour Party, this was emotionally articulated by the veteran Labour MP, Bob Edwards, who could always wind up a speech with references in ever more rolling cadences to the 1930s, the Spanish Civil War and the famously brave International Brigade. I treasure (and I asked him about this once) the story about Young Socialists, then effectively Trotskyist, seeking to challenge him on 'socialist principles' in a parliamentary selection conference. Bob had been actively involved in international affairs over the decades, especially for the Independent Labour Party, and responded, 'Comrades, that is not how Trotsky put it to me'; bending down he took out a book from his briefcase with a fly-leaf inscription to him from Leon Davidovitch Trotsky himself.

The Tribunite left agitated through the 1960 and 1961 Labour Party Conferences, and I was reported by John Ennis in *Reynolds News* for 18 March 1962 in a profile headed 'A fast-talking Welsh dynamo who *enjoys* beating the bosses':

When the 1961 Labour Party Conference came to discuss Britain's entry into the Common Market, things were not quite as they appeared on the surface. Sitting shirt-sleeved in the hall, Clive Jenkins, a small fast-talking Welshman, felt his well-developed political antennae registering intrigue, but for the moment he was unable to get a direct bearing on it. When he did catch on, he moved quickly into a piece of subtle political by-play that left his opponents awe-struck.

Three resolutions were put before the delegates: one for entering the Common Market, one backed by Jenkins for staying out and a composite resolution which advocated entry with safeguards so potent that the Europeans probably would not accept them anyway. The composite resolution was adopted. Then the chairman asked the woman who had moved the pro-entry resolution if she would remit it for consideration by the Executive. Suddenly Jenkins saw through his opponent's plan. The woman was expected to shout 'yes' and delegates would go home leaving behind them an open door to the Common Market. But the woman missed her cue. Before she could reply a male voice called 'No'.

The delegates voted and the pro-entry resolution was lost.

Then the chairman asked Jenkins if he would remit his resolution. He was expected to say 'no'. After all, he had spent his lunch hour telling his supporters: 'We are going

to fight it out.' Now, on his feet, he changed his tactics.
'Yes' he said!

So the delegates went home, leaving the door to Europe
no more than ajar and Jenkins with the right to raise his
point the following year. It took Jenkins some hours to
prove to outraged supporters that, far from turning traitor,
he had snatched victory from defeat.

This was all roughly true but my 'supporters' saw the points
quite rapidly. On the Wednesday of the 1962 Labour Party
Conference, Hugh Gaitskell made, against this background, a
devastating anti-Market speech which gave him the only whole-
hearted Conference ovation of his time as Leader. Frank
Cousins went emotionally to the rostrum and promised to
finance printing one million copies of Gaitskell's speech for the
Party. I wonder if he ever did? And did they manage to
distribute them?

George Brown's fudging supporting speech was a muddled
disaster. I do not think Cousins offered to reprint that, although
some die-hard union marketeers whispered about the possi-
bilities: the whispers faded. The MPs who did not get up were
(excepting Roy Jenkins) the nucleus of the SDP breakaway
almost two decades later.

In the wake of the marketeers' despair, Anthony Howard
wrote in the *New Statesman* in his usual misunderstanding of
trade union tactics:

> The only real reassurance, in fact, came in the defeat of
> ASSET's resolution demanding that, regardless of terms,
> the question of Britain's entry into the Common Market
> 'must be placed before the British people at a General
> Election', yet even this was scarcely a matter of substance
> – as they had already realised that this was the only logical
> interpretation to be put on Gaitskell's own speech. Any
> comfort they derived from this – the only ballot vote to
> take place in the Common Market debate – they owed
> entirely to the tactical ineptitude of Mr Clive Jenkins –
> which for once surpassed even that of Mr John Stonehouse.

He did not understand we were working for a voters' decision
and registered almost two million votes (although 2.8 were

pledged). Tony Benn later powerfully developed the Referendum proposition. Poor insecure John Stonehouse, a golden boy who was greedy, had been a chairman of our Parliamentary Committee and made a brilliant speech to our Southport Conference (we gave his beautiful wife some orchids – she said she had never had any before – as did Mary Wilson when we gave a dinner for Harold to celebrate his election as Leader of the Labour Party in 1963). When Harold Wilson appointed him to office after his 1964 Election victory, John rang me: 'I am in a telephone box in Whitehall. I have got Aviation.' Many years later, after his faked disappearance from a beach in Miami a naïve bank manager telephoned me to ask if I was the Clive Jenkins who was a co-signatory of a small bank account with a Mr John Stonehouse. I had long forgotten a fund we set up for the anti-Common Market campaign.

I now look back at the passions of those times with some surprise. I still recall Harold Wilson's satirical speech in the Commons in this period about the (im)possibilities of our 'selling refrigerators in Dusseldorf' and his bringing bundles of reprints from Hansard to a Party Conference, opening his briefcase, balanced on his knee, and giving me a handful with the request to give them to union leaders. I did.

The left trade union motives were classic. We very reasonably had reservations about the Europe of that time, the immediate past and the perceived future. The ghosts (and some physical presences) of Adenauer, de Gaulle, Franco, de Gasperi and Salazar confronted us. Later, we had the Colonels' coup in Greece and the conflict in France in 1968 reinforced us. Who could have prophesied (Red) Daniel Cohn-Bendit as the Green Deputy Major of Frankfurt, the German financial centre of the Federal Republic of Germany in 1988?

So we campaigned on all sorts of grounds. I wrote a rather jingoistic four-page leaflet, much seen, if not read, at Labour Conferences and called 'Against the Treaty of Rome: 18 Questions answered by Clive Jenkins'. Now, in the post-Gorbachev era, some of my 'answers' seem at least stilted or unforgiving:

Economic integration always means political commitment. This could be extremely hazardous. Just what will happen in France after de Gaulle? The West Germans' policies certainly would not commend themselves to most Britons. After all, both candidates for the Chancellorship of West Germany argued for the return of Silesia. This is the language of war. West Germany's eastern neighbours distrust her growing military strength and are alarmed at the inflammatory speeches made at rallies financed by the West German government.

Do we want to be committed to an enlargement of Germany's frontiers? This is a serious question of immediate concern: advertisements were recently placed in Irish newspapers by the West German Dublin embassy. These provocatively claimed that the frontiers of Hitler's Third Reich were the 'legal' boundaries to which West Germany is heir! In the Common Market – as now organised – we shall be inextricably bound to West Germany. The men behind the Common Market are in politics. They want one nation, one citizenship. And British membership means to them the weakening of a rival manufacturing and trading power. It could also dissolve the Commonwealth, break up the Sterling area and enable other 'export-hungry' European nations to penetrate into British markets.

At the time it felt right. It seems so dated now.

I even went into court to seek an injunction to prevent the government distributing informative (pro-EEC) literature through the post offices. I lost because it was held in the High Court that I was not especially disadvantaged as an individual. But it was all good mass-media fun.

My union Executive Committee licensed me to demonstrate. We even held a meeting in 1971 at Wissaint in Normandy addressed by leaders of the Communist, Social Democratic, Catholic left and managerial trade union federations, all bitterly competitive with each other. We chartered a small aircraft from Lympne and ran into trouble when we landed: one executive member had left his passport behind. But as he was Welsh and a rugby supporter, the immigration officer asked his opinion on the games to be played and shrugged his shoulders agreeably to let him through. The wine was good: we did not learn too much. The Communists were simply hostile on the basis that the EEC was a buttress of anti-Sovietism; the division of Europe would be dominated by a West Germany manipulated by the United States. The Social Democrats were dismissive, saying that French workers were not interested in wider European questions, so the floor was being left to the technocrats in *their* Europe where, overall, only twenty per cent of the workers were organised and three million foreign workers were living in poor conditions and grossly exploited. Overall, they did not want us in and warned of the cost of supporting a medieval farming system.

I shunned visits and appointments to Brussels committees for years but we asked a professional journalist working there to be our 'early warning' reader of directives and drafts to sensitise me. My apprehension and prejudices were profound.

In my constant campaigning in the period before the 1975 Referendum, I was criticised for sharing platforms with right-wingers like Enoch Powell and Lord Hinchingbrooke. I remember one particular Saturday evening in Hastings where Enoch and I (he was an extremely amusing man in private and away from immigration issues) had agreed to do a Town Hall meeting. As we were driven through the deserted streets, our spirits were low – until we got to the hall where hundreds were trying to get in and the organisers were desperately seeking overflow facilities. So we did two meetings. Hastings was passionately anti-Market or simply greatly entertained by Enoch and me counterpointing each other. I still see Enoch sitting on a table gaily swinging his legs.

As the Referendum on EEC membership loomed, Granada Television launched an ambitious expedition within their tradition of 'polling-as-you-go'. Their press release read:

A gaily Union-Jacked Lancashire bus has just completed a 3,000-miles journey of discovery in aid of European understanding. The Selnec coach was loaded up with a Granada 'World in Action' camera team and nineteen Very Important Passengers for a fifteen-day jaunt round Europe. Except that 'jaunt' is a little too flippant a word for the serious business in hand.

Fifteen of the passengers formed a carefully selected cross-section of the British people – housewives, farmers, pensioners, a car worker, a shopkeeper, a managing director. Their mission – to find out for themselves and the television viewers, at first hand, what life is like for the European man in the street.

Chipping in on the political arguments were Lord George Brown and union boss Clive Jenkins. The economic experts made up the party: Stockport driver Alf Walker was at the wheel and Granada's Mike Scott acted as 'conductor'.

The results of their round-Europe quiz will be screened in two hour-long editions of 'World in Action' as the referendum debate reaches boiling point.

Granada had sent a jet to pick me up from my union annual conference in Bournemouth. I took Greta Karpin, the head of my secretariat, and a researcher, with me. When George Brown found this out later that evening he was furious with the producers, especially David Boulton. He wanted a researcher. 'But you did not ask us . . .' The sounds of his rage came through the walls of the Windsor Hotel in Brussels before they comforted him with bottles of white wine (he was allegedly abstinent at the time). This was different in mood (and his moods changed often) from when George first joined the bus at a motorway service station, fresh from a football match, and attempted to lead the passengers in a rendition of 'I'm forever blowing bubbles, pretty bubbles in the air'.

George was always a temperamental problem. I was in the lower bar in the Windsor Hotel in Brussels when he literally rolled down the stairs into it. I was not surprised. Years earlier, when he was chairman of the Home Policy Committee of the Labour Party National Executive Committee, I was leading a deputation of airline unions arguing that state airlines ought to be able to buy hotels, sell tours and offer all kinds of services instead of simply carrying passengers. This may seem normal now, but then it was not. I kept referring to how Pan American Airways (later Pan Am) was expanding into the services area. George could not comprehend. 'Clive, I understand your argument, but what has this got to do with Panama?' and so he went on, to the embarrassment of the Committee and its staff.

Stories about George compete and jostle with each other. My favourite (if apocryphal) is when, as Foreign Secretary, he had appointed Len Williams, General Secretary of the Labour Party, as High Commissioner to a West Indian State (where he is now buried). Allegedly, and it was easy, they quarrelled in the Foreign Secretary's room in the House of Commons and as Len stalked away down the corridor, George shouted after him, 'And I hope your f . . . feathers fall out.'

But George and I put up with each other most of the time on the two-week bus trip, donning fur coats for filming the frozen food mountains and suffering excruciating frontier customs delays (which still exist). After all this, there was a television technicians' strike in Granada and the programme only just got screened: instead of on successive nights it formed two one-hour segments on the same evening.

I think opposition to entry was justified then, although eventual!y I was elected to the Executive Committee of the European Trades Union Congress. This was a frustrating experience and I still resent the politicking (allegedly to suit the West Germans and the Americans) which has kept out significant union federations in France, Spain and Portugal. The British Trades Union Congress was (and is) traditionally timorous in this area and even when I asserted that I had talked to other delegates and found there was no last-ditch opposition to the entry of the excluded union centres, I was told, 'You have been talking to the wrong people. If we force it to a vote, we will lose and put the issue back for years.' So we did not and the years still tick by. The nation states will abandon their frontiers before the unions.

In mid-1988 my union published a post-1992 agenda, 'What about the workers?' using all the nine languages on the cover. It was aimed at the British and the Irish, as the union was strong in these two EEC states. Then the proposition was put to me as President of the TUC that the recently re-appointed President of the EEC, Jacques Delors, be invited to address the 1988 Congress. This was unprecedented: Congress had been anti-EEC for so long. But it was correct, timely. I think the

inspiration came from David Lea, an Assistant General Secretary of the TUC, and long engaged in Euro-economic affairs.
So Delors came, and also helped us and Michael Rizzello, the
distinguished sculptor, to present the latter's bust of Nelson
Mandela to the African National Congress. He then made a
fluent social engineer's speech, as from a 'militant' of the French
non-confessional Catholic white-collar CFDT union federation,
which apparently irritated and perturbed the British government and its Prime Minister.

So, what a change; from fear of a totalitarian Europe to hope
that better legislation would come from Socialist influences and
Social Christians on mainland Europe which would blunt and
then reverse the right-wing thrust of a Conservative government
based on the South-East of England. The EEC has certainly
been much better for women's efforts to right discrimination
against them. I had to face up to these realities and I publicly
thanked and praised Jacques Delors, making sure he saw the
long composite motion agreed by Congress which was, and is,
an agenda for advances by all those citizens who have to go to
work. I then went to the Labour Party Conference as the TUC's
fraternal delegate in October. On the record there appears this:

Clive Jenkins (past President of the Trade Union Congress):
'Comrades, fraternal greetings sometimes empty a hall. I
am here to bring you greetings – so "greetings". But I want
to bring a set of historic messages because the Trades
Union Congress is re-estimating our thrust in Europe. This
is a hard process of learning from life itself and from 1960
many of us, many of the comrades here, opposed British
entry into the European Economic Community. But that
was the Europe of de Gaulle, the Europe of Franco, the
Europe of Salazar, the European dimension that was forced
upon us by the Greek colonels and of course, Franz Joseph
Strauss, by the great butter mountain, the rampant anti-
Sovietism and a deep distrust of the People's Republic of
China . . .

'We now have Mitterand and socialist governments in
Spain, Portugal and Greece, powerful socialist parties
poised for power in Italy, Germany, Holland and Belgium,

and a socialist Commission President in Delors, whom I had the privilege of welcoming to the TUC. Only the British government is now out of step in Europe. She may criticise Delors and the Commission for social engineering, but we are all social engineers here and therefore we reach out and extend our hand to Delors.

'We want Euro-legislation to protect workers in mergers and takeovers. We want Euro-minimum wages, the right to be consulted by management, the right to have power in companies, the rights of women to equal status by law and we look forward to the battles over the new European company law, already drafted with a social dimension which is abhorred and detested by the British government. We want rights for workers as well as for the fictional small shareholder. The workers at GCHQ could not have been victimised this way inside the EEC and I have to say to the Prime Minister: remember, there have never been any working-class spies; they all came from Eton, Harrow, Oxford, Cambridge and their secret societies. [Applause]

'Only EEC regulations will now clean up our polluted island, doused with arsenic and dripping sulphuric acid.

'But as we see the EEC cleansed of its anti-Sovietism and welcoming President Gorbachev's initiatives, I also welcome Delors' principled opposition to apartheid. At the TUC, delegates wore their badges greeting Nelson Mandela and Delors associated himself with it. The gold badge for Nelson was presented to the African National Congress, all banned persons. I was later told the badge had been taken in to him and he was wearing it in his prison room.'

So that was the end of the Labour movement's opposition to British membership of the European Economic Community. We were right in our day – but that was yesterday. I could not have behaved differently. Would the fanatically right-wing pro-EEC Labour MPs have split away? Would they have had the financial resources? Could Thatcherism have been averted because our vote would not have been split? The touchstone of 'Europeanism' now seems archaic: the left will be most vigorous in the post-1991 Community. The Labour pro-marketeers of the sixties and seventies are now all side-lined. The mainstream of the Labour Party will help set the agenda in a socially inclined EEC which may well heed Mikhail Gorbachev's plea not to build a permanent wall across Europe in 1992. What a vision!

10

The Social Contract
Era

In 1975, with prices and inflation on the increase, the unions and Wilson's Labour government reached a joint understanding on minimum wage rises which undoubtedly saved the economy. The social contract owed a great deal to Jack Jones, General Secretary of the Transport and General Workers' Union, and the most effective and influential trade union leader in the post-war years. When he in effect invented the £6 per week increase, this immensely benefited large numbers of the transport workers' membership and low-paid workers generally, although Jack recently told me that skilled engineering workers had made gains as well and their employers' federation hated it. It was a settlement that many unions had not even dared to claim in the past but Jack had the numbers and the personal stature to help to bulldoze it through. I was against it because the overall package had the effect of reducing or lowering differentials still further, so I think it probably was a minus for my own union. However, there is no doubt at all that the political advantages were immense and although looked at against the long march of history skilled technical and scientific workers managed to improve their status and their returns in others ways, this was a base.

The Labour government also appointed the Bullock inquiry into industrial democracy and I was an active member of the committee and a signatory of the sensible democratic suggestions in the 1975 Bullock Report. However, the trade union movement in a confused and reactionary way denied itself the huge potential gains that could have flowed from adopting the Bullock Committee's recommendations. They evoked a hysterical response from employers and some union leaders, who seemed not to want to see a transfer of authority to their members as employees. My own union conference rejected it after Trotskyist attacks, at least one of which was written by a leading lay member, Harry Newton, who had a guru-like influence in the Midlands and was only after his death identified as a long-time serving MI6 intelligence officer planted in the union.

I should have realised that the Report was hazarded when in a building especially rented near Congress House in Bloomsbury Square one of our meetings was interrupted by an urgent call at 11 am, for Jack Jones to go to No. 10 Downing Street. He was back within the hour, shocked, and whispered to me, 'Harold's going to resign!' 'Why?' 'He wouldn't say. Let's go down to the pub next door. He said it would be on the one o'clock news.' It was probably at that point in April 1976 when Harold Wilson resigned, handing over to Jim Callaghan, that the impetus went out of the political push for workers' democracy.

At one time we thought we might just have an agreed Report. But John Methuen, who had been appointed to the Bullock Committee when Director General of Fair Trading, was headhunted to become Director General of the Confederation of British Industry. I remember asking him why he went to the CBI, since he had a grievance about his earlier experience as a manager in ICI, and he replied, 'They made me an offer I couldn't refuse.' (Ironically, he died unexpectedly in a private sector hospital.) Until then we had counted him as on 'our side' but he later turned around from what seemed to be a reasonable progressive position to attack sharply the recommendation that workers' representatives on boards should come through the 'single channel' of the recognised trade unions.

The Bullock recommendations might have prepared us for the Social Charter after 1992 in the European Community. All of us on the committee were impressed by the sheer effectiveness of the way the systems worked in the Federal Republic of

West Germany and Sweden. Of course, in Sweden the economic problems of collective bargaining can always be sweated out in 'night mangling' sessions in the sauna. An old friend of mine who chaired the Swedish Labour Market Board and later the state corporation which controlled certain public enterprises helped our deliberations there with six kinds of aquavit, spiced sausage and meatballs, and a sauna – so the naked Bullock Committee members plus the British Ambassador argued it out in the heat.

Sir Barrie Heath, Chairman of a large British engineering company, topped this on our return from Germany by having a small jet sent for us suitably loaded with champagne. There were two pretty girls (there always seemed to be around Barrie) but he put on an apron and popped the corks (several) himself.

There was a chilling incident during that visit. Prime Minister Jim Callaghan was visiting Chancellor Helmut Schmidt and had a high-speed motor convoy sent to bring us to join German leaders for dinner at the Chancellor's old residence in Bonn, where he was waiting to move into a new, more secure building. I was having a drink with the two leaders on the patio when Chancellor Schmidt was called away. I had been talking about the problems hampering our marine insurers in the protected West German market and was giving the Chancellor an *aide mémoire* prepared by some affected British companies for me in the hope that I would meet suitable personages and press their case. We had earlier heard that a Lufthansa aircraft had been hijacked and ended up in Entebbe, and when Chancellor Schmidt came back he was grave faced. 'It is very bad news. They are separating the Jews from the others.' He added significantly that this was especially traumatic as he was a German Chancellor.

Back in the United Kingdom, powerful forces were assembling against British workers having new rights. Anthony Sampson in his book *Anatomy of Britain* wrote that the Cabinet was split, with Edmund Dell, then an ASTMS-sponsored MP and Secretary of State for Industry, attacking the concept and Albert Booth, Secretary of State for Employment, backing the unions. A Cabinet sub-committee was appointed, including Shirley Williams and Tony Benn, and a White Paper appeared in 1978.

The Callaghan government then lost the Commons vote of confidence and after the General Election of 1979 all thoughts of taking new ground evaporated. Dell and Williams, of course, left the Labour Party.

I look back on this as a major disappointment, a defeat engineered by reactionary elements in the political parties, the employers, the unions, the security services and the Trotskyist splinters who also did not trust or want workers to look after their own interest. If only we had had anything like workers' representation in management and policy-making, the sudden shocks of redundancy and mergers could have been managed better. Now we will have to await reform from the outside through EEC directives and legal structures. I hope that the trade unions will be progressive and ambitious this time.

Jim Callaghan's government did not deserve to be brought down. It could have been saved, although Jim must bear responsibility for at least three errors on his own account. In his memoirs he wrote of the 'fateful' target of five per cent for wage settlements (which was an arbitrary figure virtually plucked out of the air):

> At the final Cabinet meeting of 1977, held three days before Christmas, I summed up for Ministers my view about the outlook for 1978: if we held as near as we could to our pay policy, the inflation rate would be steadily reduced to about nine per cent. That would be a noteworthy achievement compared with earlier years, but not good enough. For the first time I put forward the fateful figure of five per cent inflation as our objective for the pay year beginning in August 1978. That would require wage settlements of the same order, recognising these by results in earnings increases of seven per cent or more. Some Ministers took a very pessimistic view of achieving such an objective, but nevertheless, I repeated this figure publicly in a New Year's broadcast. A year later, they were entitled to say (although most of them are too kind to do so) I was wrong to have set such a low target.

Well, yes. I argued for no sharp-edged figures to be published and to try to put some silk into the bargaining process. Jim continued:

> Our disabilities in trying to come to some agreement with the TUC for the 1978/9 pay rise were compounded by the fact that the leadership of the two largest unions were changing hands. Jack Jones, the leader of the Transport Workers, retired in March 1978 and Terry Duffy was elected to succeed Hugh Scanlon at the Engineering Union in May 1978. These changes materially weakened the influence of the Neddy Six, the top union leaders with whom Denis Healey, the Chancellor, had negotiated previous pay agreements. The other mistake was not to go for an election earlier.

It is well known that the six leaders on the National Economic Development Council were asked to go to see Jim to talk about these issues at his farmhouse. But he made an amusing speech to the Trade Union Congress, with a song about 'waiting at the church', and the disputes worsened. There was a drive to reach some kind of agreed document between the government and the unions, and as Jim wrote, 'it was argued the very fact that an agreed document was in existence would keep open the line between the Government and the TUC: there was an explicit recognition of the link between pay and prices increases and the document might ensure a hoped-for-neutrality from the TUC as a whole.'

This all went badly wrong because a number of people didn't come to the key General Council meeting at which the document was presented. Moss Evans of the Transport and General Workers' Union was so certain it would sail through that he went on holiday to Malta. Why? He had been at the Finance and General Purposes Committee on the previous Monday where the recommendation had been 'almost unanimous'. He had taken Len Murray, the TUC General Secretary, into a corner and asked if he should cancel. He was advised it was not necessary, so he went off. Len Murray has since said that he had had no confidence in the negotiations and was not sorry the document had not carried. It did not seem like that on the day. He looked deeply downcast.

Jim records that disappointing meeting when the document was not adopted:

> The Government was to be denied even this. We had anticipated that when the Neddy Six presented the document to the full Council of the TUC in November 1978, it would be accepted. Their own negotiators had spent five weeks hammering it out and expected no real difficulties. All of us were wrong. There was strong resistance, some of it very misguided. At the end of a long discussion the document was put to the vote and the result was a tie: 14:14. The Chairman, Tom Jackson, was in favour of the document and by convention was reluctantly forced to give his casting vote against it. So it was lost.

My memory is different. I recall Tom Jackson simply declaring the document 'Not carried'. He did not give a casting vote against it. There was no such convention. I wonder how this silly story got circulated. Of course, he could have given his 'deliberative' vote even before the casting vote. If I had been in the Chair, I would have firmly given a deliberative and a casting vote for the document without any doubts at all because it was clear that a Thatcher government would be a very positive threat to trade union activity. The other problem that day was that so many people were simply not there: a turnout of only twenty-eight is tiny for a General Council meeting. To recall the General Council was not a political possibility, although some of us did all we could to salvage some sort of accord.

I remember being amazed by Moss Evans when we met in the Marquis of Granby, the traditional pub across from the Transport and General Workers' Union, and learning that his union's Executive Committee had made the lorry drivers' wildcat strike official 'in order to control it'. I think that this was clearly a strategic error, even though Moss believes the drivers' substantial increase was largely 'self-financing' and therefore within the five per cent limit.

I thought the agreement with the government should have been approved by the General Council. At an earlier meeting on the morning of the 14 November, we were given assurances, and in the marginalia on my agenda I noted, 'We are away from the five per cent, we are not setting out a framework of rules or sanctions of any industrial Court. We do not have to support a union opposing the five per cent limit but neither do we have to condemn.' The previous weekend there had been a number of ill-judged speeches. Bernard Dix, Assistant General Secretary of the National Union of Public Employees, spoke at a Tribune Rally in Birmingham in defence of a claim for a rise of nearly fifty per cent for the (badly paid) 1.1 million local authority workers and a claim flagged by 250,000 National Health Service ancillary workers, with another claim from miners for forty per cent coming over the horizon. Bernard very properly insisted that:

> the first job of trade unions is to look after the interests of their members. This means above all else, you endeavour to negotiate improvements in wages and conditions. If unions cannot do this because the government has imposed a limit on wage increases, your ability to act on wider political, economic and social issues will also be reduced, because they will have lost their bargaining power and with it the support of their millions of members.
>
> The Tory Party would welcome such a situation but it would be an absolute disaster for the Labour government. It is a matter of historical fact that a Labour government can exist only if unions can give support to the Labour Party financially and otherwise. If a Labour government weakens the unions by using sanctions to impose pay limits and prevent free collective bargaining, the unions will have few resources and less power to support the Labour Party.

He continued, dangerously pessimistically, that this meant 'the prospects for a Labour government are virtually non-existent'.

He was only half right. It turned out that the unions did lose a great deal of their power to influence social and economic issues. But some of the union bargaining figures were also plucked out of a void and it is now clear to me that much more will have to be done between the unions and government in the future because Labour, on taking office, will have to have an incomes policy for the unemployed, the aged, the sick and the students. The whole of the national income will have to be taken into account in a much more sophisticated way than ever before. This underlines the importance of the Labour Party's concept of a National Economic Assessment.

The drama before the fall of the government was played out over the following weeks with pay norms effectively eliminated, but the damage had been done, and the situation was further inflamed by the decision of the Labour Party Conference against the five per cent target limit. There was also a general feeling of antagonism against automatic sanctions such as suspending purchases by government departments from companies which breached the guidelines. The last but one draft that I saw of the statement by the government and the TUC on collective bargaining costs and prices had some mutually contradictory paragraphs. One of them stated that the government reaffirmed its position as given in the White Paper, 'Winning the Battle against Inflation', including the maximum level of settlements consistent with the agreed objective and discretionary action necessary to support it. This was clearly a threat in anyone's language. But in the next paragraph it was stated that 'the TUC remains committed to voluntary collective bargaining and believes that adherence to its guidance to negotiators . . . will result in settlements . . . consistent with the agreed objectives . . . It also believes that the threat on the use of sanctions in these circumstances is neither necessary nor desirable.' So at the heart of the statement was this worm. I voted for the document because I wanted to save the government and also because we had been given numerous assurances that there was going to be a lot more discussion and no more *fait accomplis*.

Paragraphs 11 and 12 sketched an outline of how it might be done:

> Progress towards the agreed objectives of any action that may from time to time be needed, will be discussed at monthly meetings between Ministers and representatives of the TUC, which will cover all relevant economic issues . . . For the future, the government and the TUC will

CLIVE
JENKINS

IAN
MIKARDO, MP

9a With Ian Mikardo at an ASTMS conference teach-in satirising the
Heath Government's industrial relations proposal, 20 June 1971
(Hulton Picture Company)

9b Tony Benn and Barbara Castle during the
Labour Party Conference in 1976 (Hulton Picture Company)

10a With members of my executive during a weekend at Wissant,
France, to discuss the industrial effects of the Common Market
with French union leaders, 14 March 1971
(Hulton Picture Company)

10b With other ASTMS union leaders and the Mayor of New York
on a visit to look at US labour law and health care
(Dick de Marsico)

11a Salmon fishing in Vancouver with Lawrence Daly, General
Secretary of the National Union of Mineworkers, during a TUC
delegation to Canada in the mid-1970s

11b In North Vietnam during the making of a TV documentary,
standing on the one bridge which the Americans failed to
destroy with their bombing

12a In front of a union slogan during an
ASTMS press conference on recruitment in 1979
(Hulton Picture Company)

12b At the press conference for 'The Secret Policeman's Ball' in
1979, in which I had a walk-on part. With me, left to right, are John
Cleese, Rowan Atkinson, Billy Conolly, Anna Ford and Peter Cook
(Hulton Picture Company)

13a Michael Foot addressing the ASTMS conference
just prior to the General Election in 1983 (Jack Blake)

13b Following a swim at the ASTMS college, Whitehall College in
the early 1980s, with Ron Todd, Moss Evans of the TGWU and
Geoffrey Drain of Nalgo

14a The General Secretary of the TUC, Norman Willis,
during the 117th annual conference in Blackpool in 1985
(Popperfoto)

14b Consulting Terry Duffy and John Boyd of the AEU during the
Labour Party Special Conference in January 1981 at which the
electoral college for the election of the leader was created
(Laurie Sparham)

15a On the way to Aberdeen with Robert Maxwell to address
British Airways helicopter workers and reassure them that,
following his purchase of the company, Maxwell would grant them
a share in equity and would not be an asset stripper
(Bill Rowntree/*Daily Mirror*)

15b Giving the TUC Presidential Address, September 1988

16 One of the photographs as General Secretary of ASTMS,
taken for the National Portrait Gallery in 1982 (Liam Woon)

make arrangements for annual discussion of the whole range of social and economic matters which are a common concern, including a common understanding on the prospect of pay and prices.

It wasn't just official words. On the Economic Committee top paper for 14 November I noted in the margin, 'This buries five per cent and *sanctions* and any incomes policy policed by the General Council.' Promises were given of comparability reviews on wages and salaries between groups of workers to avoid damaging disputes.

There were unsolved issues, of course. I noted Tommy Jackson asking, 'Can a price increase brought about by pay increases be cancelled by the Prices Commission?' Alan Fisher was concerned about comparable work and comparable pay: 'Do you compare, for example, hospital catering and laundry workers with commercial laundries and catering?' Tony Christopher of the Inland Revenue Staffs' Federation warned that there were big increases on the way for civil servants even with staging over a period and this was likely to heighten the temperature of the brew. My position was that, with misgivings but reinforced by all the Ministers' oral promises, I was for it. It seems to me now that what Tommy Jackson said at the time deserves to be reproduced: 'The trade union movement has lost its way. It is not socialist. I would prefer an incomes policy.' I was against *that*, but who is to say that, now, he was wrong on this issue?

The first draft of the 'TUC Guidance for Negotiators' had an unacceptable paragraph which read:

The General Council do not believe that it is practicable or desirable to attempt themselves to 'vet' claims or to act as watch-dogs in the process of negotiation or to scrutinise settlements. They believe, on the contrary, that negotiators should themselves accept specific responsibility both in the framing of claims and in the process of negotiation to ensure that the guidance both in spirit and in letters is respected.

I wrote a series of amendments to this, seconded by Harry Urwin of the Transport Workers, so we ended up with a revised

Of course, he didn't. Jim goes on:

A debate took place on a Conservative call to abandon any sanctions against companies which broke the five per cent guidelines. When the vote was taken both Liberals and Scottish Nationalists voted with the Conservatives and against the government. On the other hand, nearly all the left-wing Tribune Group, which was opposed to the five per cent figure pay policy, voted with the government, although a few abstained. We were defeated with a narrow margin of two votes – 285–283.

Jim Callaghan then asked for a vote of confidence and the Scottish Nationalists changed sides because they could see the possibility of further progress on devolution being lost. So the Labour government won by 10 votes. But out of that came a softening in the government's attitude and Jim notes: 'The CBI came to see me to thank the government for dropping the threat of using sanctions against its members, adding that there would not be a pay explosion in the private sector provided the government was resolute in resisting pay claims from the public sector.' I have never seen a real pay 'explosion'. The market stops that; just as I have never identified a single company that has collapsed simply due to wage costs or the pressure of unions for high wages/salaries.

There were some last efforts to reach an agreement. The TUC Economic Committee and its employment policy committee laboured away and a few of us were asked to meet the Prime Minister with Michael Foot, Denis Healey and Albert Booth in the Cabinet Room at 10 Downing Street. Jim said, 'That's the Chancellor's chair, Clive. You've always wanted to sit there.' He said that the two failures to reach agreement in the summer meant that the current discussions were the last chance. I posed the question of whether Labour's social aims and its claim to halt inflation plus an increase in productivity could all be married together. 'Can we recreate the successful partnership?' Jim was concerned, and my note reads: 'Can we risk a Budget without it being mangled? We are going to have to make this estimate soon.' He quite reasonably pointed out that there was public dissatisfaction due to some rather inhumane incidents in the course of some of the public sector disputes, particularly in hospitals and cemeteries. He was willing to consider low pay and acknowledge a pay freeze was 'out', with a relationship across all government pay scales so as to deal with gross discrimination in pay in the community as a whole. But he wanted new guarantees of maintaining essential services and balloting in strikes, and closed by saying that an agreement was needed within two weeks.

So we had another go at it, with Lionel Murray explaining that we had all moved on from pay norms, there could be no renegotiation of these. This was the background to an early undertaking for some kind of three-part settlement with us to deal with local government manual workers' low pay, an inquiry into analogues between groups of workers in that sector and a phasing-in over a period so there was no special jump in rates in taxes. Jim said, 'We can't borrow more than £815 million at the moment. If we had some industrial calm and a code of practice in industrial disputes, a declaration that we all want to bring down the rate of inflation, we can hold on.' Moss Evans acknowledged that one particularly irritating freeze order had been abandoned and he saw an end to the road haulage disputes; in the various areas there had been agreements covering 150,000 workers.

I decided to follow on with all this work against the background of the earlier meeting of the General Council on 24 January; there was a genuine feeling for trying to make some more progress as the time ticked away to a General Election. The General Secretary, Lionel Murray, undertook to have a short paper prepared and the two key committees both had special meetings arranged before the next meeting with the Prime Minister, to be preceded by a meeting with the Chancellor of the Exchequer.

At this stage, the Party and Cabinet managers clearly decided to involve more members of the General Council in order not to have a repeat of the débâcle of the previous winter, but not enough General Council members had thought it important enough to be present. Before I went off to Downing Street I made my position clear, insofar as I didn't want any new pay boards and no pay targets, as all had been provocative, but did desire vigorous government action, particularly in the field of import controls and social engineering, plus normal inquiries into pay. My handwritten notes record that 'we will stretch every effort to provide a platform for the General Election for the Party'. The heart of our document, 'a pay graph for a TUC/ Government agreement', was in the last paragraph. 'An Agreed Economic Assessment', it covered most of the economy: 'imports and exports, public expenditure, nationalised industries, social and fiscal policy, manpower measures, productivity projections, price developments including the new Prices Bill and role of the Prices Commission, profits, productivity, prices and earnings and unit costs for the next twelve months, three-year forward look, transition from present situation, handling of current issues.' I thought this was a useful programme.

After I had been promised that there would be no 'targets' for earnings, the Lord President, the Chancellor of the Exchequer and the Secretary of State for Employment, Industry and Prices and Consumer Protection came to talk to the Economic Committee at a special meeting on 26 January. We were entertained to lunch at which there was a patter through the document. My handwritten notes record:

> The Ministers were cagey, repeating, 'The government cannot emphasise enough the extreme urgency of the present situation. While the pound has remained strong up to now despite current industrial troubles, the financial situation is delicately poised, and if it did start to slide the government could be forced to take measures which would be unpalatable both to itself and to trade unions . . . The government's position in the Commons is tenuous and there is a clear possibility of defeat at any time. There are varying assessments of the Parliamentary situation and it would be wrong to make any assumptions about the date of the General Election.'
>
> Ministers pointed out that the position in Parliament would become extremely difficult after the Referendum on 1 March. If current industrial action was to continue, or even intensify, the government had little hope of electoral

success. If, on the other hand, the government were able to go back to Parliament with a list of agreed propositions dealing with the economic situation, including pay as a means of achieving the agreed objective of containing inflation, then the situation could be transformed. There was not the slightest doubt that the joint understanding reached in 1975 had saved the economy and the government, and whilst the government appreciated the circumstances had changed, and the context of any new agreement would be different, the object should be to restore the sort of relationship that had existed in 1975 and to make good the ground that had been lost since then.

While Ministers would like to reflect over the proposed framework for an agreement before detailed discussions projected for the following week, a first impression was that it covered all the issues of importance in the right order as well as achieving a broad understanding on economic policy as envisaged by the Liaison Committee.

We were all very sympathetic to this but it had to be said, and it was minuted:

The existence of a pay norm for all settlements, focusing attention – and not least by the media – by crude comparability with everyone else regardless of justification – was just not appropriate after three years of restrictive pay policy and it would be in the government's interest to consider some means of transition to a more flexible system where settlements could be made on a basis that was internally consistent, as well as taking into account general economic considerations. If the right framework and climate were achieved, it would be possible for unions to negotiate in a sensible and responsible way . . . It was clear that the government and the TUC were not going to be able to reach total agreement and on all the issues that day the government hoped that progress could be made urgently. The TUC agreed.

So, Ministers met the Economic Committee yet again, on Wednesday, 31 January. I recognise in one Minute a number of my comments put together: 'It was agreed that there was a need to have an early reference to the changes in the nature of jobs, resulting from technological developments; market forces could not deal with these changes which would place great strains and responsibilities on workers.' (This was discussed in my book with Barrie Sherman, *The Collapse of Work*.) There was a clear need to direct attention to the potentialities in terms of the creation of new jobs, including expanding services, and the terms of reduced hours of work, rather than to the loss of jobs in vulnerable areas. There was a discussion of the role of pension funds in relation to provision of capital, and it was agreed to make the general point that the whole of the nation's institutional funds should be available to support industrial development.

The heads of agreement were painfully hammered out, and I tried to respond to Jim Callaghan's request. I talked to our members in the National Health Service who were of critical importance in the pathology laboratories and on 2 February 1979 I wrote to Lionel Murray:

> Arising out of our conversation the other day, do you think the draft for the meeting with economic ministers on Monday might possibly contain the following paragraph?:
>
> 'The TUC General Council is willing to undertake the new and difficult responsibility of counselling and reinsuring the efforts of affiliated unions in the life or death areas of the National Health Service and other parts of the social services area. The General Council accepts this is a difficult and unenviable task, but one which it feels it ought to attempt so that workers in this vital part of our society should not have to undertake industrial action in order to bring their legitimate problems to public attention.'

We had a special combined meeting of the Economic Committee and the Employment Policy Committee at 10 Downing Street on Monday, 5 February, and had a detailed discussion before the Prime Minister, the Lord President of the Council and the Secretaries of State for Employment, Industry, Social Services, Prices and Consumer Protection joined us; I presume because of some of the difficulties on picket lines, the Home

Secretary was also there. At our preliminary meeting I wanted the draft strengthened and made more explicit, and I watched carefully the subsequent Minutes which recorded what I had said. Looking at them with the Prime Minister, I not unreasonably kept sharpening my trusty hatchet, welcoming the recognition that there was no precise mathematical relationship between a price target of five per cent and a particular level of settlements, and the affirmation that the best way to keep prices down was by increasing the role of productivity with the aim of ensuring a high income, high productivity, low cost economy. I had added that, whilst there might be a need to warn against the dangers of pay escalation, any overt reference to current difficulties would make life really quite difficult for unions in disputatious situations. And so we talked our way through. (I have, incidentally, never ever been offered beer and sandwiches at No. 10, although the writers of newspaper editorials apparently think this is all that is ever on offer.)

The Minutes have a very odd comment from Denis Healey, who

> drew attention to the reference to the position of workers in essential services, and suggested that further attention needed to be given to whether, in return for guarantees on pay, such groups would forgo the right to take industrial action. For the TUC, it was stated that there was a willingness to examine this question – though the intention would be to have voluntary arrangements which would not deprive such groups of the right to strike; what was needed was to create the conditions under which it would be unnecessary to resort to strike action.

I was a derider of this proposition as I didn't see how it could possibly be drafted, let alone work.

The process speeded up and the two committees had another special meeting at No. 10 on 7 February which focussed on the document now entitled 'The Government, the Economy and Trade Union Responsibilities', which had been re-drafted following the debate at the meeting on 5 February. The Prime Minister and the various Ministers concerned joined our meeting and Jim Callaghan said that he thought it 'had more substance than previous drafts', and on this basis was generally acceptable to the government. After tightening up the document they decided to have yet another meeting on 9 February, also at 10 Downing Street.

There is no doubt that Jim Callaghan took all this very seriously and he started off the discussion against the background of the previous day's decision to raise the minimum lending rate to fourteen per cent. This had disconcerted us because, while clearly there was no obligation whatsoever to contemplate consulting us, it did have an effect upon the whole document and it therefore had to be looked at again in respect of monetary and fiscal forces. Ministers stated that they had taken the decision on MLR with the object of avoiding being forced into more drastic action at a later date. In any case, we had a text to take to the General Council on 14 February, slightly muddied by at least one semi-literate circular letter from a junior minister who was eventually to end up in the Social Democratic Party.

All of these efforts failed. But I set them down in order to see whether there can be more work done on a flexible and sophisticated framework for Ministers to interact with leaders of unions and their members so that there are no sudden or startling jolts in economic policy. I repeat that I think Jim Callaghan made mistakes but then, who has not? He had an immensely loyal supporter in Michael Foot, and as the calendar leaves turned over towards Election Day, Denis Healey levelled and was more open and frank and helpful than at any other time. I was fascinated by his belated attempts to re-structure the market.

When Jim Callaghan invited me to sit in the Chancellor's chair in the Cabinet Room I wonder if he recalled, when he sat there, that he had trounced me at the Labour Party Conference when I was advocating devaluation. In Hong Kong, a few weeks later, I read with disbelief that he had done just that. The first note of congratulations he received on the platform was from Tom Jackson, who later would not give the key casting vote which might have saved his premiership. If so, there might have a political innovation. Jim was contemplating an idea of mine that he might summon, and preside over, a Conference of the Nation, in Church House (Bob Hawke held his in the Australian Parliament) for all organised groups. A senior civil servant told me, 'We all carried bulging briefcases home for weeks. Then the government fell.'

11

Intimidation and Infiltration

I was perturbed in the mid-1970s by the bullet hole in the conservatory window of my house on the Regents Canal in St Mark's Crescent, Regents Park. The bullet had splashed against the concrete wall, above a settee. I was not near but I heard it. The CID came and investigated. 'Do you think it could have been a duck hunter?' With the opposite canal bank eight foot lower? And a hunter after mallards with a small calibre weapon? 'Do you have any enemies?' That was trickier – but why should anyone want to *kill* me?

I asked this question of the Special Branch Officers who came to see me a few years later in my office in Half Moon Street at their request. They explained that they had informants who had reported that there were assassination plots to murder Jack Jones, Hugh Scanlon and me. Separately? Together at a meeting? They could not say, but they insisted it was serious. They arranged an armed guard protection for me, and presumably for Jack and Hughie. This extended to railway stations, journeys and handovers at airports (I treasure the memory of the very burly civilian who winked at me very broadly while patting himself under the arm when we were landing at Glasgow airport). I was enjoined not to mention this threat publicly. I didn't but Hughie Scanlon, after the 'crisis' was over, whatever it was, blurted it out on television.

This was when the *Daily Mail* sent a photographer around to my house. He clicked away at my two small children in their nighties, who had curiously gone to the front door. I was furious. Not a violent man, I seized his camera, but lost my grip, although I tore the strap off it. He was undeterred, and went to the bridge over the canal in Regents Park Road to take strategic pictures of the house. I was ablaze with anger because I thought my children were being put at risk and when I saw his car across the road – I was sure it was his because there was a cowering girl inside – I stormed towards it in an ungovernable rate and started to kick in its door panels. I then telephoned David English, editor of the *Daily Mail*, and demanded the photographer be withdrawn and his photographs not published, or I would personally go to the *Daily Mail* building or David English's house and kick other door panels in. He urged me to be calm: I declined. There was no publication – but fancy attempting it?

The attempt to harm speakers at the Washington 'March on the Pentagon' at the height of the Vietnam War had, however, been very real. The platform party of which I was a member were all on the steps facing the reflecting pool and an enormous crowd of several hundred thousand. I was the only foreign speaker who had not been turned back by immigration officers and the Chairman said, 'You're a crowd pleaser, you go first.' After I had started to give my greetings, I saw from the corner of my left eye a group which had broken through (or was let through) a police cordon established behind the platform to protect us. They had bicycle chains and knives, were uniformed and in a flying phalanx. I moved sharply to the right, and the first man missed me, hit the speaker's podium and caused it – with the many microphones linked to it – to tumble noisily down the steps towards the massed television cameras. There was pandemonium. The huge crowd was in tumult – they thought their leaders were at risk. I picked up the nearest microphone – remarkably it was live and linked into the public address system in the trees – and continued to speak, while around me the muscular Rev. Sloan Coffin, Chaplain of Yale, and the paediatrician Dr Benjamin Spock, who was an impressively large man, wrestled two of the assailants to the floor and sat on them. Apparently they were American Nazi Party adherents and they were eventually arrested and taken off to gaol.

The pictures of the attack went around the world and resulted in a footnote in Norman Mailer's chronicle of the march 'Armies of the Night' about the union official who was assaulted. I was driven back to New York to be queried all night on the telephone from London by newspapers who seemed put out to find I was only bruised.

Equally disconcerting was the time I was on a visit to New York to speak at a rally for the progressive *National Guardian* in a hotel ballroom off Times Square. I was seated on the platform alongside a populist, inflammatory black activist named H. Rap Brown who had acquired a sudden violent notoriety. A note was passed up to him. He unfolded it and showed it to me. 'We have a grenade here for you.' 'Is it, this, real?' I asked. He shrugged. I calculated that a grenade thrown at him would see off the rest of the platform party as well. It *could* have been real: so many black activists have been killed.

I remember, too, with interest the small finned bridge across a stream to an odd latrine hut in North Vietnam near the 'Demilitarised Zone': an oil drum filled with water was useful. It had the largest floating spiders I had ever seen. The metal bridge had United States Army Airforce stencils on it so I presumed it was an unexploded bomb. But defused? No one knew. But we had to go to the loo – that was more immediate. The Americans dropped so many bombs it is probably still there.

There have been other odd dangerous incidents. I used to drive a pillar-box-red open Alpine sports car. The police were told that I had run down and killed a dog without reporting it. Reprehensible – except that I was in New York and the Alpine was privately parked near Heathrow Airport. But I was firmly identified as the driver. Then there was the report that I had damaged cars in a narrow street near Sergeants Inn. I was, again, firmly identified, by two men including a painter decorating the front of a pub. The police telephoned. I *had* been there seeing my lawyers. I had just given up my favourite Alpine for a Ford Zephyr. I took it to the police station and invited the police to inspect it: not a scratch. 'It could not have been you, then, sir.' Well, no. I do not really believe in coincidences. I snorted with disgust in later years at the idea that Peter Hain should be accused of stealing banknotes from a bank counter in public and in daylight. It was clearly a dirty tricks operation to discredit him. By whom? In his case the finger must point (as an anti-apartheid campaigner) to the South African (BOSS) secret service. In my case, who knows?

The tapping of my telephones went on with the familiar sound of a replayed recording, even after remonstrances to the chairman of the telecommunications system (and sympathy from his knowing engineers, two of whom deliberately broke into my telephone conversations – 'being bugged, Clive'). Congress House was also affected and I gave Len Murray when he was General Secretary of the TUC a letter I had received from someone in the security services (with references to MPs who knew him) who was angry about a bug planted there.

It may well be that ministers can say that the secret intelligence services do none of these things, except when authorised by a Home Secretary's warrant. But it is also well known that there are numerous private agencies that are employed to do such work directly, and therefore, they are deniable. When the ASTMS head office was in Jamestown Road, we had some odd interruptions of our telephone calls, which were so clumsy that clearly friends were warning us. I brought in experts from a group of our members working in secret undertakings who were outraged that there should be attempts to have a surveillance of their union's head office. They swept my office and checked our switchboard, and came to the conclusion that there *had* been an operation mounted, but it had recently been dismantled. They decided to make me an apparatus which they housed in an old portable radio set and which would scream if there was a transmitter nearby. I offered it to Tony Benn who was having the same problems.

It was clear to me that there were all sorts of attempts to tap into my telephones, both at two different offices and my home. There were at least two incidents when a telephone conversation was interrupted by a voice. I took it that this was a tapper who was unhappy with his task. My presumption is that widespread tapping still goes on and it was well known that when British

Telecom was publicly owned there was a substantial secret operation there. But now that British Telecom is privately owned, who does it? Who pays for it?

I was irritated, like Tony Benn, at hearing a tape of a previous conversation played back to me on lifting the receiver. But there was worse – surveillance of in-office conversations. One incident that brought this to light was when I met Victoria Preston, an artist who had developed a special tapestry-like weaving using newspaper photographs and clippings. It seemed that she had done me holding up a voting card with 147,000 written on it at a Labour Party Conference; she had already done Roy Jenkins, the Queen and President Reagan. She wanted me to look at this, which I did, and after we had it and finally settled upon a price, I bought it. I then had a telephone call from the television presenter I had been talking to earlier who said, 'You gave that artist a very hard time.' When I asked what she meant, she said that when she had telephoned me back on my desk telephone she could hear the entire conversation in my office. I complained to the chairman of British Telecom – again – about some of these events, and he denied all knowledge of them but had my house and the junctions outside it reviewed by engineers. I failed to get any satisfaction but it was quite clear that something was going on. I was told that the local telephone engineers held a meeting and decided that if they came up with hard evidence that I was being tapped at home they would hold a stop-work meeting and demand that it ended.

Our members also swept the office of another General Secretary who was deeply involved in anti-apartheid and other political activism. His bug was on top of his television aerial. Who does all this? And why? Do they *want* you to know?

It was clear, too, that there was targeting of individuals. My colleague, as Joint General Secretary of MSF, Ken Gill, had reported to him quite precisely the conversation that he had had with his sister in his own kitchen. This had been about whether he could help her buy the council house that she had lived in for many years. It seemed that the intelligence services thought that to have a progressive left-wing person willing to help buy a council house was in some way an enormous betrayal and could be used against him, so someone planted a device in his home.

As far as I know, my only direct contact with the CIA was when it was announced that I was going to North Vietnam to make a film and I was contacted by an attaché at the American Embassy in London, who said he wanted to talk about it. He came down to my cottage at Muttow Row in Essex, with a gallon jar of bourbon. He said that he was acting on behalf of the 'missing in action' families associations in the United States, and wanted me to try to find anything about the American servicemen who were listed as missing in action, about whom they could discover nothing more. I asked him, 'Are you in the CIA and is this just a device to find out where the camps are?' He said, 'Of course I am in the CIA but "in the liberal wing".'

What does the British Labour Party and the British trade union movement do about all this intense activity and interest? As far as I know, there has only been one occasion where it might have been alleged that a middle-class officer of a middle-class union was actually talent-hunting for a foreign power. He could not have been very good at it because he left his briefcase with a list of names in a restaurant. Somehow or another, this was retrieved and given to Vic Feather, then Deputy General Secretary of the Trades Union Congress, who seized control of the situation with the rapidity of a Panzer general and the man concerned was virtually excommunicated at once (on grounds of ill health). The British trade union movement is a very patriotic organisation.

In another rather odd incident an American psychiatrist accidentally, I thought at the time, became a friendly acquaintance in Britain and America. His wife later wrote me a distraught letter which implied that he had either responded to a CIA lure or he had approached them to write 'psychological profiles'. She said this had gravely strained their marriage and he had abandoned whatever he was either contemplating or started upon. The message from her was clear – there was a profile of me; his eyes *did* gleam as he looked at me contemplatively. Whatever did they want it for? Whatever would they have done with such an analysis? Perhaps they were simply underspent on the departmental budget for foreign political psychological profiles? Since I am anyway convinced that the most venomous academic and professional disputes are between psychiatrists (with historians as robust runners-ups), this simply confirmed my view that psychiatrists are all slightly disturbed and interested in money and factioneering. Of course, I would like to have read the profile if only to know what I should, or was going to, do next.

Recently I talked with Philip Knightley when he was promoting his book on Philby in Launceston, Tasmania, and he said he thought there were many 'freelance' bugging and surveillance operations paid from UK taxpayers' monies, but they were private and freestanding operations so that ministers could deny them. The Yorkshire TV programme, 'The Walls have Ears', was transmitted in Tasmania on 12 June 1989 and the testimony of David Richards, ex-British Telecom, and David Coughlan reflected my personal experiences: the figure of 450 telephones admitted to be officially tapped in 1986–7 may seem large (who were they?) but it is a fraction of the total.

They were exposing part of the MI5 Zeus operation, but whatever has happened to the millions of words recorded (and transcribed) near the old Passport Office in Petty France? Oddly, many senior intelligence officers lived around there during the war. A hostile reviewer of an exposé book by a female operative intimate with the heads of secret services in St James and, apparently, some famous comedians during World War Two wrote that, 'Some time in 1944 she pulled up her knickers and went on with the war'. That would be nice. Clearly some officers did not and carried on with their private class war – as Harold Wilson was to find out. He assigned Colonel George Wigg to keep an eye on them. After a long, unblemished political career he was, it was alleged, seen 'kerb crawling'. This seemed quite out of character.

A civil service union official said that before an arbitration case affecting 'composite signals' operators, his members effectively 'swept' the trade union side room in the old industrial court building in Abbey Gardens, Westminster. They did not trust their government employers.

There were, and are, problems where civil libertarian ministers head departments. One of our union members who was an important local politician in London came to me and said that he had been offered a position by a minister at the Department

of Energy, on one of the consumer councils which was remuner-
ated. This was quite common and Labour and Conservative
ministers alike provided for locally elected councillors to play
their part in this process. But having been offered the post at a
meeting with the minister, he had then been told that the offer
was being withdrawn. It was his opinion that as he had once
been an unhappy MI6 officer, they were still pursuing him. I
offered to go to see Tony Benn, which I did. He found it quite
remarkable that this could happen inside his department and
promised to look into it. I gather that there had been some
blackballing of this councillor which Tony Benn, as Secretary
of State, put right, and the offer of appointment was re-made
and our member was appointed. But how could Tony not have
known about this?

I believe that there is a paid informer on the Executive
Committee of all the important unions. This is extremely
difficult to cope with, although libel action sometimes brings
out hints and clues. One surprising event was after the sudden
death of one of our members called Harry Newton who had
been actively involved in the leadership of our West Midlands
Divisional Council; it was found that he had been an MI6
officer. This gives rise to all sorts of other questions. He had
been involved in the quite venomous strike at Fircroft College
outside Birmingham, which seemed purposeless at the time,
and a clash of personalities. However, as a result of it, Fircroft
College was effectively lost to the Labour movement and one
wonders whether this was fomented, and what for? Newton had
also boasted that he had written some of the speeches delivered
at ASTMS annual conference which resulted in the defeat of
my union's support for the Bullock Committee's recommendations on industrial democracy which I had signed. As I had
been an active member of that committee, this would seem to
me significant. What was he doing arguing against the sensible
democratic suggestion of a Labour government-appointed
inquiry? Was this, again, a dirty tricks operation to undermine
the authority of the Labour government? I wonder, too, who
replaced him?

The British Labour movement is so open and democratic that
foreign intelligence services are always trying to penetrate it.

There have been virtually no working-class spies, for spies have always come from cliques in the upper classes. There might have been an exception in the case of Jeffrey Prime at the government's monitoring station in Cheltenham. When I remarked to a senior official of a civil service union, 'Thank God he wasn't a member of a trade union,' his reply was, 'Oh. It's more complicated than that. He tore up his union card. This is because he was dissatisfied that we didn't get him an increase in his Russian language allowance!' I surmised that perhaps his Soviet controller was also dissatisfied if he couldn't get an increase in his English language allowance. I remember retailing this story to Sir Harold Wilson at the Soviet Embassy in the company of the Soviet Ambassador. Neither of them were greatly amused.

It is quite easy to become obsessed with the idea that various secret intelligence services are watching all the time.

12

Working and Investigating for the State

It was Tony Benn who, as Minister for Industry, gave me my first state appointment in 1974, when I joined the board of the National Research Development Corporation. This was despite, or perhaps because of, a supposed exchange that Tony published in *Office Without Power*, his diaries for 1966–72, where he recorded for Tuesday, 3 October 1972:

> I went to the Post Office unions' party (at the Labour Conference). Clive Jenkins was there and I remarked to Clive that I inevitably felt inadequate for the job I was doing. He said, 'What do you mean, inadequate?' 'Well, I don't feel I am as good as the job requires.' 'I never feel inadequate,' he said. I said, 'Well, I make mistakes.' 'We all make mistakes, but I don't feel inadequate.' So I replied, 'Well, the credibility of a man who admits his mistakes is slightly greater if, in advance, he has confessed he was inadequate.'
>
> He laughed, 'Oh, I must write that down.' He then turned to Ray Buckton, General Secretary of ASLEF, and asked Ray, 'Do you feel inadequate?' Ray said, 'Yes, of course I do.' He asked Muriel Turner, ASTMS' National Officer, if she felt inadequate and she answered, 'Of course I do.' Clive got very agitated. He repeated, 'I don't feel inadequate.'

I do not remember this exchange. It is true that I have never felt inadequate, and I don't get agitated. I have sometimes felt frustrated and sometimes have been defeated, but inadequate? When I asked Muriel Turner if she recalled the exchange, she did not either, and it would be remarkably out of character for her to say she felt inadequate since she has always been more than adequate for the tasks presented to her or those which she has decided to tackle.

I went once or twice to Tony's Sunday faction meetings at his house in Holland Park but the style did not suit me although gifted people attended. One time he escorted me to his front gate facing the Bayswater Road and said, 'Would you like to go on the Board of the National Research Development Corporation? Industrialists and Nobel Prize winners. You could shake it up.' So I was appointed and spent six very informative years there.

The board of the NRDC (which still exists, much truncated, as the British Technology Group) met once a month, when we would approve, or not, an immensely wide range of projects from Linear motor research and special tunnelling equipment (one of the tunnels consequently built exists under London) to herbicides and pesticides and even a plan to breed a pure line of monkeys for research (which was not done). It had some successes, mainly in the field of pharmaceuticals, and also helped to develop the hovercraft and literally hundreds of other projects.

I found the work fascinating, and it gave me my first groundings in the handling of cash flows, loans and options. It was also not without humour. One executive presented a case for developing a new kind of synthetic cladding for buildings which would be impermeable, light-weight and very strong. He had brought a panel in with him and to demonstrate its strength he jumped on it. It cracked in half. I later found that he had jumped on it several times the previous day so perhaps that had affected the stresses. We did not fund it.

The board was full of thoughtful people and included Lord Todd, the Master of Christ's College, Cambridge, the Managing Director of Vickers and the Chairman of Croda International, Sir Freddie Woods, plus the very forceful now Lord Marshall, who was then at the Aldermaston Weapons establishment. It was quite a mix. I recall Sir Keith Joseph, when he became our sponsoring minister, coming to see us and being quite anguished in pursuit of some of his enquiries; I found it startling when he put his head on the table.

Two years after joining the NRDC board, I had the particularly pleasurable task of helping to organise a fiftieth anniversary celebration of the 1926 General Strike. This might have been the splendid notion of the printer and author John Gorman, who produced the erudite and beautiful book about trade union banners *Banner Bright*, now used around the English-speaking world as a bible of reference. Or it might have been due to Tony Banks, then General Purposes Committee Chairman of the GLC, later the last Chairman of the Council and now MP for Newham North-West. A passionate collector of Labour movement memorabilia, including commemorative porcelain, he is one of the only two persons who owns a mint-condition plate commemorating the successful late nineteenth-century strike on the Tyne for a nine-hour-day. It features engineering leader Burnett in the centre as 'king of the nine-hour-day movement' and was produced as a congratulation by W. Snowball, a local haberdasher who thoughtfully decorated the rim with admonitory verses such as 'a bird in the hand is worth two in the bush' and his current prices for cotton, bombazine and winceyette.

The other mint example belongs to a collector who cannot be named because of burglary risks, but he showed his amazing collection to Michael and Jill Foot at my request and gave us roast beef on a beautiful dinner service marked in blue with a gold rim that commemorated the Queen Victoria's Golden Jubilee. His collection is so great that is has separate sections for all the commemoratives: royals, politicians, wars, railways, ships, and includes unique curiosities such as china for Tsar Nicholas II, with a small red hammer and sickle additionally fired alongside the manufacturers' identification on the back after the Great October Revolution. My own cracked Burnett plate could hardly compare, but I learned that Burnett later became the first union officer to join the civil service as a specialist in union affairs, working as some sort of liaison officer at the Board of Trade.

I gave a lunch for the commemorative enthusiasts and Tony

Banks obtained a grant of £20,000 from the GLC to underpin the 1926 exhibition as a 'London tourist' activity. Most importantly, he arranged for us as the self-appointed organising committee to have the use of the disused great Floral Hall in old Covent Garden which was waiting to be redeveloped. I asked ASTMS to give £2,000 and at a breakfast meeting with Joe Gormley in the Miners' Union grand old office in Euston Road, he promised £1,000 and miners' support. We were away.

The National Coal Board lent a pit cage and although I could not get the gun used to intimidate pickets or the famous motorcycle-mounted machine gun (it had apparently been permanently fixed in place at the Hendon museum), we had a mass of brilliantly illustrative material. Before the opening, Jack Jones, Joe Gormley, Ray Buckton and I toured Central London on the top of a 1926 London omnibus – an open double-decker bus – to advertise the event. The foreign tourists flocked in as well as the British public.

At this time Jon Snow, the television correspondent, rang and offered me a collection of printed ephemera from the ten days which shook the nation. There were 400 national newspapers, including the TUC General Council's *British Worker*, the Winston Churchill-edited *British Gazette*, the British Union of Fascists' penny sheets, transcripts of BBC News broadcasts and versions of all national magazines and local newspapers. They had been collected as a task set by Bishop Snow when he had been a house-master at Eton College and were in two tuck boxes, almost airproof and certainly light-proof. I seized on them to add to my own collection, and had them collated. It took me almost twelve years to find the proper home for them. Lord (Martin) Charteris, former Private Secretary to the Queen and Provost of Eton, who was the Chairman of the National Heritage Memorial Fund and a wise, courtly and sagacious figure there, wanted the collection back for his newly created museum at Eton. But that did not seem absolutely right. (At the National Memorial Heritage Fund, Lord Charteris later supported a request that I also backed for a grant to restore beautiful old trade union banners.)

The opportunity eventually came when I was President of the Trades Union Congress in 1987–8 and was asked to chair an inquiry into the National Museum of Labour History, which had been generally (and in a worried way) approved by the TUC as a repository for documents and objects. It had been housed in disused baths in East London, evicted by a hostile incoming anti-Labour council and finally and generously offered a home in the splendidly refurbished Mechanics Institute in Manchester – where the first tiny congress of the TUC had taken place. I opened this later in 1988 at the invitation of the Manchester City Council and the adjoining local authorities (all credit to Manchester's leader, Graham Stringer, and an enthusiastic councillor, Jack Flanagan). The inquiry's report was briefly that the Museum needed reorganisation and restaffing. When this was done I donated the 'Clive Jenkins-Bishop Snow Collection' to it – a heart-hardening account of pitiless government hostility, with barefoot children combing coal tips, relieved only by the warming solidarity of hungry ordinary people.

The collection is the largest of its kind anywhere and commemorates that the coal miners *were* abandoned and the trade unions suffered a major defeat, which led to the 1929 Labour government, its betrayal in 1931 by Ramsay Macdonald and an interregnum of appeasement. Only in the crisis of early victories by the Fascist powers nine years later were Labour leaders to be in the wartime government, followed by their overwhelming 1945 General Election victory. Macdonald was the MP for my home constituency of Aberavon: as a child I remember singing to the tune of 'Men of Harlech', 'He's the man who came from Scotland, shooting peas up a nanny goat's bottom.' I have forgotten the rest – and the rationale. He went, leaving scattered amongst the matrons of the constituency, top-hatted pictures of himself in an aspidistra-decorated studio, beringed and with a silver-topped cane across his lap. He retreated to Seaham Harbour, losing coherence in his speech and defeated in the 1935 General Election by Emmanuel Shinwell. After this the unions, with rearmament under way and munitions jobs being created, rebuilt their strength. But it was a slow progress.

The Labour Museum foreshadows all of this except the thirty million deaths of World War Two. I hope that the plates, cups and saucers produced by the Conservative Party after the

Munich Agreement of 1938, celebrating the dismemberment of helpless countries and depicting Neville Chamberlain with adulatory slogans such as 'from this nettle danger, we pluck this flower, peace', are displayed as emblems of shame.

It was the year after the 1926 General Strike commemoration that I had to go into hospital for a rather nasty operation to remove a pigeon-egg sized gallstone, which was followed by pleurisy because I had decided it was my duty to go to the General Council meeting at the time of the Fire Brigades Union strike in the winter of 1977/78. I had been told by friends that mine might be the crucial vote in deciding support for the firemen, who had an injustice being done to them. So I got out of bed and went along to Congress House. We lost and although I was still quite ill, I later went to Blackpool for the Labour Party conference. I was using a stick and knew that all the Fleet Street gossip columnists had assured each other that I had cancer and it would not be long before I was off for good. I walked into the Imperial Hotel bar (this was before it was tarted up with pictures of all the Prime Ministers who had stayed there) and saw, sitting on a bar stool, Hugh Chevins, for years the doyen of the Fleet Street industrial correspondents, although he had had some competition from Eric Wigham of the then respectable *Times* and the great Sir Trevor Evans of the *Daily Express*. Hugh had retired years earlier to Wissaint in Normandy and must have been well into his seventies, so I greeted him with some surprise. 'You are my reason for being here. The *Telegraph* brought me back from France to update your obituary.' I was slightly put out by this, but he put his hand on mine and reassured me, 'It's all right, dear boy, don't worry. It was very kind.'

To the disappointment of some, I lived, and the next year I was appointed to a second state post by Tony Benn, with the British National Oil Corporation. The actual suggestion was made after an ASTMS parliamentary lunch by Dr Dickson Mabon, who was Tony's Minister of State at the Department of Energy and who later became a member of the SDP. He gave me the only political advice I ever had in any of my political appointments: 'Let, or don't object to, the West Germans buying into the North Sea, they are feeling deprived', and he guided me towards a deal coming up. It seemed right, and I noted it being nodded through. As a member of the Board I used to go to brief Tony as the sponsoring minister, but he never called *me* in. I understand this to be true of Board members elsewhere in the public sector. I even went to the Prime Minister once when I was unhappy; Jim Callaghan appreciated it and on one occasion asked me to undertake a mission to another government to pass on my amateur knowledge. I prepared, although it was not in the end necessary. Is it perhaps right that ministers should select people on what they believe to be their merits and not have them as listening posts on various Boards? I don't think so. I made every effort to volunteer information because I thought ministers should be as well informed as possible. I think that this relationship is not yet properly spelled out.

The BNOC was making very large surpluses and creating a 'mature oil province'. Its chairman was Lord Kearton, who ran all the board meetings as socio-economic seminars, and with his long experience in public enterprise and great private companies, he was always worth listening to. He occasionally had a vivid turn of phrase. When we were having trouble with a small entrepreneur he said, 'The trouble is that he has got us by the stocking tops.' We all knew exactly what he meant. The board was unusual because it had two senior civil servants on it who were meant to keep open lines of communications to ministers, which I believe they did. One of them went on to head a nationalised industry.

A very hard man on the board was Sir Dennis Rooke, chairman of British Gas, who continually had to declare his interest because the Gas Corporation had found oil as well as gas. He strongly defended the public interest, even though it was rather difficult because of his other responsibilities, but he certainly did his utmost all through the controversies which eventually led to this huge public asset being 'privatised'. Gavin Laird, the General Secretary of the engineers' union, and I fought against this act, just as we fought to make sure that BNOC bought British equipment and argued for all sorts of financial arrangements which would overcome the difference in price between building platforms in Scotland or in South Korea or Taiwan. We also held secret meetings with International Computers to preserve orders for them when some technical things had gone wrong and the IBM-trained engineers wanted to junk the contracts. We succeeded, but it meant all sorts of lobbying and secret breakfast meetings in St James's hotels.

It was useful to me to recall the investment patterns I learned about when serving on Sir Harold Wilson's committee to review the functioning of financial institutions in 1977–80. (Harold complained that it should have been a Royal Commission because as chairman he would have got a silver inkstand). The Wilson committee commissioned a study of how the exploration and extraction of oil in the North Sea was funded. The funding did not show up in the balance of payment figures because the major oil companies did their borrowing elsewhere and it was explained to me that 'the money really did not cross the exchanges at all'. Since then I have been highly sceptical of balance of payment deficits and wonder if there is really anything of true importance in them.

After the defeat of the Labour government in 1979, there were a number of difficulties in replacing the chairman of BNOC; and Tommy Balogh must surely have been wrong to resign as deputy chairman and clear his desk immediately after the electoral defeat.

Following a pitched battle with the sponsoring minister, Sir Philip Shelbourne was appointed and trouble started at once. A brilliant financier and board member, Alastair Morton (now chairman of the Channel Tunnel project and other enterprises), had had a bitter battle with Shelbourne when they worked together in banking in the past. I too found him a difficult man and I don't doubt he thought the same of me. Still, he had me to dinner at his gloomy house where I recall him having Turkish Delight after dinner. The Government had sent him into BNOC as a hatchet man and he fulfilled that role. I did my damnedest to stop him but the Conservative Whips had all the numbers and planned everything through. When some board members were resisting in every way possible the government's determination to sell off BNOC, Shelbourne said from the chair, 'I will

carry out the government's wishes even if mine is the only vote.'
And he did.

But the Corporation was very concerned environmentally and
helped to fund officers who worked with the Royal Society for
the Protection of Birds. There was always a special report to the
board if there had been any spillage of oil anywhere, even if it
was not strictly our responsibility.

We also certainly had good lunches at BNOC, in the former
London home of Lord Beaverbrook. In the board room there, I
pondered that Aneurin Bevan, the Bollinger Bolshevik, would
almost certainly have sat with the Beaver. I expect the conversation was better then as well. We had one odd cameo at a lunch
when Philip Shelbourne brought in some of his staff and said,
'Here are the people who are cooking for us. Do they look
unhappy?' I did not understand this until somebody later said
that some scurrilous publication had been alleging that he had a
poor relationship with his servants.

Many years later in 1988, it was divulged that after British
Petroleum had taken over Britoil, they had raised Philip Shelbourne's salary from the £60,000-odd that I had agreed for him
at BNOC (as a member of the board committee on remunera-
tions) to £130,000. BP re-hired him as a 'consultant'; his pay-
off deal was quite lavish. Some other businessman criticised the
fact that he was permitted a lunch allowance of £92 a day in
addition to a salary of £40,000 for three days' work a month. His
contract included four tickets for the centre court at Wimbledon
every year, four for the Royal Opera House, a chauffeur-driven
car, health insurance, and free travel and hotel expenses. Even
the delegates at the Confederation of British Industries conference in Torquay were surprised by this. One delegate remarked,
'I hope he chokes on his oysters.' Or his Turkish Delight.

When the Conservative government sold off BNOC, Gavin
Laird and I wrote a half-page denunciation of the looting of our
national wealth for the *Guardian*. It was the end of a magnificent
and highly profitable public enterprise. Gavin salvaged a huge
scale-model floating in a glass tank of water that portrayed the
most advanced technology and it is still, I am glad to say, in the
engineering union's museum in Peckham Road. It has some
very special features to enable it to ride out the enormous

pressures of the North Sea where a single wave could bend a steel banister. When I agitated the model and said, 'Look it is unstable,' one of the engineers said, 'Yes, but that is the kind of storm which only occurs once in ten thousand years.' I asked, 'When did the ten-thousand-year clock start ticking?'

At this time I went to see Norman Tebbit, the Secretary of State for Employment, to explain our union training work in my role as chairman of the TUC's Education Committee, to which I had been elected in 1979. There was some threat to the TUC's educational grant, which was jointly funded by the Department of Employment and the Department of Education and Science headed by Sir Keith Joseph.

I had first met Norman Tebbit in the early seventies after the return of the Heath government and the rather jejune attempts to intrude into industrial relations. The controversy over the new proposed laws had meant that all the current affairs programmes were looking for disputants and Andrew Boyle, the editor of the BBC's flagship sound news programme, 'The World at One', telephoned to ask if I knew any Tory to debate with me, apart from the much-used Ray Mawby, MP for Totnes and supposedly the only trade unionist on the government benches – a pleasant ex-electrician who was chagrined at finally being displaced from that safe Conservative seat. I had heard that the newly elected Conservative MP for Epping was an active member of the British Airline Pilots' Association in BOAC. This was Norman Tebbit. (I later asked him, at the US Ambassador's house, if I had seen him in his First Officer's navy-blue gabardine raincoat, fraternally demonstrating in support of other pilots being oppressed by an arrogant management at British United Airways. He denied it and moved away. But . . .)

We met at the BBC in Portland Place and went in to see Andrew Boyle (who was also a distinguished biographer and unraveller of mysteries around the Burgess, Maclean and Philby affairs), and William Hardcastle, former editor of the *Daily Mail* who felt out of sympathy with that paper's proprietors and moved to become an incisive presenter in sound radio. This was Norman's first national broadcast and he was nervous. As we sat, side by side, facing Bill Hardcastle across the green baize table, Norman drummed with his fingers; this could cause an earthquake of sound through the sensitive microphone, so I put my hand over his to signal restraint. The first time and the last time. 'You were very professional, thank you,' said Bill Hardcastle.

Perhaps Norman had not forgotten. When we explained our TUC educational work, he jovially accused, 'You are just creating Bolsheviks.' As we developed our case, he said, 'If you think I am difficult, you should see the other feller' (referring to Keith Joseph). We kept our grant. He proudly showed us his outer office, almost exclusively occupied by women. 'No discrimination here.' After our meeting, monitored by a senior member of his Private Office who wore fetching white knee-length socks, he politely took us to the lift. So we did not have to see Keith Joseph. When I once asked the latter to read a book I had written, he responded by agreeing as long as I would read one of his pamphlets. I did and asked him to dinner at Jack Straw's Castle in Hampstead. He started a very entertaining evening by saying, 'I have never been in Hampstead before. I am a Chelsea man.'

Another Conservative MP whom I had known for some years and for whom I have the warmest affection is Norman St John Stevas, even though he once did me damage by making a speech in which he referred to me as 'an orchid in the sea of parsnips which is the Trades Union Congress'. That cost me thousands of votes. When our ASTMS office was in Half Moon Street (I used the room where Sapper had written the 'Bulldog Drummond' books), there was a problem in GEC's Marconi plant in Norman's Chelmsford constituency and I either rang him or he rang me. I invited him to lunch, to which he said with an elegant hauteur in his voice, 'Where do trade union officials have lunch?' I said, 'Let's go somewhere local.' 'What is local to you?' 'What about the Ritz? It is at the end of our street.' So we went to the Ritz. I remember Norman limping in (he had damaged his ankle) and the maître d'hotel recognising me because I ran an account there but not recognising Norman, to his irritation.

It was Norman, I gather, who was behind my appointment by Prime Minister Thatcher to the National Heritage Memorial

Fund in 1980. I had three interesting terms there, and helped to spend a hundred million pounds of taxpayers' money. I think that my appointment came about as a result of being invited to put a 'socialist' point of view to the annual conference of the Historic Houses Association, which was made up of historic house-owners quite apprehensive of my labour movement interest in them and their possessions. I spoke to them in one of the rooms at the Festival Hall and explained that I thought there was enormous merit in state support for this part of our heritage and also for people still to live in such houses, helping to look after them – provided that they made useful and interesting contributions, not attempting to disperse important works of art, and making special arrangements for school-children to come in. I had developed a theory on this and was greeted with sustained applause. Norman, who was the next speaker, came on to the stage while the applause was still in progress and I was charmed by his fast reaction. He said to the audience, 'Thank you very much for that warm reception!'

We stayed on friendly terms over the years and after seeing his little jewel-box of a house in Holland Park I gave him a set of Victorian song-sheets with Queen Victoria on the cover: what else could you give to Norman? I once also persuaded the BBC to give us champagne in paper cups in the canteen at Lime Grove when Labour had lost and he had narrowly hung on in Chelsmford. When I was facing some unjustified criticisms inside the union which a journalist had blown up out of all proportion, he sent me a gentle letter which contained the words, 'My Dear Boy, They should be on their knees every day thanking the Lord for having you.' I rather liked that.

Many years later we celebrated the first time we went to the Ritz together with a lunch with Sherie Naidoo and Carol Stone, the producer of 'Any Questions', of which he, like me, was a repertory company member. I had a very gracious letter of thanks delivered to me that afternoon. He had obviously gone out into the Ritz lobby and procured a sheet of their elegant note-paper and sent it along.

It was Sherie Naidoo who suggested that we ask George Thomas if he would give a Speaker's Reception in his elegant rooms in the House of Commons when we were looking for a place to bring together a distinguished group of supporters of Amnesty to spread further the good word that imprisonment and torture were hugely repugnant. I have always had a soft spot for George, who once interrupted his conducting of the hymn singing at a Labour Party Conference Welsh night on my entry into the crowded ballroom in the Blackpool Imperial Hotel by melodramatically pointing at me and saying, 'When we have a Labour government he should be Prince of Wales.' When we went to him with our request, George asked us in, gave us tea and showed us around his grand rooms, telling us about the antique buckles on his Speaker's patent leather shoes and how they squeaked. He asked if we wanted drinks served for the guests. He was a leading Methodist and teetotal. We said, 'Yes, we thought so.' 'Mixed drinks, full bar?' 'Yes.' 'Who will pay for it?' 'We will.'

The event was a glittering success. David Blunkett, the blind leader of Sheffield City Council, came with his guide dog, dog food and a feeding bowl. When he asked George if the dog could have his supper in the kitchen George grandly replied, 'Kitchen? He can have it in the State Dining Room.' So he did. The first dog to eat there?

Who paid for the reception? George never sent us a bill.

In 1983 the Economic Committee of the Trades Union Congress elected me to the National Economic Development Council, although beforehand Len Murray, the General Secretary of the TUC, had come in briefly to a buffet lunch and said, 'I can't support you for election to the NEDC. I think we need to have someone from retailing.' (i.e. Anybody except you, and Bill Whatley of USDAW is the best hope, despite the fact that there was no private sector white-collar representative there.) So I said, 'Len, I will run anyway.' When it came to the election Len counted the committee heads and did not make any recommendation, so Rodney Bickerstaffe of NUPE and I were elected to fill two vacancies.

On being elected I was quite astonished to find that we were asked to sign the Official Secrets Act. The NEDC monthly meetings in the Vickers Tower on the Embankment were virtually mass meetings. The government, the TUC, the CBI, the nationalised industry chairmen and the consumers' representatives sat round a large table and were perhaps outnumbered by all their advisers and Press people on the outside. The minutes of meetings and the papers would come in double envelopes and we were required to sign for their receipt. This receipt, which would make us open to prosecution under the Official Secrets Act, was in respect of material which was readily available in the Press. So I refused to sign, or to become involved in what I thought was an absurd rigmorale.

I had signed the Official Secrets Act on my appointment to the National Research Development Corporation in 1974 (with a written caveat that this was only in respect of my NRDC work and not my other political and industrial activities). I had done so then because the NRDC held patents as part of the Wilson government's arrangements for research in the public sector which resulted in patentable discoveries being offered up to the Corporation in the first instance. (This was abolished by the Thatcher-led Conservative administration, to, I think, the great loss of both researchers and entrepreneurs and persons who need an organisation to protect their patents in the courts of the world.)

On the NEDC I was surprised to find that all my predecessors, left-wing and right-wing, had gone along with all the Official Secrets nonsense. Rodney Bickerstaffe, however, had simultaneously a similar view to mine and also refused to become involved. I certainly never learned any secrets at the NEDC – or anything very interesting, except for Lord Marshall telling Mrs Thatcher that he had personally stopped Harwell research on irradiating food to prevent decay, as he had reservations about it. She seemed surprised.

Mrs Thatcher was also surprised on a later occasion when the Prime Minister of the Chinese People's Republic, Zhao Ziyang, came to the United Kingdom and she gave a banquet for him at No. 10 Downing Street. It was a glittering assembly which included ministers, Nicholas Ridley (who had to abandon his chain-smoking for the course of the dinner; I once got him to stop smoking in the Neddy Council Chamber in the Millbank Tower), Lord Young, Lord Weinstock of GEC, Sir Eric Sharp of Cable and Wireless (who had started to make his major

advances into telecommunications in the Chinese People's
Republic and who had brought me back my first 'chop': a
marble embossed stick with Jenkins translated into Chinese
characters; apparently it meant 'House of Gold'), Admiral Sir
John Fieldhouse who commanded the British forces at the time
of the invasion of the Falklands, a distinguished sinologist, Dr
Joseph Needham, and various industrialists. There were only
two trade unionists, Eric Hammond and me, and one Labour
MP, the former Prime Minister, James Callaghan. Mrs
Thatcher introduced a number of guests to the Chinese Prime
Minister as they arrived, saying of me something like, 'This is
Mr Clive Jenkins, one of our better trade union leaders.' The
Chinese Prime Minister, through his interpreter, said, 'Yes, I
know him well.'

I had been to the Chinese People's Republic only twice, the
first time when Mark Young and I went together after persuading the Chinese Embassy in London that we genuinely were
going to pay for ourselves and asking for facilities to be given to
us to see people. A senior Chinese diplomat in London was
astonished. When we arrived in Beijing we were greeted by two
large black limousines on the tarmac and swept off to the
Chinese Federation of Trade Unions which had recently been
re-established after the Maoist excesses of the cultural revol-
tuion; it seemed that we were the first contacts with the West
since their re-establishment. They were astonishingly hospitable
and gave us a programme that they had prepared for us. When
we asked, 'How much is all this going to cost us?' (fingering our
travellers' cheques), our friends were puzzled and said, 'What
is cost?' and hugged us to their bosoms. What was cost? No
cost.

Back in Britain I reported in detail the culture shock I had
had in confronting the administrative problems of ruling over a
billion people and put down, as frankly as I could perceive
them, the difficulties and successes. My Chinese friends decided
that I was a 'sincere, candid friend' and invited me to the thirty-
fifth anniversary of the declaration of the Chinese People's
Republic by Mao in Tianamen Square, where I saw the largest
parade the world has ever seen of ethnic nationalities, industries
and the armed services, and was deeply impressed by Mr Deng

standing in an open car touring amidst the army, navy and air force representatives, saying over the loudspeaker, 'Are you alright, Members of the People's Liberation Army, Navy, Airforce,' to be greeted with the response, 'Yes, how are you Uncle Deng?' In the utterly remarkable banquet that followed an incredible firework display, there were very few non-Chinese faces. I saw the British Ambassador, Sir Peter Matthews of Vickers, the former German Chancellor Willi Brandt and Prince Sihanouk. An interesting feature was the separate table for physicians; the elderly Chinese leaders were obviously so valuable and respected that this medical resource was necessary.

I had blazed the trail for a TUC delegation to China and brought back an invitation. The group which went included Moss Evans, who was asked if I still had 'that coat'. I had worn a Moss Bros black broadcloth with a beaver collar and a mink lining. It was very grand and I resembled a Victorian undertaker. Moss said, 'No, it was rented.' Incredulous, the Chinese said *'Rented?'* 'Yes, and if I know Clive he has got sub-tenants in it by now.'

The most disappointing of my public sector work was an attempt to create a centre for small businesses and incubators for even smaller ones in a very large disused former London bus garage in Notting Hill. Why there? Because a property developer had had his eye on the site for years and there was over fifty per cent black youth unemployment in the area. The Greater London Enterprise Board set up by the Greater London Council supported the concept and established a company named London Enterprise Developments to handle this and other similar projects. It was a public-private sector project. I was invited to become chairman on a five-year contract. But it was overshadowed by the government threats to the continued existence of the GLC and by a lack of expertise of board members and executives. I was put in to blow the whistle any time necessary.

I did, but people did not want to hear. I was not happy with some of the transactions: it takes skill to manage millions of pounds in urban development. So I talked to the chairman of the GLEB (a senior trade union official now retired) and to a leading member of the Board (still a senior trade union official), and had a meeting with the chief officer of the GLC, and the councillor who was chairman of the funding committee. I also saw the GLC leader, Ken Livingstone. I blew the whistle again and again. Only Ken took my warning as somberly as I would wish; he took a memorandum from me, handwritten by the private partner, outlining the problems I had encountered.

Later, when cleaning out his leader's room in an empty, echoing County Hall in the last days before the GLC's demise, he took it out of a desk drawer and gave it back to me. 'I would not want to leave it here!' Essentially it was a history of cost over-runs and errors drafted by the dismayed private partners, who were also imperfect, and matched by a lack of expertise among the councillors and shortcomings in the GLEB professional staff.

Ken, who had once been one of our union members at the Medical Research Council where he developed his interest in herpetology, came to speak to my union's Executive Council about the problems of providing adequate services in a crowded multi-ethnic capital: they have been much worse since London lost its central government – the only major city in the world without such a democratically elected focus and desperately dirty with an appalling public transport system.

Afterwards I took him to my adjoining office for a drink; this was in the period when the leadership of the Labour Party was being discussed and I was known to be for Neil Kinnock. Ken was the first person to say, 'Neil Kinnock and Roy Hattersley – *that* is the dream ticket.' But he could not, would not, intervene in GLEB, although he blessed and presided over transfers of power and land to Londoners in a rush before dissolution. I recall congratulating him on the brilliant media campaign to preserve the GLC. 'It's not that hard,' he said. 'Find a good advertising agency and appropriate four million pounds.'

Ken had fun in office as the GLC leader and shared it with London's citizens. As County Hall started to empty, he remarked, 'I feel like a Caesar towards the Fall of the Roman Empire and the legions are not responding to me.' He had an elegiacal plate produced that mourned the GLC's passing and together we presented one to Victor Sassie, the presiding master-class-of-service owner of the Gay Hussar restaurant in Greek Street, who arranged a formal drawing back of red velvet curtains to unveil it in the main restaurant. It must be the only fashionable literary, media and political restaurant to display not only its patrons' books, but a TUC Tolpuddle Martyrs' Centenary commemorative plate and a framed teatowel printed with the *Daily Herald*'s front page announcement of Labour's victory in the 1945 General Election. I presented them both.

(The Gay Hussar's top-floor 'belfry' room was used for secret intimate meetings by Labour ministers in the 1966–70 government and I recall being summoned by Barbara Castle to one of these agreeable, hectoring, persuasive events when there was a problem in the Health Service. As we passed through the aisle between the tables on the ground floor, the newspaper editors there commented, 'Barbara is having another one of her secret meetings'.)

Aside from the elegant lunch to which Ken took me (paid for with his own money), as a result of my whistle-blowing activities with London Enterprise Developments I was removed from office as chairman, survived an attempt to remove me as a director and was later reinstated as chairman. It is always useful to have political support (and lawyers – who even got their costs). But it was an unsatisfactory and unpleasant experience and although heads later rolled it did not reflect well upon the image of a job-creating public enterprise. It attracted too many amateurish ideologues and unqualified, inexperienced local politicians.

The only satisfaction in an unsatisfactory episode is that I was compensated for the unexpired portion of my contract. I could not possibly keep the money, which was enough for the TUC, at my request, to provide for two travelling bursaries of £750 each every year in perpetuity for young trade unionists. I rather liked being the largest ever single personal donor to the TUC. Ever since my applications were rejected (to be fair, I was only in my mid-teens) for every Labour movement scholarship, college entry or bursary, I have been sensitive to providing help for potential leaders. I ended up decades later chairing some of the bodies who refused me help, including the TUC's own Education Committee.

It is hard to draw lessons from GLEB's failed enterprises: many private ventures also failed. Another disappointment to me at this time was Sadlers Wells, the historic theatre in north-east London which was under threat of closure because of finance: the threatened GLC also meant that substantial theatre funding was at risk. The redoubtable Frances Morrell, former political adviser to Tony Benn, and Tony Banks (who was also on the National Theatre Board) entrusted me with being involved with the Wells and I was asked to be a governor representing the interests of the GLC together with Frances.

The arts-conscious councillors decided to go to the ruling Labour group and get a 'tombstone' legacy for deserving causes. This was planned (and, I thought, decided at a breakfast I gave at the Waldorf Hotel). The responsible staff were instructed to prepare a paper but, alas, it foundered mainly due to lack of time and too little political drive. The great ballet company has now moved to Birmingham, leaving its historic site over which so much hard work was lavished.

For this Frances Morrell was undoubtedly not to blame, but my experiences with the GLEB left me with a nagging concern that elected local government does not have enough training. Magistrates get guidance on sentencing but how to guide councillors in making substantial investment of ratepayers' capital? There was and still is a Labour Party commitment to create a Staff College to incubate and groom public sector entrepeneurs who can identify good propositions and assess the downside risk. Should MPs also be trained or – perish the dogma – qualified? Democracy is a rough, rude instrument. But clever people can make it work and defend it.

13

The Labour Party
Leadership Contests

When Jim Callaghan resigned as Leader of the Labour Party in 1980, David Basnett, General Secretary of the Municipal Workers' Union and later Lord Basnett, Mostyn Evans and I went to David's central London pied-à-terre office in Duke Street to talk it over. It was clear that the main contender was Denis Healey, whom none of us wanted because we thought he was too aggressive and would split the Party. (As we all know now, the Party was split anyway.) I suggested Michael Foot and both Moss and David thought this was a good idea. Moss said, 'You're an old mate of his – you go and ask him.' This was on a Thursday and I found that Michael was delivering a Dean Swift Anniversary lecture in Dublin. I could not track him down.

I talked with Ian Mikardo, who was warmly in favour of seeking to persuade Michael to stand, and I therefore asked my head of secretariat Greta Karpin to compile a list with me of everyone we could think of in leading union positions in local constituency parties whom we could contact to urge support for Michael. Greta worked her way through a long list and the basic message we sent was: 'We think Michael Foot might be persuaded to run for the leadership of the Labour Party. If you want this you have to be in touch with him now. Send letters or telegrams or messages by hand to him.' We took the liberty of disclosing Michael's home address. The approach might not have seemed entirely spontaneous, but hopefully Michael would welcome the pressure. We got a magnificent response but we still did not have Michael Foot himself. Ian Mikardo took on the responsibility and brought his inimitable powers of persuasion to bear. He telephoned me back to say: 'Michael asks whether we can put together some people to have supper with him on Sunday, after he returns from Dublin.' Mik assembled some parliamentarians and I managed to get hold of Alan Fisher of the public employees' union, Alec Smith of the tailors and garment workers' union and Arthur Scargill of the miners' union. More would have come but it was remarkably short notice – in some instances just a few hours. Jill Foot had made a casserole, Mary Mikardo brought over a sweet and I took a case of quite reasonable claret. At the end of the supper, we went upstairs to the Foots' sitting room, where the mantelpiece was dominated by a beautiful lustre jug decorated with a royal figure holding a sword erect as his horse went through blue water, above a slogan reading 'No surrender'. Remarkably, this was a purely decorative item for the Foots, who did not know that it commemorated King Billy's victory over the Catholic armies at the Battle of the River Boyne. I knew because I had one just like it but not as grand, and I lusted after it.

There were not enough seats for everyone to sit down so I, in an uncomfortable and unaccustomed pose, propped myself up on an elbow on the floor near Michael's feet and in the debate about how to stop Denis Healey argued from there that I wanted Michael absolutely on his own spendid merits. We all agreed and each of us in her or his own way left to campaign for this.

It did not prove to be very difficult. There were some unlikely candidates. Peter Shore was being pushed by Terry Duffy, then President of the engineers' union, on grounds which are now quite unclear. But no one was with him and he said to me, 'So I gave up, didn't I? If you have not got the numbers, you have not got the numbers.' John Silkin was convinced that he *could* win, which I did not believe. He came to my office and when I told him I was totally committed to Michael, he said, 'Are you really sure he is going to run?' Since there were still some confidences to be maintained, I replied that I was pretty sure of it. John left me all of his telephone numbers and spoke to me later when I was lying in bed on a Sunday morning: 'I cannot find out what Michael is going to do. Do you know?' I said I did, and told him that Michael was going to run. John sighed saying, 'Poor Michael. He is going to be so hurt.'

I was in a BBC TV news studio when the quite remarkably good result from the MPs voting came through, and I let out a whoop of joy. I now know that in a House of Commons Committee room, Neil Kinnock had done the same thing. Later that night some of us (for a reason which now escapes me – was it some kind of working party or what were we plotting?) met at the St Ermin's Hotel. This hotel was usually the nest for the hatching of bitterly right-wing conspiratorial plots: there is still a group named after it. Judith Hart was in the chair at the dinner and when Michael came in we burst into applause. I think we were recognising a link with all the struggles of the past but the feeling of relief that we had managed to elect a Leader was quite colossal.

There was one unpleasant administrative aspect to the start of Michael's leadership. Until the provision of slightly larger state funding – the 'Short' money, named after the Chief Whip Ted Short who helped to bring it about – Labour Opposition Leaders had had to rely in part on individual and trade union donations to finance the considerable staff and general office costs. During Jim Callaghan's office as Leader of the Opposition, administrative services had been provided by the electricians' union and when Michael Foot was elected, the office books were promptly audited and returned by the electricians, and all aid was cut off. Sir Tom McCaffrey, the head of Jim's office (and then Michael's), told me: 'They even took the golf-ball typewriter away. We don't know how to do pay-as-you-earn tax deductions.' I volunteered ASTMS support and our Finance Officer at once went in to help. Our financial administration subsequently looked after the necessary details throughout Michael's leadership. It was not a very graceful act on the part of Frank Chapple.

Although I had been in favour of Michael Foot and not Denis Healey as Leader of the Labour Party, I was opposed to Tony Benn contesting Denis for the deputy leadership in 1981. In spite of my friendship for, and appreciation of, Tony's talents,

I thought this was a divisive stand and I was determined to try to abort it.

As a friend (and also a patron – Tony had been responsible for my appointment to the NRDC Board and also the BNOC), I asked him to lunch in my office in Jamestown Road, Camden Town. I devised a plan. I knew that he liked strong tea and would carry his own enamel mug, given to him in the People's Republic of China, to political meetings around the country; I also knew he had a minor interest in commemorative china. So I asked one of our officials in the Stoke on Trent area who knew the management and artists in a plant that made high-quality porcelain if he could have a few mugs produced with an appropriate slogan. On seeing the sketch I had done, the artist said that what we should produce was a gold-rimmed loving cup, with a handle on each side and written on one side in black lettering 'Don't do it, Tony' and on the other 'Elections can also be poisoned chalices, Tony'.

Tony duly arrived and, as always very polite, finished his pipe on the pavement outside before coming up the stairs. An excellent local Kosher Jewish restaurant provided us with egg and onion, chopped liver, salt beef and sweet and sour cucumbers, and after we had finished eating I offered him tea. One of my colleagues brought in the porcelain loving cup. Tony lifted it by the handles and was amazed to see the inscription. I had never before, and have never since, seen him genuinely surprised. He turned it round and burst out laughing at the inscription on the other side. 'No one else is going to ask me not to run quite as elegantly as this, Clive,' he said.

But he did run and his representatives stormed my own union's annual conference, which, I confess, I disliked because of slightly hysterical speeches. The delegates voted to instruct the Executive to nominate and support Tony, although many of them, particularly in the finance sectors, were not in favour of the policies he was putting forward. It was a good exciting rally on the day. I tried to stop it and failed. But a vote is a vote, is a mandate. When the first rumours swept the Labour Party conference that Tony had actually fractionally beaten Denis Healey, my feeling was of profound disappointment because I could see years ahead of internecine strife. (Michael Meacher was delighted with this information.) But we then found that there had been a scrutineers' slip and Tony had lost. It was a bitter blow for him but while a first-class Minister and patriot, I think he was a dangerously divisive politician for the Labour Party and helped to keep us out of office.

Tony has a quality of brilliance. I still remember his excellent short speech in the emergency Suez debate in the House of Commons in 1956 (I was waiting in the galleries for a scheduled discussion on some civil aviation questions). He put forward and worked for important political ideas like the referendum on continuing British membership of the European Economic Commission and support for the Electoral College to choose Party leaders, as well as his earlier campaign to enable hereditary peers to renounce their membership of the House of Lords. I am also quite sure that the approach he took in seeking to safeguard British control of oil and gas being produced from the UK continental shelf was absolutely correct. As a minister he was undoubtedly very good indeed, although I am still surprised that in respect of the two Boards to which he appointed me he never made any query as to what I was doing or about the general atmosphere inside these public corporations.

There is no question that he was absurdly and disgracefully treated by the British press and justified in carrying a tape recorder simply to make a record of his interviews with them. But he and Eric Heffer were a very distracting influence in the Labour Party National Executive Committee and, without doubt, provided material which enemies could use against us. I nevertheless always sought to deploy resources and volunteers to him in his often difficult parliamentary election campaigns. I recall one in which he was speaking outside an aero-engine plant in Bristol and things were not going well when I arrived with volunteers to help. He greeted me with the words, 'Ah, Blücher. I now know, to paraphrase the late great Duke of Wellington, it will not be a damn close-run thing!'

I am fond of Tony but his contradictions still puzzle. In his first volume of diaries *Against the Tide*, he writes: 'I remember a note coming to me in 1969 or 1970 about Jack Jones being a security risk and I sent Harold a Minute on Jack Jones and on this case; it might precipitate some examination of procedures, though the Security Services would never forgive me for doing it.' Tony had given me a pre-publication copy of his book and the day I read this I met Jack at a farewell reception for Fred Jarvis, the retiring General Secretary of the National Union of Teachers. Jack had not seen the diaries. I asked, 'Did you know about the incident?' 'Yes, at that time they were saying I was a Communist.' 'So Tony told you?' 'No, Barbara Castle.'

I found Tony's diaries quite difficult to evaluate. I was one of a group of trade union leaders who helped form a protective screen around him and telephoned ministers and Party friends whenever he thought he was likely to be sacked or worse. Yet he could write on Friday 17 March 1972 in *Office Without Power*:

> Went to see Clive Jenkins and tried to win his support for the Referendum. He is a shrewd guy, very bright. He runs his union rather like an American political machine with a lot of bosses who work round him. His driver is a former Communist. It is a left-wing union but is appealing to a right-wing group of people – the white-collar workers. I say right-wing, but that is not quite true – people who, if they are politically interested, are left-wing, but who are normally thought of as being in the centre of politics. He told me about the amazing growth of the union and I asked him what he would like to be doing in ten years' time. Would he like to be in a Labour government? He very quickly assumed that I was offering him a job in my Cabinet. He then said, 'Of course, when Harold goes we'll have to have a chap who's just on the left of centre, like you.' It was like talking to someone at an American convention without any pretence of principle.

Not very agreeable and based upon a complete misreading of me. I also wonder what the motivation was for including this ungracious reference to Michael Foot at a No. 10 meeting on 21 September 1976. '. . . Michael, who looks more and more like a moth-eaten suit on a hanger, was very worried.'

Years later at a January 1985 meeting in the Shadow Cabinet Room, after a sour, and long, speech from Tony, Neil Kinnock passed me this note: 'I have now reached the stage in my political development where I think Tony should not be impeded in his statements. On most things.' But Tony is a valuable camera man and recordist – on most things.

In January 1981 the special Wembley Conference of the Labour Party decided on a new voting formula to elect its leaders. In a significant extension of the franchise, the unions were allotted forty per cent of the votes, MPs thirty per cent and constituency parties thirty per cent. The furore which surrounded this conference was remarkable, and outrageous accusations appeared in the press that I had plotted and engineered the final vote for the 40:30:30 formula.

But there was no plot, and no 'smoke-filled room' in which it supposedly took place. If there was any plot at all it was an old-guard attempt to frustrate change and leave the election of the Leader principally in the hands of Members of Parliament; such an attempt went, happily, awry. I did have a suite to entertain union leaders for the Saturday lunchtime break. I detest smoking, so Tom Jackson of the Post Office Workers leaned out of the window to smoke his cigar. There were no secret agreements: the left, centre and right were there. I simply wanted to monitor any changes in voting patterns and keep an eye on other lobbying to see what was best tactically to bring about change to enlarge the franchise. The night before, I gave a dinner for a cross-section of those actively involved, prudently including the talented David Warburton, a national officer of the Municipal Workers who was also a numbers man for the centre right.

Journalists, however, wanted a plot, so they invented one. The *Daily Mail* for 28 January ran the following feature credited to Gordon Greig, Robert Porter and Anthony Bevins (although I have reason to believe that two of the journalists were innocent of intent to mislead and one wrote an accurate account which was junked):

> The rotund and generally genially smiling figure of union chief Clive Jenkins stands today at the centre of the Great Labour Voting Mystery. Or to be more precise: was Jenkins the mastermind behind the voting coup which gave

the Left its most outstanding victory in Labour Party history?

'No' declared Jenkins yesterday, with an evaporation of his normal geniality. He went further. Stories that he had been at the centre of any wheeler-dealing were 'straight-forward goddam lies' he said.

Jenkins is not usually a man who is backward in coming forward in the honours stakes. Yet despite his refusal to accept credit for what the Left regard as a brilliantly engineered coup, moderate union leaders still insist that the marks of his negotiating ability were there.

Most moderates would not be drawn into a public attack on Jenkins because of the damage an open row would do to the trade union movement. But electricians' leader Frank Chapple had no such inhibitions. 'Anyone who follows Clive Jenkins deserves all he gets,' he snorted. 'What happened at Wembley on Saturday was a surprise only to naïve people – and there are plenty of those in this movement.'

What happened at Wembley, in fact, was that a carthorse became a Trojan horse with a very clever manipulator indeed at the reins. A resolution of USDAW, the shop-workers' union – a reliable but far from volatile organis-ation with something of the TUC carthorse image about it – was used to burst into the citadel of Labour Party privilege. What was once an obscure USDAW amendment was elevated by the might of union block votes to a law which puts 70 per cent of the power in picking a Labour leader – and if the party are in government a future Prime Minister – outside the ambit of Labour MPs. Labour's special conference at Wembley gave 40 per cent of the choice to the unions, 30 per cent to MPs and 30 per cent to constituency parties.

That result, which set Right-wing dissident Neville Sandelson dancing in a jig of fury in the gallery of the Wembley Conference Centre and put a smile of exultation on the glistening face of Anthony Wedgwood Benn, had at least part of its roots in a dinner at the Crest Hotel in

Wembley on Friday night, according to the union moderates.

There, in the Medallion Restaurant, where the wine waiter extols the virtues of the Château Mouton Rothschild 1964 (at £27.60 a bottle), Clive Jenkins dined with a foursome including transport union leader Moss Evans. But as they sliced their way through roast beef from the carvery, was there something else on the menu? Did the subject arise of tactics of manoeuvres needed to push the USDAW formula through the next day's conference?

'Definitely not,' says Jenkins categorically. And the leader of the white-collar workers' union added: 'There was nothing secret about it. We dined in the public restaurant in full view of everyone. We were simply a group of friends together. We never even discussed the conference. We each knew that our views on the subject were different.'

Moderates are unconvinced. They hand to Mr Jenkins the accolade of first realising that the Left was unstoppable, provided it backed the USDAW 40:30:30 formula. And that was the message they accuse him of spreading so assiduously on Saturday morning when he made a determined tour of the Wembley Conference Centre seeking out Left-wing union/leaders.

The exact statistics of the coup were engineered, it appears, not by 'four trade union barons in a smoke-filled room' (Shirley Williams' description) but in the executive suite of the Crest Hotel. Certainly a number of big union chiefs adjourned there for drinks and discussion during a break in Saturday's conference, with Clive Jenkins playing host. Jenkins, an outspoken critic of the Labour Party's administration, organisation and the way its finances are handled, had for some time been determined to bring about change. Accounts of what happened at such a closed and vital meeting as that of Saturday lunchtime necessarily vary. There are accusations that Jenkins first pledged his vote one way and then persuaded others to join him in voting another – something that he categorically denies.

By then most of the party and union hierarchy knew

how unions were committed to vote first time round. But few had much idea of what individual unions would do when their votes were released from official commitments in the second and third ballots.

At the lunchtime meeting and before the first of the conference's ballots, Jenkins made it clear in an aside to Moss Evans that he was backing the shopworkers' formula. Would Moss Evans do the same? The transport workers' leader nodded in agreement. The scene was set.

Back at the conference centre, the Labour Party's Executive formula – for a 33:33:33 share of the say in electing a leader – ran a sad third on the second ballot and vanished from the agenda. Up until then Moss Evans had been committed to support it, the official party line. Now he was free to put his millions of votes where he chose.

David Basnett, the municipal workers' leader, who masterminded the Foot 50:25:25 compromise formula, had fully expected Evans' support. The shopworkers' formula had been kept alive by backing from NUPE, the white-collar workers and the firemen. As amendments fell, votes snowballed to the USDAW solution. Then to Basnett's horror, the transport workers swung the biggest vote of all behind USDAW. Terry Duffy, the engineers' leader, was impotent to help despite his union's 928,000 votes. He had been mandated to vote against every proposal which did not give MPs 51 per cent or above.

Nothing could be done. The 40:30:30 formula went through. The Labour Party's history had been changed.

It was the moment when the Labour movement was confronted with something so many had heard about but few actually witnessed – the Great Union Fix. The trade union barons, so long the traditional paymasters of the Labour Party, had decided to become its Kingmakers too.

I angrily wrote at once to the editor of the *Daily Mail*, referring to the article:

. . . when you say, 'At the lunchtime meeting and before the first of the conference's ballots, Clive Jenkins made it clear in an aside to Moss Evans that he was backing the shop workers' formula. Would Moss Evans do the same? The transport leader nodded in agreement. The scene was set.'

This is a lie. This aside (and nod) did not happen. *How could you print this? It is a malicious fabrication. Are we likely now to have an apology? You ought to because I gave the facts to your industrial correspondent* (Robert Porter) *at his request last Sunday. He must have told you – so how could you print otherwise?*

The only lobbying in which I was vigorously engaged was to make sure we had a clear-cut decision last Saturday so that we could sweep this reactionary government from office and rebuild adequate employment for all our people.

Receiving no response, I fired off several urgent reminders:

For the immediate and personal attention of the Editor of the *Daily Mail*: Are you going to publish my letter or do I have to announce now that I am referring you to the Press Council?

Attention Deputy Editor – immediate please: Have you a reply to the telex timed at 17.48 – or do we release our complaint to the Press Council to the PA now? Immediate reply please.

For the immediate and urgent attention of the Deputy Editor: Are you going to publish tomorrow, or not?

I then got this, saucy extraordinary reply:

Clive Jenkins: Regret printing unions' attitude to new technology makes impossible publish letters on day of receipt. Strongly urge patience and calm. Deputy Editor: *Daily Mail.*

Another reminder from me produced the following exchange:

Clive Jenkins: Can only repeat previous advice. Not normal practice to reveal contents of tomorrow's paper. But on humanitarian grounds can say that decision to publish taken this morning so now safe to shut down your telex for the night – Deputy Editor, *Daily Mail.*

Attention Deputy Editor: As I am not entirely certain you are human or humanoid, I shall soothe our telex and even or especially read the *Mail* tomorrow. So watch it, mate.

What tomorrow's *Mail* contained were two letters. One was mine, which began as I had written it, quoting the press article's paragraph: 'At the lunchtime meeting and before the first of the conference's ballots, Clive Jenkins made it clear in an aside to Moss Evans that he was backing the shop workers' formula. Would Moss Evans do the same? The transport leader nodded in agreement. The scene was set.' But then it was cut. Out had come 'This is a lie' and my other all-important comments (italicised in my above-quoted letter).

The second letter was from Moss Evans. He, too, began by quoting the *Mail's* paragraph about our lunchtime meeting, and he continued:

You go on to say: 'Up until then Moss Evans had been committed to support the official party line (that is 33:33:33). Now he was free to put his millions of votes where he chose.'

May I make it clear beyond any shadow of doubt that I do not choose, and never have the authority under our constitution to choose, where to put the 1,250,000 votes of the Transport and General Workers' Union.

On 4 December last, at a Press conference, I said clearly, to avoid any confusion or rumour, that the Executive of the TGWU would recommend to our Labour Party Delegate Conference, which has the final say, that the TGWU should support the formula 33:33:33 and not support any motion that would give more than 40 per cent to any constituent body. That is, we would be prepared in the last resort to support the 30/30/40 formula.

On 23 January 1981, our Delegate Conference gave support to the Executive recommendation but, because of similarities between our amendment and that put by the Labour Party NEC, which called for equal representation and an electoral college, it was decided to withdraw our option in favour of the NEC's so that there would not be too many amendments on the agenda.

In the event of the NEC option not getting through the ballot the delegation agreed to support the 30:30:40 formula. Our delegation also decided in the event of that option being eliminated that we would support the 50:25:25 formula. That was the situation to which we consistently adhered.

I did tell my other trade union colleagues that the TGWU delegation had decided that if in finality the 50:25:25 formula was the only option left we would cast our votes in favour of that option, rather than have what is termed a 'hung conference'.

Therefore you will appreciate that the way in which you have represented to your readers what appears on the surface to be an authoritative statement, is completely misleading and, to a certain extent, smacks of fabrication.

Under these two letters was printed a note by Gordon Greig:

It is hardly surprising that Messrs Jenkins and Evans should protest at our reconstruction of how the deal over the Labour Party leadership was cooked up. As Mandy Rice-Davis once said, 'They would, wouldn't they?'

Our story made it clear that there were several different versions of what took place – hence we styled it 'a political whodunnit'. Readers may judge for themselves who did what, where and to whom.

Outraged, I wrote to David English, the editor of the *Daily Mail*:

I am greatly disturbed that you should have cut my letter rebutting your version of the Wembley Labour Party conference without any reference to me in spite of the flurry of telexes exchanged on the afternoon and evening of 27th January. This is so outrageous that I am referring the matter to the Press Council because as you know I informed your newspaper through your Industrial Reporter Mr Robert Porter as to the facts.

What *did* he write? I trust that you have a copy of all the copy submitted to you so that we can find out who is being faithful to the truth.

Incidentally, the offensive piece by Mr Gordon Greig is quite deplorable and I propose to raise this as well.

I am referring all this correspondence and telexes to the Press Council as I believe you have behaved in a thoroughly reprehensible way.

What was appearing in the papers – and the *Mail* was not alone, the *Guardian* and also the *Sunday Telegraph* and *Observer* had all published accounts on similar lines – was so insulting and misleading that I put out a press statement announcing that I had asked the Press Council to investigate my complaints about the 'malicious and untrue' accounts of my activities at the Wembley Conference and 'the entirely reprehensible role of those parts of the media in seeking to portray a conspiratorial situation at the Wembley Conference when none existed.'

The Press Council took until October to deliver an adjudication (Oh! for a prompt decision and compulsory publication.) It read:

The original article headed 'Clue by Clue . . . a great Labour Whodunnit!' to which Mr Clive Jenkins took exception was, in the Press Council's view, ambiguous. Readers could differ about whether its description of exchanges between Mr Jenkins and Mr Moss Evans over lunch was offered as speculation or a factual report.

The footnote broadly quoting Miss Rice-Davis' well known answer 'they would, wouldn't they?' which the newspaper added to Mr Jenkins' and Mr Evans' letters removed the ambiguity. It made clear that the newspaper itself intended the account as a factual one, despite saying there were several different versions and readers might themselves judge who did what, where and to whom.

In essence the question was an invitation to disbelieve Mr Jenkins' and Mr Evans' denials.

The newspaper did publish an account of an alleged conversation which is unsupported by evidence and its reply in the footnote was unethical. To this extent the complaint against the *Daily Mail* is upheld.

The Press Council does not agree that Mr Jenkins' letter

was improperly edited and that complaint against the *Daily Mail* is rejected.

I told the Press Association I was not satisfied with the quality and depth of their investigation and the time it took. I pushed it further in a letter to Kenneth Morgan, the Director of the Press Council:

I am not satisfied with your adjudication. I repeat that there was no exchange between Mr Evans and me at a lunchtime meeting. I gave the facts to Mr Robert Porter.

I want to put to you a specific question. Mr Bevins has requested that his name be withdrawn 'because his contribution had nothing to do with the relevant conversation'. Have you asked to see the original stories written by Mr Greig and Mr Porter?

I repeat that the allegation of collaboration is a straightforward lie and I would like to know if either of these correspondents represented it as being a fact as I specifically and in detail contradicted it to one of them.

So what copy did they supply to their editor? And did you ask to see it?

You will realise that the heart of this question to you is whether you have investigated this complaint in detail.

Kenneth Morgan eventually replied:

I am sorry you are not satisfied with the Council's adjudication: the *Daily Mail* may well be even less so, of course. As we both know, parties to a dispute are often less than satisfied with its adjudication by a tribunal or arbitration.

When a member of the public makes a complaint against a newspaper it is for him or her, not the Council, to assemble and produce the evidence to support the complaint. You did this; the evidence you produced and the comments you made were represented to the editor and, through him to the three journalists named in the by-line for them to respond.

The narrative in the Council's press release reports that the newspaper told the Council it did not wish to comment further – i.e., in response to the complaint – as the Council told you in its letter of 23 July 81. The press release reports Mr Bevins' request that his name should be withdrawn. The Council does not, nor did it need to, rule on this. The newspaper and the journalists were free to produce copy of other material to the Council in answer to the complaint if they so wished. They clearly did not, and the Council judge the matter on the evidence before it – all of which was supplied by you save for the newspaper's statement that it and its journalists wished to make no further comment.

As the newspaper made no further attempt to substantiate to the Council a conversation which had been denied publicly in its letters column by both the alleged participants, there was no obligation on the Council to investigate this allegation further.

So, with this pusillanimity, we closed.

Perhaps it might be thought that this was behaviour to be expected from the *Daily Mail*. But other newspapers of different reputation also behaved badly and grudgingly retracted. Peter Jenkins, in a *Guardian* feature, wrote:

Whatever the electoral fortunes of the breakaways over the next few years, it is probable that the events of this weekend will become a milestone in the realignment of British party politics which is now in progress. Wembley, coming after Blackpool, marked what seems to be a decisive stage in the disintegration of the Labour movement as we know it.

Some trade unionists – and Mr Clive Jenkins was one of them – have no qualms about extending direct trade union control over the party – but other prime movers in the affair, notably Mr David Basnett, believed themselves to be engaged in saving the Labour Party and were tragically unable to see that they were being duped into a process which would destroy its independence.

The scales fell from Mr Basnett's eyes at around four o'clock on Saturday – too late. Mr Jenkins had taken him to the cleaners and made him look a fool. 'I think David has rumbled Clive at last' said one of Mr Basnett's advisers, somewhat wearily. Not only was Mr Basnett duped, and duped from the very day he initiated the commission of inquiry and embarked along the fatal road which led via Bishops Stortford to Blackpool and Wembley: so was Mr Callaghan and so was, most humiliatingly of all, Mr Michael Foot.

What happened on Saturday made it perfectly plain that Mr Jenkins was hand-in-glove with Mr Benn. By moving their supporters in behind the USDAW motion, Mr Jenkins and Mr Benn ensured that that union could not escape the hook on which it had impaled itself . . .

I wrote to Peter Preston, the *Guardian* editor, by hand on 26 January, saying that Peter Jenkins' piece was 'both lying and meretricious'. 'There was no consultation with Tony Benn or any discussion whatsoever. The only time we met over the weekend was in public at Central Hall when we had a vigorous difference of opinion over another political issue.' And, I continued:

I flatly deny the absurd charge that I sought to lobby Mr Moss Evans and Mr Alan Fisher . . . they had their own decisions and views. Anyway, either the ASDAW or the ASTMS amendment would have survived through that balloting stage. The only minor surprise is how much generalised support existed for the proposition which was finally adopted.

As far as my union and I were concerned we would have embraced any extension of the franchise. There were no secret dinners or parties. I *did* lobby hard, but only for the proposition that we did not wish an indecisive conference. In my speech I made it clear that we would not 'cry into our beer' about any decision. We simply wanted to reaffirm that we supported our Leader and Deputy Leader in their current roles and in leading us into the coming General Election.

A snowstorm of communications followed, when my letter appeared – *cut*. On 27 January, however, this letter from me appeared:

I am surprised and disturbed that you should have cut my letter of 26 January without telling me or your readers. I accused Peter Jenkins' piece of being 'both lying and meretricious'. Why can't your readers know this? He accused me of similar offences and I declared the accusations to be baseless. I trust this letter is going to be printed without any cuts.

The *Guardian* added this footnote:

The laws of the land and common courtesy mean that we do not print allegations of lying without first informing our correspondents. Mr Peter Jenkins was away when Mr Clive Jenkins' letter arrived. He has since been consulted and is happy to allow the other Mr Jenkins the adjectives of his choice – Editor.

Also published was a letter from Moss Evans:

It is completely misleading for Mr Peter Jenkins to suggest that 'by moving their supporters in behind the USDAW motion, Mr Jenkins and Mr Benn ensured that that union could not escape the hook on which it had impaled itself. NUPE and the TGWU were made to realise that defeating the NEC's 33:33:33 formula was the only way of achieving the defeat of the Basnett 50 per cent. It was a brilliant piece of manoeuvring, the only clues to which were the open Bennite support for what was not most obviously the most Left-wing solution.'

You will know that at a press conference following our general executive council, on 4 December, attended by your Labour Editor, Keith Harper, I reported that the TGWU Executive would recommend the TGWU Labour Party delegate conference to support the formula 33:33:33. In the event of that formula being eliminated, the TGWU would support the 30:30:40; then they would support any formula which did not give more than 40 per cent to any one section.

This was agreed by the TGWU delegates conference on the morning of 23 January, but with two significant changes. That the executive recommendation should be supported but – because of the similarities between our amendment and that put by the Labour Party NEC which called for equal representation and an electoral college – we should withdraw our option in favour of the NEC's so that there would not be too many amendments on the agenda. And if in finality the 50:25:25 formula were the only option left to conference, the TGWU would cast its vote in favour of that option rather than have a 'hung conference'.

What an effort it was to try to put the record straight, although perhaps the *Guardian's* response was the most gracious in the end.

This could not describe the *Sunday Telegraph*, which reported without a by-line (did they just rewrite other newspapers' copy?):

Angry TUC moderates protested last night that behind the scenes conduct of the white-collar union leader, Mr Clive Jenkins, may have cost the Labour Party the next General Election.

The row erupted immediately it became known that Mr Jenkins, Left-wing General Secretary of the Association of Scientific, Technical and Managerial Staffs, had, with the active encouragement of Mr Wedgwood Benn, canvassed the backing of Mr Moss Evans, Transport Workers' leader, and others for the shopworkers' union formula for electing Labour's leader . . .

I wrote to J. W. M. Thompson, the editor of the *Sunday Telegraph*, on 28 January:

I must strongly protest at the report which appeared in last week's newspaper in which I was accused by a *Sunday Telegraph* reporter of 'behind the scenes conduct . . . (which) . . . may have cost the Labour Party the next General Election'.

It was alleged that I 'canvassed Mr Moss Evans, the Transport Workers' leader, and others for the shopworkers' union formula for electing Labour's leader'. This is a lie. My own union decided at the beginning of November on its 40:30:30 formula. So where on earth does 'Mr

Jenkins lulled them into a belief that he would support the formula backed by Mr Michael Foot' come from? Either the USDAW or the ASTMS amendment would have survived through the balloting stages.

To put the record straight for your readers, though I fear this fleet-footed lie may never be arrested, I would say this. As far as my union and I were concerned we would have embraced any extension of the franchise. There were no secret meetings. I *did* lobby hard, but only for the proposition that we did not wish an indecisive conference.

Your article was entirely defamatory. Is it too much to hope that your reporters might in future test out their highly damaging allegations on their victims before committing themselves to print?

Thompson had to be nudged by telex during that week but eventually he printed my letter on 1 February after our checking that there would be no cuts.

But who were these moderates? I suspect spurious, invented ghosts, which is why there was no attribution to a journalist. The truth is that after my delegation saw how the voting might go as the National Executive Committee's proposition was losing, we met outside the hall doors and decided to vote for the USDAW proposition. I went down the aisle – Bill Whatley and David Basnett were sitting diagonally across from each other – and said, 'I want you both to hear this. We are going to announce our vote for USDAW.' They said, 'Why not?' So I went to the rostrum and did just that. Others coalesced behind us. So was the electoral college – a great success in democracy – set up.

I later said to Moss, 'If we could do that with a nod and an aside, what would have happened if we had laughed?'

Ronald Butt in *The Times* sought to sum up at the end of January 1981, and how oddly his words now read. I did not mind his comment: 'Still, Parliament survived the rotten boroughs of the eighteenth century, so why should it not survive the use of union block votes in the appointment of a Labour leader? It survived the borough mongering of the Duke of Newcastle: why should it not survive Mr Clive Jenkins?' But I found this rich following praise for 'Mr Sid Weighell, of the railwaymen, an honourable trade union leader who genuinely seeks to represent the opinions of his rank and file, [and who] declared the block vote was suspect. "I know, because I've got one in my hand."' As it turned out later, it was a use of the block vote which cost Sid Weighell the General Secretaryship of the Railwaymen and brought forth the engaging Jimmy Knapp.

After all this I was astonished to read in Denis Healey's memoirs, *The Time of my Life*:

> I made a blistering attack on the trades union leader, Clive Jenkins, at the party conference in 1974, which was all the more effective for relying on ridicule rather than abuse. It won me a standing ovation at the time; but another union leader warned me that I might live to regret it.
>
> I remembered his words in 1980, when Jenkins persuaded David Basnett to support a new system for electing the party leader, and later pushed Michael Foot into premature resignation just after the 1983 general election, so helping to stitch up the succesion for Neil Kinnock.

How could he have thought this? David Basnett was never persuaded, and Michael is not and was not a pushable man. Did Denis think that I could harbour a grudge over all those years to prevent him becoming Leader of the Labour Party? I don't even remember the 1974 Conference. Well, I suppose you have to have someone to blame but this seems excessive. He continued:

> Again and again in the critical years after the 1979 election, incoherence or incompetence in the trade union leadership led us to disaster. With the retirement of Jack Jones and Hugh Scanlon, the party had lost its ablest supporters in the TUC. Their mantle should have fallen on David Basnett, the leader of the mighty General and Municipal Workers' Union. But Basnett seemed to find the mantle uncomfortable and embarrassing; it was in any case too heavy for him. He proved weak and vacillating in our years of travail, and was too much influenced by Clive Jenkins, the maverick left-wing leader of a professional union whose

members mainly voted Tory . . . and our next ordeal was the special conference of the party at Wembley in January 1981, which was an even bigger shambles than its predecessor. This time the conference was confronted with five separate ways of composing an electoral college. Basnett proposed the original Bishop's Stortford formula, which gave 50 per cent to the Labour MPs. It would have been carried easily but for the fatal purism of the AUEW; Terry Duffy wanted the Labour MPs to have 75 per cent and had decided not to support any motion which gave them less than 51 per cent. So his union abstained. Clive Jenkins acted as the catspaw of CLPD by swinging his union behind a motion which gave the Labour MPs only 30 per cent, as against 40 per cent for the unions and 30 per cent for the constituency parties.

One would not think from these sour grapes that the electoral college has worked rather well. It even, narrowly, elected Denis once. And in 1983 it did indeed elect Neil Kinnock.

The Friday morning after the literate, generous and supportive sage Michael Foot and the Labour Party were defeated in the General Election of 1983, I went into my office early, having not been up so late the night before at the Labour Party Headquarters because it was apparent that we had received a horrendous defeat. I have no doubt that if Michael Foot had become Prime Minister many of the privations and ugly social developments that the British people have suffered could have been avoided. There could have been a massaging of the changes in the workforce that were undoubtedly going to take place and which I had personally been preaching in books and articles for some years.

Michael Foot lacked only one quality. He could not be angry with Labour Party colleagues and he lacked a divine impatience. He once defended David Owen to me in the course of an industrial dispute, when Owen, as Minister of Health, was quite clearly wrong, saying in his Commons room to both of us: 'Ah, Clive, you were too professional for poor David there.'

He had great courtesy, particularly to young people, and

would always listen to new ideas. So, of course, does Neil. I treasure the time when I was the chair of a TUC-Labour Party Liaison Committee and Neil was talking about the need for people to change their jobs, to be re-educated, to have different life styles; I interrupted to say, 'Neil, but I have written books about this,' and he turned to me, smiled beatifically, and said, 'Yes, Clive, and I used to teach from them.'

On that morning after the electoral defeat, the question was, what to do? I knew that Moss Evans was usually in his office before 8 am and would be at his desk drinking his favourite Oxo. So I telephoned him on his private unlisted desk number and we wept over the line to each other. I then reminded him that the Labour Party had called, as it does annually, for nominations for the posts of Leader, Deputy Leader and Treasurer. According to the timetable of my own National Executive, we would have to take some decisions the next day to fit in with the Party's closing dates. This was the monthly Saturday meeting and, for purposes of convenience, our full delegation to the Labour Party conference, which was made up of National Executive Council members, lay delegates elected nationally and certain national officials of the union, was meeting on the Sunday. So I said to Moss, 'We are going to have to do something.'

He said, 'Well, what do you have in mind?' I said that our debt of gratitude to Michael Foot and our respect for him was so deep that we would, naturally, nominate him. Moss paused and said, 'What if he decides he doesn't want it?' 'In that case, I think we ought to jump a generation and nominate a young man.' Moss said at once, 'I think I know who you have got in mind. Are you saying that Neil Kinnock is a possibility?' He rapidly added, 'You know he is a TGWU member as well?' I said, 'I don't think this is necessarily a disadvantage under the circumstances.'

Moss had been the man who worked with me when we discussed Michael Foot's candidature at the time that the franchise was restricted to members of the Parliamentary Labour Party in the House of Commons, and he said, 'Well, you ask him, because if he wants it we will nominate him again, of course.' Greta Karpin found Michael at home and I explained that we had our Executive Council meeting on the Saturday and that they would normally consult with the delegation at the Sunday morning meeting but that we were still for him.

There have been all sorts of mis-statements in books and newspaper reports that Michael had decided that he was going to 'resign' and that this was discussed in a train on the Saturday morning when he was returning from a Miners' gala in Northumberland. I do not believe this to be true.

What happened was that Michael said, 'Let us talk. Come to supper tonight [Friday].' So later, having canvassed others, off I went to Pilgrims Lane. A mythology has grown up around a pleasant little supper party. When we had finished Jill's casserole, Michael had his favourite small amount of whisky in a little silver mug and we went over the question of the leadership of nominations in detail. I repeated to him that the recommendation of ASTMS would be absolutely flatly for him. I also told him that Moss and the TGWU would do the same. He then asked me the question that Moss had put. 'What if I were to decide not to accept the nomination?' Jill Foot, who is a very percipient and shrewd observer said, 'I know what he will do.' She paused and our eyes met. 'He will go for Neil.'

Michael looked at me and I nodded. He thought for a while and said that in that case he would gratefully decline the nomination. 'I had better tell him now.' He put the telephone alongside him on the table and, not needing to look up the telephone number, rang Neil. It was obvious that he was taken aback. (I have to say that Neil does not recall this incident: at least he did not when I mentioned it to him first of all, but it did happen.)

That over, we did a little more planning. I took the view that I would have to go through the formal procedures at the ASTMS National Executive Council meeting and formally invite Michael to stand. I would then raise the question as to what we would do if Michael were not to run, and would offer to go out and go through the gesture of consulting him.

At the Saturday meeting I therefore duly telephoned and explained the situation, and he then formally declined, with gratitude, the offer. I went back into the Executive and said, 'with appreciation he has decided not to run', and I developed the idea of jumping a generation and proposed Neil Kinnock. This was agreed without any dissent from a group with mixed political viewpoints, subject to our consulting with our delegation the following morning.

I returned to Pilgrims Lane on the Saturday evening to report back, something which I had forgotten until Dick Clements reminded me that he had met me on the pavement outside after having declined an invitation to go in because he was 'knackered' after the election campaign and the Saturday trip to the Northumberland gala. When I queried his memory, he said, 'You had a pot of fuchsias in your hand for Jill.' You cannot invent a cameo like that.

Overnight I drafted a press release with the objective of clearing it with Michael and aiming it for the radio programme 'The World This Weekend' to pre-empt other candidates. Our Labour Party delegation liked the scenario of first speaking to Michael and then tracking down Neil. Neil was in the studio of the 'World at One' and we had difficulty in getting him out because the BBC could not think what could be that urgent. Other journalists, including Adam Raphael, present at the time subsequently claimed that they were aware of a machination going on and made appropriate guesses, but I doubt it. When I spoke with Neil, he said, 'I am pleased and proud to accept your nomination,' and we arranged for him to come into my office the next morning to analyse support and discuss the mechanics of his campaign.

In the meantime, I edited a press release and spoke with Moss Evans at home so that he knew that the plan was in place and running. He recalls taking my call sitting on the stairs in Hemel Hempstead (had he been in the bath?) and thinking, 'I can put this to our impending Biennial Delegate Conference and have our Labour Conference delegates mandated by our supreme policy making body.'

So off I went explaining to the media that we had a vigorous, young, articulate, cultured candidate whom I did not doubt would be elected. I was also careful to underline our debt to Michael. The news was a bombshell, and I was glad Greta Karpin had come in to the office especially to handle calls. Roy Hattersley has said since that while watching David Basnett and

Terry Duffy discussing the candidates on television, 'for one hour I thought I was going to be Leader of the Labour Party'. Roy is a gifted politician who writes like an angel but he was not our candidate on that day. Neil was our spontaneous choice.

Neil came into the office on the Monday morning with Robin Cook MP, one of his campaign managers, and we looked at the campaign. Neil said that, in his opinion, it would come down to him or Roy Hattersley and that they should decide, ethically, not to outspend each other in the leadership election campaign and that they should both keep accounts. They both did. I volunteered our print shop to help get the campaign up and running and Neil in his beautiful italic hand headed a sheet of paper with the words 'The Neil Kinnock Campaign'. That piece of paper was in our print shop in half an hour and we delivered several thousand sheets and imprinted envelopes to him within the course of the afternoon. We also needed photographs for union journals. They were taken on my patio – after Neil had prudently taken out all bulky objects from his pockets: the man had style even then!

A duty press officer at the Labour Party Headquarters had made a number of enquiries on the Sunday night and I am told, after consulting Sir Tom McCaffrey, Michael's 'Chief of Staff', that she expressed disbelief that Michael Foot was not standing and explained that he would be very angry at my announcing it on his behalf. This, of course, was nonsense. When Michael and I went to the cinema together to see the *Ploughman's Lunch* in Notting Hill on the following Wednesday, the Press was puzzled: he did not seem cross at all. When Michael got up to leave it was heartwarming to see the audience looking up at him and then breaking into spontaneous applause.

In the meantime I had been telephoning all the sympathetic union people and other opinion formers, and there were many of them. It was not hard; everyone came up with Neil's name. In fact it seemed Alan Tuffin had also raised the issue of a Kinnock run inside the Post Office Workers' Union on the day after polling day. (We both bet that he would be elected on the first ballot. We won.) The move had captured everyone's imagination and as history will have it we started early, we started vigorously and out of that I have no doubt will come Prime Minister Kinnock.

14

Inside the TUC

After Len Murray decided to step down as General Secretary of the Trades Union Congress in 1984, a group of large and middle-sized unions tried to draft me. I knew that Len had to go. In the key committee discussion over Eddy Shah and the *Messenger* group dispute with the printing unions in Warrington, he had attacked the very moderate motion whch I had put forward expressing sympathy for the print workers' unions and which the committee voted for. His reaction was extreme; usually mild-mannered, he exited from the Congress House committee room after the vote swearing at me, 'If you want my . . . . job go down to my . . . . office and take it now.' He went to put his personal point of view to the press waiting outside on the pavement lit by television cameras. The Committee's vote was reversed at the General Council meeting, which demoralised the print unions but also doomed the General Secretary of the TUC. You cannot lose the support of so many significant people, including many of the Committee Chairmen on your General Council, and stay in office.

Len confided his decision to retire to the then President of the TUC, Ray Buckton of the Locomotive Engineers, who then confided in me. Mostyn Evans arranged a dinner at his favourite subterranean Italian restaurant, L'Amico, near Transport House and a group of us sat and debated the situation over our saltimbocca. I did not want the General Secretaryship; it was a treadmill and would have prevented me doing the many things outside the trade union movement that I found valuable and interesting. When it came down to it my candidate was Rodney Bickerstaffe of the National Union of Public Employees. But Rodney was not persuadable, mainly because he doubted whether all the votes that were promised to me were capable of being transferred to him, but also because he had not been in office very long and felt that he had major work to do inside NUPE, including seeing a national minimum wage established. So it was left that evening that we would all think about it a little more – except for me since I had declared myself out of the contest.

When we came out of our private room in the restaurant, another diner deduced that there had been a dinner to decide who should run and we were counting up the votes: he telephoned a newspaper, which printed a speculative piece. There was obviously great interest in the succession and information inevitably leaked out. The speculation effectively aborted the planned idea to have one agreed personality as a candidate. In the event, Norman Willis was elected. ASTMS did not nominate him, but we believed in unity and subsequently voted for him. We did not think he had the weight, the gravitas for the job; too many jokes were ultimately erosive of authority.

To be the General Secretary of the British national trade union centre, which has an international role to play of great importance, is a huge and bone-breaking task, not helped by the unwieldy old-fashioned bureaucracy of the TUC. The spirit of Lord Citrine, General Secretary of the TUC for over twenty years until he left to head the Electricity Board set up by the nationalising Labour government of 1945, still lay heavily on Congress House. He was the author of the classic guide to chairmanship, which was based on the London County Council's Standing Orders, and his selection of the colours for the coding of committee documents was still in existence. So too was the very odd idea, until I managed to reverse it in 1974, that you were not given an agenda for a committee meeting until you arrived at the meeting. After a great struggle the bureaucracy finally compromised with me and issued what they called a draft agenda, with the right to provide another agenda to put in front of your chair for you to read on arrival at the meeting.

The General Council, when it met monthly on a Wednesday, had laid before them the Minutes of the previous Monday's meeting of the Finance and General Purpose Committee, a key body. Before I became a member of this august committee, the so called 'Inner Cabinet', I always got there well before ten o'clock in the morning to read what had happened. At one time the system had been that the Deputy General Secretary actually read out the entire Minutes of the previous Monday, so that people could be taken right through it. Some of us eventually ridiculed this practice and threatened to hold up ice-skating judges' cards awarding marks for style, performance and content. The practice went, but that was not until 1976.

Lord Citrine retained an enormous interest in Congress affairs and, well into his eighties, would come to the TUC Annual Congress and sit behind the curtains in the wings of the platform occupied by the General Council. Until shortly before he died he would be found there using his own code of personal shorthand to make notes. I wonder what for? Norman Willis used to joke (and this one I liked) that if there was a major row over procedural questions at the TUC, when someone would inevitably say 'Well, according to Citrine', he could always reply 'No, I don't think that is right, and by the way we will consult Citrine' – at which point the silver-haired gentleman would be brought on to the stage from the wings.

Lord Citrine was a hard act to follow as General Secretary and Sir Vincent Tewson was not up to it. He left in 1960, partly under the pressure of George Woodcock who, it was said by Congress staff, disdained to verbally address his chief for months on end. George Woodcock achieved eminence in the press with confused lofty statements. He had the attention of, and played the guru to, a group of industrial correspondents and editors who were entranced with him, although I don't know why or how. I cannot think of any substantial achievement, any glittering phrase, although the Fleet Street pundits thought there was great depth in one of his questions at a Congress to himself: 'What are we here for?' He went on to make a remarkably muddled statement about function, structure and purpose. He was one of the most arrogant men I have met: when I had been invited on to a television programme with him to discuss some of the Wilson Government's industrial relations, he insisted to the producers that I be put into a separate segment, or sent home, because my union was too small. It may be that I am still resentful of his role in the quarrel over the recognition of white-collar workers in the British Steel Corporation. George Woodcock had come from a small craft union and was still part of the whole blue-collar frame of mind on the General Council. He could tolerate white-collar workers being organised in the civil service and the Town Halls as this has had happened a long time before, but the idea that they should be represented in industry, services and finance was, I think, quite alien to him.

Consequently he was absolutely the wrong choice as Chairman of the Labour-created Commission on Industrial Relations. He simply had no feel or appreciation for the growth of the white-collar workers or even the reasons for unhappiness and discontent in the skilled blue-collar unions whose members were sensing that there were many changes in technology going on around them. Barbara Castle told me she appointed him 'to get him out of Vic Feather's hair'. The Commission was a monument to futility, although it had some persons of integrity on it. There was Leslie Blakeman, who had been the head of industrial relations at the Ford Motor Company, which had resisted recognition of my own foremen's union for many years. Will Paynter, who had been the Communist General Secretary of the National Union of Mineworkers, oversaw one of our claims for recognition at the CIR. He had no comprehension whatsoever of what we were talking about, he had never heard of incremental scales and merit payments, and, while a man of great integrity and charm, was the wrong choice. One of the senior staff at the CIR, later to go much further in the civil service, said to me of George Woodcock: 'He does not really trust us. He locks his office door at nights when he goes home.' In George Woodcock's period of office there, and in Congress House, nothing really important happened.

The only General Secretary of the TUC who had a feel for

wider developments was the greatly underestimated Victor Feather, who succeeded Woodcock in 1969. He was hard, tough, shrewd and flexible. At the time of the Heath government's drive in the early seventies to have unions 'registered' and the title of 'union' taken away from any collective bargaining body which had not registered, I went to see Vic because I was concerned about the frail organising basis of my own small union. After I had explained the problem, he said, 'Well, we will have to call ourselves the Congress of Industrial Organisations then.' This was of immense importance because previous (and subsequent) General Secretaries had been afraid of somehow exposing the national centre to legal action of any kind. It was their virginal horror of this which led to the problems of Len Murray over the Warrington *Messenger* dispute.

I found Vic a complicated and interesting character (including his masterminding of the exposure of the ETU ballot riggers). He was intensely interested in art and in his office there were canvasses stacked against the walls and a marble relief on an easel. According to what I think is an almost true story, when Vic was appointed in the mid-thirties to a junior TUC job he went out with the money in his pocket to buy an early Hillman Minx car and came back with a Jacob Epstein bust of Paul Robeson. This was the bust that we had under a spotlight at the rally I had helped organise as chairman of the Free Paul Robeson Committee in the late 1950s. Vic's son Sandy Feather, who is an officer of The Iron and Steel Trades Federation, told me in 1988 that the bust was in his mother's front room and he was kind enough to drive to Northampton and bring it back to lend to me for an opening of our new MSF building in Dublin (which had previously been the American Embassy).

Vic was hard working and modest, and when I asked him to speak to our Executive Committee on a Sunday morning in Eastbourne he readily agreed to come. I only found out later that he had been in the north of the country and had had to spend hours at Victoria station in order to be with us on time. But we all owe him more than that.

The TUC's obvious need for its own college was something which I had to propose – and I got my union to become the biggest lender. Quite remarkably there had remained an atavistic resistance to seeking state aid for education of trade union representatives and there was a shock wave in the Education Committee of the TUC when I suggested that that was the norm for European union centres of every political affiliation. As a leftist trade union official explained, 'The government will want to interfere with our teaching. They'll get their hands under our skirts.' 'In that case,' I said, 'we'll put a dotted line around their wrists first and then cut their hands off.'

We reached an agreement on funding of £400,000 from the Labour government in 1977 and the General Council made an application for capital funding in August 1977 but did not get a meeting with Shirley Williams, the Education Minister, until October 1978. We had hoped for a capital sum of a million pounds; this was a petty sum in Europe – the Swedish unions were getting the equivalent of £120 million a year. The responsible ministers dallied and then, alas, Labour lost the 1979 General Election. I blame Shirley Williams, not a very progressive lady, for failing to do all that was necessary, as with the 1975 Bullock Committee recommendations on industrial democracy. It has now become a standing joke, but there were so many occasions when Shirley arrived late. I remember once waiting around to see her at her ministry when she was Secretary of State for Education and on walking past her office door, which was open, saw her simply sitting there contemplating her desk. When she came (late) to a conference we organised on genetic manipulation, she had two civil service minders, both female, who said they were deployed to try to get her to meetings more or less on time.

In 1980, after the Labour defeat, the TUC General Council went for self-funding, and ASTMS lent £250,000 and provided banking contacts for a 'soft' loan. My earlier proposal was for ongoing annual funding, and under the Conservative government this brought me into contact with Norman Tebbit ad Keith Joseph to put our case for an ongoing grant. In August 1984 the National Education Centre was opened, on the site of the old Hornsey College of Art, with the aim of training full-time union officers.

The whole structure of the TUC is badly financed. When it

became obvious that Congress House itself would have to be 'refurbished', I argued for selling it because it was on a prime site – millions of people pass its doors on the way to the British Museum – and it would obviously have attractions for developers. The money could then be used to create a purpose-built, high technology centre linked directly to union head offices and TUC regions. This proved too terrifying an initiative and instead money had to be provided for rebuilding Congress House, which had won a prize for street architecture but had become quite impractical in terms of people working there.

A number of us urged that computer technology be put in, connecting with union head offices so that, instead of information being posted in weighty bundles, it could simply be relayed by computer. I believed, for instance, that if we had a data bank that recorded all the cases of industrial decease or injury pursued by affiliated unions, it would be possible to predict where new hazards of poisoning or infection were going to occur. I set up a system whereby my own union sent a weekly return to the TUC of all our legal cases. As far as I know, no other unions did and no one at the TUC zealously pursued them to do so. Some unions pleaded financial constraints or manpower problems, which I never understood because if you are instructing solicitors to proceed in a case you have a return from them. We still do not have such a data bank and I very much regret it because it would be an analytical and predictive tool to use for the safety of workers.

The trade union movement has, however, never really believed in analysis and has always derided theory, which meant that its representatives were using those crumbs of yesterday's theories which had now become accepted. There had never been a concept of the trade union officer as a specially stressed and interesting social engineer. Perhaps he, and now she, may be taking that view as 1992's 'Social Charter' approaches. Conservative politicians certainly did not have this view. Relatively sophisticated centrist ministers in the Heath government, and Ted Heath himself (who came to lunch with ASTMS – out of office; Jim Prior and Lord Carrington entertained us while in government) had never been members of unions. Of course they had not. They must, therefore, since they were not ideological men, have been ascribing to the unions and their leaders behaviour patterns from within the large organisations they knew best, like manufacturing corporations, banks and big firms. Unions were seen as having hierarchies and command structures which could be dominated, but which in fact they did not ever possess, and this led ministers to a basic incomprehension of the role of the trade union officer.

I remember, with fascination, sitting alongside Maurice Macmillan when he held the Labour Ministry under Heath and making a point to him about how the TUC thinks: I saw him laboriously copy down 'Trades Union Congress'. I wrote at the time in the *Spectator*:

Do they really appreciate that every professional union bargainer sits on a pinnacle of institutionalised indignation? He is vocationally a gladiator as well, because the work of the union is basically defensive. It really is quite remarkable that one of the most moderate (and economically successful) trade union organisations in the world should be the subject of a national debate about extremism. Of course, unions do go to war from time to time but until recently this has almost always been in three basic ways. There is the 'defence of the job' which has mostly been in industries suffering from structural decline, such as shipbuilding; there is the 'monotony and strain' strike which is so much in the foreground of motor manufacturing disputes. Then there is 'the change of union leadership' strike where shifts in personalities over a period lead to a reappraisal of the union's performance and often a sense of dissatisfaction.

The miners' strike falls into this category. The astonishing point about the miners' union is that it has so rarely used its power, that it has so understated its argument. There is even the case for saying that by tempering their demands over the years and providing such cheap fuel the nation has been done a *disservice* and that the present strike could not only have been foreseen but is necessary.

I have increasingly come towards the view that most unions have been incapable of seeing into their own future, and most unions do not have trained leaders. In the Thatcher era, unions in print, sea transport and mining were outgeneralled. The remarkable feature of the National Union of Mineworkers was that it had *so many* officials, so much money, and yet stayed in the organisation of the coal workers, the coal-face hewer as the king. The Transport Workers Unions was therefore able to organise open-cast mining, and other unions organised people producing gas, electricity and oil.

I find it difficult to write about the NUM because I am deeply sympathetic to the miner and have bitten my tongue frequently in meetings when invited to appraise the industrial and political strategy of the leadership. Arthur Scargill is a man of immense personal charm and one of the funniest re-tellers of anecdotes from Yorkshire about work, life, death and sex as one could ever wish to have a drink with. He also does quite a passable imitation of me. (As did Jeremy Thorpe, who once invited me to lunch in a private room in the Reform Club with the Parliamentary Liberal Party and as I opened the door I heard a voice which was uncannily familiar; I realised that Jeremy was imitating me to his fellow Liberal MPs and, intuitively knowing I had come in, he swung around with feline grace saying, 'Clive, I am just telling them about my Welsh auntie!')

But I think Arthur got it almost all wrong for almost all of the time. I met him after the very first of the miners' strikes when he was on the same Soviet ship going to Leningrad with a party of miners, their wives and children; he was still almost literally at the coal-face. He was not really interested in training union officers and created a most unwelcome precedent for trade union pension fund trustees by insisting that decisions had to be in accord with policy decisions, instead of simply putting his hand very properly on his heart and declaring, 'I believe as a trustee this to be in the interest of the pensioners.'

It was only after a series of colossal industrial defeats that the NUM decided at its annual conference in 1988 (at which I spoke as President of the TUC) that it would seek amalgamation with other unions. The first motion was amalgamation with a view to creating an 'energy union', but this was dropped in favour of bargaining a merger with some organisation somewhere. At this conference Neil Kinnock had brought the Labour Party's fraternal greetings the previous day and I saw a photograph of

Arthur Scargill presenting him with 'a rose-bowl of Sheffield Steel filled with socialist fundamentalism'. After my speech, as Chairman of the TUC, Arthur charmingly explained that the leader of the union movement should have a similar gift. It felt light for steel: I turned it over in the train on the way back and found it was silver-plated copper. There may be a deeper psychological explanation. Anyway, just for fun, I presented him with a Filofax absolutely devoid of any fundamentalism except days, weeks and months.

By this time in the TUC it was obvious that my relationship with Norman Willis was awkward, because I thought his presentation of issues lacked depth and was confused and obscuratory. I found this very embarrassing at the National Economic Development Council because it suited the Thatcherite ministers to have a diffuse, jokey case presented to them. I sought to constrain him at the General Council and other committees, which he reacted against. In the past we had been friendly and sometimes he had stayed with me in my home in the country, but this petered out because he perceived me as someone who did not think he was up to the job. As a result his wife could not bring herself to talk to me, and neither could Mrs Murray. The situation made it very difficult with the media. You certainly don't feed information to journalists, who generally take delight in knocking the trade union movement – as do their proprietors.

This recalls the trade union joke related to me by David Basnett, General Secretary of the municipal workers. After a heated debate about leadership during a Trades Union Congress, a noted TV journalist and his crew descended on a leading lay delegate. 'Will you give us your opinion of your General Secretary?' He looks nervously around the Blackpool Wintergarden and starts: 'Not here.' They take him out on to the Promenade and he looks from side to side, 'far too public here,' so they end up in Stanley Park with the camera rolling. 'What do you think of your General Secretary?' 'Well, actually, to be honest, I don't think he is doing such a bad job.'

David Basnett, Geoffrey Drain of NALGO, Moss Evans of the transport workers and I used to lunch every month at the Reform Club before the TUC's Finance and General Purposes

Committee. 'Congress House' deeply resented our camaraderie, which affected 'fixes' on policy and administration. After all, we had read our papers, or our researchers had – and provided briefs and questions pinned to the agenda papers. Moss, Geoffrey (later the agreeable chairman of the Reform Club itself) and I always had our obligation to report back to our constituents. David said he didn't. 'I fill in the voting form at the TUC and Labour Praty (for the various elections) and I don't have to show it to anyone.' That 'right' has now been invaded at the Labour Conference to the point that ballot casting now has to be published. David hated that reform: so he might. He was quite unreliable in terms of voting agreements. I thought he had agreed to vote for Muriel Turner when she first ran for election to the General Council and when we met in a concourse in the Winter Gardens in Blackpool after the votes had been cast and not counted, I thanked him for his support. 'We didn't vote for her.' 'Why? I thought you promised – we voted for your candidates.' 'Well, you know how it is.' No, I did not. He was an ally sometimes on issues but quite unreliable in terms of *realpolitik*.

I once gave him a painting of the Mersey docks and its grain elevators (a painting I had beaten Vic Feather to at the Liverpool Trades Council's centenary celebrations) because he said he had spent years looking at that view from the Municipal Workers' office where he had been employed as part of the family nepotism which deeply penetrated that union for many generations. So I took it off my wall (keeping its partner – both by a painter now celebrated). 'That's nice,' he said, and that was that. On another occasion, when he was running for the General Secretaryship of his union and had asked for my media help, I arranged for him to go to a dinner with Hugh Cudlipp of the *Daily Mirror* in an upstairs room at Kettners in Soho. They had never met. There was some crisis on and Hugh had two proofs of an editorial brought in for approval. The paper's industrial relations editor, Geoffrey Goodman, was also there. Hugh agreed to have the *Daily Mirror* support David during the election campaign. It did, David won, and never, ever, referred to this seminal meeting again.

But on one issue he was supportive. After a distinctively

frustrating meeting of the TUC's 'inner cabinet', as we drank in David's Duke Street pied-à-terre office, I expressed my boredom with the repetitive pettiness of our internal TUC discussions on finance and services. 'Why not have our own bank? The Germans, Israelis and Scandinavian unions benefit from owning their own financial institutions. Why not have our own?' 'Let's do it,' he said, 'I will talk to Lewis Lee [Chairman of the Cooperative Bank].' Lewis had us to lunch in his City office and was willing to try, ambitiously, to expand an otherwise mildly becalmed bank traditionally servicing most British unions.

Out of this, eventually, came Unity Trust, the 'union bank'. For some months I was the largest shareholder in the sector of shareholdings confined to individuals. I happened to have a £500 cheque for some journalism so I handed it over to the manager, Terry Thomas, who eventually ended up running an enterprise which has bid to outgrow its parent as it absorbs the head office accounts of the major unions and the TUC. It was always a prudent investor – chastened further by a visit to Frankfurt to see the operations of the German trade union bank on the day it effectively collapsed. The German bank was taken over by a German insurance giant because of its exposure in housing support loans, and alleged culpability of leading trade union officials, which resulted in changes in the election order of the West German trade union leadership, starting that day. Unity Trust, though, was sound to invest in and prudent with a mandate in Britain.

It was also David Basnett, Geoffrey Drain, Moss Evans and I – this time meeting at the Market Street Wine Bar in Brighton during a TUC Congress – who agreed that Frank Chapple should, as a token of collegiate disapproval of his behaviour, be removed from certain key committees when the internal 'Committee to Select Committees' met after Congress. So, over the lobsters, he was removed. Len Murray as General Secretary opposed it. But Chapple *was* removed, although he became President of the TUC by seniority and the General Council members' devotion to longstanding precedent. This precedent was, however, later challenged, by Jack Eccles, an ageing municipal workers member of the General Council with a jovial laughing exterior and a colder interior, who attempted a coup against the election of Ray Buckton of the enginemen's union – whose turn it was. When I learned of this, I saw Len Murray behind the curtains on the platform and warned him of this disruptive activity. 'I should look up the precedents,' I suggested – not that I thought it was needed. They were all so clear: one even moved around the General Council year by year as one's seniority accumulated. But, to my astonishment, Len hedged and raised doubts. A few hours later, at the traditional meeting of the Council to elect its Chairman (and thus the President of Congress) and its Committee to Select Committees, Ray was challenged. He won handsomely. But there is no doubt in my mind that he should not have been challenged in the first place. I had taken the precaution of warning friendly Council members that morning and canvassing those who might otherwise be surprised or taken off balance. When in doubt, canvass.

As part of my personal diplomacy in the run-up to my own TUC Presidency in 1988, I booked a box at Covent Garden, through being a GLC-nominated Governor of Sadlers Wells, and invited the electricians' union leader Eric Hammond and his wife for ballet, champagne and civilised discussion. We all enjoyed it, although Eric is one of the most reserved, inwardly tense and controlled personalities I have ever encountered. But not without a certain gallows humour. When he was appealing to the General Council against a decision affecting his union, he had to move from his General Council seat around the table to one facing the President – the traditional place for appellants. As it happened this seat was normally occupied during that year by Arthur Scargill, who vacated it, and as Eric sat down behind the nameplate, he remarked, 'With that name and my case, I wouldn't give much for my chances.' He was right: the complicity of his union in the Wapping Affair was clear enough and did enormous damage to his union's integrity, let alone the harm done to the traditional print unions.

The run-up to my Presidency was not without some odd incidents. During the course of one inter-union dispute, colleagues of mine thought that the astonishing depth and rapidity of attack on my union by the Congress House bureaucracy was inexplicable over a disputed trade union Membership award unless somebody somewhere wanted ASTMS suspended from the TUC so that I could not become President. In any event, I was elected in 1988 and used and enjoyed my year of office, although I was becoming jaded with some of the endless rounds of committee meetings. The Standing Committees of the General Council met in most cases every month and their output of material is all detailed and worthy but they work on the basis that the General Council members would spend a great deal of their time, apart from being busy union executives, going into Congress House and providing approval for material which then goes on to the transmission belt to the General Council itself every month. The diary dictated the way the business was approached. I suggested that this was essentially self-defeating. Other great trade union centres, notably the Scandinavians, had no such system and had Congress every three or four years instead of in the British seemingly 'democratic' system where, as soon as one Congress was over, preparation began for the next. A few meetings were subsequently pared out here and there but the system survived and now is clearly obsolescent.

It can be an honoured, graceful year as the TUC President. The Congress House staff work is very supportive and from month to month at the General Council meetings an uncertain chairman can always be rescued. But the TUC Congress itself is very different! Once you are in the President's chair, much is up to you in a very exposed way in the hall and on television. The senior staff take you through a carefully briefed dress-rehearsal on the previous weekend – day by day. For every session they provided a newly updated version of the programme of Business ('it was harder before the computer'), plus a thick, soft-lead pencil to mark downwards through the business and stage directions. 'Turn left to take the badge', 'turn right to present it'; everything except 'smile' and 'stay in camera axis'.

There are the physical problems of drinking tea and water under the hot TV lights, which raise the question of liquid retention. My colleague Ken Gill, General Secretary of TASS, advised me, 'No coffee with your breakfast'. So how did the First Secretaries of the former great European Communist

Parties speak for five hours? I had a prostate problem that had just been treated by the skills of Mr Neil Paynter, chief surgeon of the trade union Manor House Hospital. It went further than surgery: it *is* possible to pee on the platform always provided you have been suitably equipped. Perhaps everyone who cannot be relieved by a colleague is suitably relieved in this way!

A tradition that I found rather absurd was that the previous President mans the warning lights for rostrum and platform speakers. (At my own union conference an officer did so – no favours, keep precisely to the published speech time limits.) My predecessor, Fred Jarvis of the teachers, the indefatigable Ada Maddocks of NALGO and I tailored the lights in a thoroughly pragmatic, i.e. helpful, way. If we were running badly behind and we had heard it all before, we would put the red light on, and the delegates didn't mind. They were *en rapport*. (Control perhaps came particularly easily to Ada: when she was score-keeper at the traditional General Council v the Press cricket match, the Press never won, although, magnanimously, she sometimes let them draw.)

I enjoyed the monitoring to the extent that in support to my left would be the General Secretary and the Deputy and Assistant General Secretaries – though after a time I looked up to see in astonishment, there was no one there. When I queried what had happened, one of them said with a certain hauteur, 'You seemed to be in control.'

One's personal style matters. By imperiously swatting away the mosquito-like cloud of photographers, I was able to maintain an impressively glacial calm for Eric Hammond to try to provoke when he made his 'appeal' against expulsion for his union's greedy and undisciplined breach of fundamental TUC rules. It meant that I could also turn off the sound for the President of the engineers' union when he tried to pre-empt, on an absurd constitutional point, the full debate on the electricians' expulsion.

An incident that had arisen during my presidency was over the proposition that we present the Gold Badge of Congress to imprisoned Nelson Mandela, which I presumed we would hand to his representatives in the African National Congress and Black African trade unions at the Congress. I was then advised by my friends that there was a plan somewhere inside the TUC to give it to a 'family' member; it seemed that there was a relative working in Europe. At the General Council meeting I therefore said that the badge should go to the ANC representatives and the Congress of South African Trade Unions. This provoked a row that ended with Norman Willis in the corridor saying to me, 'Well, you will have the badge in your hand so you can do what you like.' Which I did. I still do not know what forces were at work which were seeking to deny the African National Congress a televison platform, though shortly before the actual occurrence Norman Willis came up to me and said, 'Alright, I surrender.'

I had the idea of putting Mandela's face on the delegates' badges to celebrate his seventieth birthday and they became a collector's item from the first morning of the Congress. We had a deeply satisfying, and very emotional, part of our Congress when, for the first time in history, political representatives other than from the Labour Party spoke from the General Council platform. And I am still delighted that the persons who were being pursued as targets for assassination were seen to be united with us and that the symbolic act I made of passing the badge to the unions and the African National Congress resulted in it ending up in Nelson Mandela's lapel in his prison cell.

Epilogue

The time came to consider leaving. Ken Gill, General Secretary of TASS, and I had led two competitive unions for decades. For every specialist officer in one industry or occupation, there was a watchful equivalent in the other. TASS had evolved into a multi-skilled vertical union in the metalworking, aerospace and electronic industries, partly as a result of mergers with what would once have been termed skilled blue-collar unions but where many of the collars were becoming bleached. Anyway, many office workers were in the equivalent of factories and suffering from industrial diseases, including the newer RSS (repetitive stress syndrome) of the fingers from hundred of key depressions.

I had deliberately sought in ASTMS (over angry internal protests) to diversify and expand out of engineering, chemicals, health services, universities and aviation into financial services. Early in 1985 at a 'think tank' of our Executive Council in Whitehall College, I laid out the case for more mergers to form a new kind of union which would mirror British society, and in which any new member knew she or he could always remain – no matter what changes in jobs or skills.

TASS was the prime partner. Ken Gill and I had two glasses of white wine at the Crest Hotel after a General Council Meeting and, quite suddenly and easily, agreed to start the process. It was not that difficult and we actually got it to ballot in September 1987, in the largest vote of its kind the world had ever seen. It was a resounding affirmative. Manufacturing, Science and Finance (MSF) was born.

People matter and people's aspirations matter. If Ken and I had been ten years younger, the merger might not have happened, but we two old foes worked absolutely happily together as Joint General Secretaries – until we struck a snag. The Government's new intrusive legislation, forcing regular elections and re-elections upon unwilling union electorates, gave us a problem. I was just inside the period before normal retirement when an election was not mandatory (an impertinence, in any case, when I had been confirmed in office so often in merger votes), but Ken, because he was rather younger, was caught by the legislation. He could not run for his own job because the rules we had adopted, before the legislation was passed, provided for a sole General Secretary! A conundrum: so I went on an Australian government fellowship to work with the environmental movements for a year. There is always instability and jockeying whenever the chief post in any organisation is likely to be vacated, and I did not wish to see any artificial law-induced instability in an organisation I loved. But it was a wrench and, alas, MSF seems to have been politically sidelined since I left. I always saw it as central to the British labour movement.

I have a regret that I will not be participating in the European fusion of unions which I helped start: that must be the next decisive work for the union. I look forward to MSF 1992 with a mainstream leadership. Meantime, in the words of D. H. Lawrence:

> If you make a revolution make it for fun.
> Don't make it in ghastly seriousness.
> Don't do it in deadly earnestness.
> Do it for fun.

Well, I did, most of the time.

Index

Abbott, David, 118, 119, 121, 122, 124
Aberavon, 3, 4, 173
Adenauer, Konrad, 43, 133
Advisory, Conciliation and Arbitration
  Service (ACAS), 88–9
Aeroflot, 42, 43, 44, 45
AFLO-CIO, American, 68, 73, 75
African National Congress, 138, 139, 228–9
Agar, Tom, 13
Air Transport Licensing Board, 57, 102
Airways National Advisory Council, 30, 31,
  32
Amalgamated Engineering Union (AEU), 27,
  29, 49, 96, 106, 145, 175, 228
Amery, Julian, 62
Amnesty International, 181
Anastasia, Albert, 76
anti-apartheid, 139, 163, 164
anti-semitism, 107, 108, 109, 143
'Any Questions' (BBC TV), 79, 82, 180
Armstrong Siddeley Hurricane motorcars, 61
ASLEF, 169, 214
Associated Electrical Industries (AEI), GEC
  take-over of, 108–9, 110
Association of Engineering and Shipbuilding
  Draughtsmen (AESD), 60, 96–7; see also
  TASS
Association of Scientific, Technical and
  Managerial Staff (ASTMS), ix, 179, 204,
  211, 226–7, 172, 230; administrative
  support for Michael Foot, 190; advertising
  campaigns, 117–25; anti-Common Market
  campaign, 135–7; BSC refuses to
  recognise, 110–12; Bullock Report rejected
  by Conference, 142, 167; collapse of
  British Eagle, 100–3; GEC take-over,
  108–9, 110; financial sector membership,

113–15; health and safety office, 128;
income and assets, 129; increased
membership, 117, 129; journals, 128; loans
to TUC for education centre, 218–19;
merger of ASSET and AScW into (1968),
97–100, 117; merger with TASS into MSF
(1987), 98, 129, 230–1; NEC, 119, 124,
134, 150, 230; paid informers, 167;
Pearson Court of Inquiry, 111–12; post-
1992 agenda, 137; Prudential Assurance
Male Staff Association joins (1970),
113–15; research department, 128; Rolls
Royce/RB211 crisis (1971), 125–6; training
of officials, 127; Whitehall College, 127–8;
see also ASSET; Jenkins, Clive; MSF
Association of Scientific Workers (AScW),
96–7, 114; Jenkins joins (1942), 11–12, 13,
14, 97; merges with ASSET into ASTMS,
97–100
Association of Supervisory Staffs, Executives
and Technicians (ASSET), 13, 14, 21, 30,
87, 96, 114; Airways Council, 30, 31, 32;
Annual Conference (Filey, 1951), 31–2;
annual dinners for airlines managements
given by, 37; De Havilland Aircraft
Company dispute, 60, 96; delegation to
Soviet Union (1957), 42, 43–5; engineers'
strike against International Computers
(1964), 59; first major national dispute with
airlines (1951), 30–7; genetic manipulation
issue, 55; 'The Gold Plate Handshake'
executive policy paper, 79; ICI delays
recognition of, 56–7; Jenkins appointed
Assistant Midlands Divisional Officer
(1947), 14–16; Jenkins becomes Acting
General Secretary (1960), 46; and General
Secretary, 16–17; membership in airlines,

233

Index

Index

Greater London Council (GLC), 171, 172, 184–5, 187
Greater London Enterprise Board (GLEB), 184–5, 187
Greece: Colonels' régime in, 91–2, 133, 138; Jenkins' visit to, 91–2; release of pilots, 93
Greek Cypriot community in London, 39
Greig, Gordon, 194, 200, 201, 202
Grisewood, Freddie, 79
Guardian, 177; report on Wembley Conference (1981), 201, 203–6
Gullet, Frank, 128
Gummer, Selwyn, 127–8
Gunter, Ray, 50, 59, 104

Hain, Peter, 163
Haines, Joe, 93, 94
Hammond, Eric, 183, 226, 228
Hannington, Wal, 41
Hardcastle, William, 178–9
Harper, Keith, 205
Hart, Dame Judith, 89, 190
Hattersley, Roy, 185, 212–13
Haughton, Dan, 126
Hawke, Bob, 159
Hayter, Sir William, 44
Healey, Denis, 145, 152, 157, 158; as contender for Labour Leadership (1980), 188, 189; elected Deputy Leader of Labour Party (1981), 190–2; *The Time of My Life*, 208–9
Healey, Gerry, 66–7, 81
Heath, Sir Barrie, 143
Heath, Edward, 51, 126, 178, 218, 220
Heathrow, London Airport, 30, 106; ASSET dispute at, 33–4
Heffer, Eric, 192
Hendy, Jack, 84
Hepburn, Katherine, 40
Hinchingbrooke, Lord, 135
Historic Houses Association, 180
Hoffa, Jimmy, 67–8, 69, 70–5, 78
Horner, Arthur, 25
House of Commons: ASSET Parliamentary Committee, 47–8, 51–2, 54–6; Private Members Bills, 48, 51–2, 82; Suez debate (1956), 192; Ten-Minute Rule Bill on redundancy, 48
Howard, Anthony, 132
Hoyle, Doug, 62
Hughes, Howard, 106
Humperdinck, Engelbert, 100
Hungarian uprising (1956), 43
Hurn, BOAC Flying Boats at, 41
Hutt, Allen, 128
Huxley, Julian, 10

Ibn Saud, 70
ICI, 56–7, 142

Independent Labour Party (ILP), 4, 131
Industrial Court, 31, 35
Industrial Society, 113
Industrial Tribunals, 52, 91
inflation, 17, 141, 144, 152
Ingham, Bernard, 88
International Association of Machinists, 126
International Brigade, 29, 130
International Chemical Workers, 75
International Computers, 55, 176; computer engineers' strike (1964), 59
International Labour Organization, 56–7
International Transport Workers' Federation, 68
Iron and Steel Trades Federation, 112, 218

Jackson, Tom, 146, 149, 158, 194
James, Madam Miriam Joseph, 4–5
Jarvis, Fred, 193, 228
Javits, Senator Jacob, 126
Jay, Peter, 94
Jenkins, Clive: books published by, x, 90–1, 94, 104, 124, 156; birth (1926), 1; family and childhood, 1–8; death of father (1952), 3, 7–8; leaves Port Talbot County School, 8; works in aluminium sheet plant, 8–10; studies metallurgy at Swansea Technical College, 9; passes City and Guilds exam, 9; joins Labour Party (1940), 10–11; wins prizes for essays in Workers' Eisteddfod, 11; joins AScW (1942), 11–12; works as night-shift foreman at Eaglebush Tinplate Works, 12–13, 14–15; appointed Assistant Midlands Divisional Officer of ASSET, 14–16; member of Communist Party, 29, 37, 66; appointed Secretary of Airways National Advisory Council, 30; elected to St Pancras Council (1954–60), 38–41; 'free Paul Robeson' rally, 39–40, 218; leads ASSET delegation to Russia (1957), 42, 43–5; takes photographs of Oxford Street bus disaster, 42–3; Acting General Secretary of ASSET (1960), 46; and Secretary of ASSET Parliamentary Committee, 47–8; not selected as Labour candidate for Shoreditch and Finsbury CLP, 49–51; issues libel writ against Matthews, 50, 106–7; trip to Copacabana, 60; visits French Concorde at Toulouse, 62; visits to USA, 66–76, 81, 84, 107, 161–2; and meetings with Hoffa and Gibbons, 68–74, 78; Fellowship at Woodrow Wilson Center, 76; TV and radio appearances, 78–80, 87, 101, 117, 124, 127–8, 178–9, 180; and *Tribune* column, 79, 85–6, 89, 98–100, 103; visit to Cuba, 80–1; stays at Cuernavaca with Belfrage, 81; 'Light and Liberty Fund' established

Index

Index

Index

Williams, Sir Robert, 55
Williams, Shirley, 127–8, 143, 144, 196, 219
Willis, Norman, 215, 216, 223, 229
Willis, Robert, 88
Wilson, Mrs Mary, 133
Wilson, Harold, xi, 25, 47, 82, 93, 104, 166, 168, 178; Common Market debate, 133; Leader of the Labour Party, 48, 53, 133; Open University proposed by, 54–5; President of the Board of Trade, 21; Prime Minister, 62, 87, 133; resigns as Prime Minister (1976), 142; *see also* Labour Government
Wilson Committee on financial institutions, 176
'Winter of Discontent', xi
Wolfit, Sir Donald, 40
women: ASSET union members, 58–9; insurance workers in ASTMS, 115
Woodcock, George, 22, 64, 216–17, 218
Woodrow Wilson Center, Jenkins' Fellowship at, 76

Woods, Sir Freddie, 170
Woolwich Arsenal, 108
Workers Eisteddfod, Jenkins wins first prizes for essays at, 11
Workers' Revolutionary Party, 67
'The World at One' (TV news programme), 178–9, 212
World Federation of Trade Unions, 65
'The World This Weekend' (TV news programme), 212
Worsthorne, Peregrine, 107
Wurf, Jerry, 65–6

Young, Lord, 182
Young, Mark, 85, 91–2, 93, 106, 183
Young Socialists, 130–1

Zagri, Sidney, 71
Zaharov, Lieutenant-General Nikita, 43–4
Zeus operation (MI5), 166
Zhao Ziyang, Chinese Prime Minister, 182